Ten Fundamentals for Durable Peace and Prosperity in the African Great Lakes Region
(Rwanda, Burundi, Uganda, DRC)

Understanding the True Role of the United States of America, the Belgium, the France, and the United Kingdom

VOLUME I
True Knowledge of 'Self' and the Land
English Version

Br. Paterne Muhaya Bengehya

With Preface of
Thomas D. McFarland, PhD.
Illustrated by Paulin Engambe

Africa: A Clay Pot
You need healing otherwise we will lose you!

Oh, Mother Africa!

You are very sick.

You are moving towards the graveyards.

But do not fear although your many illnesses

A generation of your lovely children has come to life;

The best they can do is to make sure you do not collapse.

They need to fight hard, not against your contaminators;

But against whose diseases to make you healthy again.

You're a clay pot of milk that refreshes minds and bodies

And the powerful are drinking from you to live better,...

Can they do it peacefully to avoid your collapse to death?

They should know you are fragile for made in clay.

That is why you are crying for you are suffering.

Oh… Africa! Do not fear; you will live long.

You will not die soon; you will be okay.

Get ready for your happiest days.

Straighten yourself for your,

Time is coming soon!!!

Contents

Acronyms and Abbreviations

9YBE: Nine Years Basis Education
ACLED According to Armed Conflict Location & Event
     Dataset
AD: Ano Domino (Christ Era)
ADF: African Development Fund
AfDB: African Development Bank
AFDL: Alliance des Forces Démocratiques pour la
     Libération du Congo/Alliance of Forces for
     Democratic Liberation
AGLR: African Great Lakes Region
ANAPI: National Agency for the Promotion of
     Investment (Agence Nationale Pour la Promotion
     des Investissements)
APROSOMA: Association for the Social Promotion of
     Masses
AU: African Union
BBC: British Broadcast Corporation
BC: Before Christ
BDK: Bundu Dia Kongo
BUCECO: Burundi Cement Company
CAADP: Comprehensive African Agriculture
     Development Program
CAMS: Credit Accumulation and Modular Scheme
CAR: Central African Republic
CEI: Commission Electoral Independent/Independent
     Electoral Commission
CIA: Central Intelligence Agency
CIP: Crop Intensification Program

CNDD-FDD: Conseil National pour la Défense de la Démocratie-Forces de Défense de la Démocratie/National Council for the Defense of Democracy–Forces for the Defense of Democracy

CNDD-FDD: National Council for the Defense of Democracy-Forces for the Defense of Democracy/Conseil National Pour la Défense de la Démocratie–Forces pour la Défense de la Démocratie

CNDP: Congrès national pour la défense du peuple/ National Congress for the Defence of the People

CNDP: National Congress for the Defense of the People

CNDP: National Congress for the Defense of the People

COMESA: Common Market for Eastern and Southern Africa

CP: Conservative Party

CSMN: Comité gouvernant Militaire du Sauvetage National/Military Committee for National Salvation

DGE: Directorate General of Energy

DGEE: Directorate General for Water and Energy

DHER: Direction General de l'Hydraulique et des Energies Rurales/General Office of Hydraulic and Rural Energies

DP: Democratic Party

DRC: Democratic Republic of Congo

DRH: Directorate of Water Resources

EAC: East African Community

ECHO: European Commission Humanitarian Aid

EDF: European Development Fund

EPSP: Enseignement Primaire, Secondaire, et

Professionnelle/Primary, Secondary, and Vocational Education

ESU: Enseignement Superieur et Universitaire/Higher and University Education (ESU)

EU: European Union

FAC: Forces Armées Congolaises or Armed Forces of the Congo

FAO: Food and Agriculture Organization

FAO: Food and Agriculture Organization

FDC: Forum for Democratic Change

FDLR: Forces Démocratiques de Libération du Rwanda/Democratic Forces for the Liberation of Rwanda

FDLR: Forces Démocratiques de Libération du Rwanda/Democratic Forces for the Liberation of Rwanda

FNL: Forces Nationales de Libération/National Forces of Liberation

FOREX: Foreign Exchange

GDP: Gross Domestic Product

HRW: Human Rights Watch

IBE: International Bureau of Education

IBEA: Imperial British East Africa Company

ICC: International Criminal Court

IDA: International Development Association

IGAD: Intergovernmental Authority on Development

IMF: International Monetary Fund

ISSP/OU: Higher Institute for Population Sciences of the University of Ouagadougou

Km: Kilometer

KY: Kabaka Yekka (The King Alone)

LRA: Lord's Resistance Army
LRA: Lord's Resistance Army
LRA: Lord's Resistance Army
MAFAP: Monitoring African Food and Agricultural
    Policies
MAS: Ministere des Affaires Sociales/Ministry of Social
    Affairs
MDR-PARMEHUTU: Rwandese Democratic
    Movement/Party of the Movement and of Hutu
    Emancipation
MINAGRIDER: Ministry of Agriculture and Rural
    Development
MINEDUC: Ministry of Education
MONUC: Mission de l'Organization des Nations Unies
    en DRC/United Nations Organization Mission
    in the Democratic Republic of the Congo
MONUSCO: The United Nations Organization
    Stabilization Mission in the Democratic Republic
    of the Congo
MONUSCO: United Nation Organization Stabilization
    Mission Mission de l'Organisation de Nations
    Unies pour la Stabilisation en RDC
MPSVE: Ministry of Primary, Secondary and Vocational
    Education
MRND: National Revolutionary Movement for
    Development
MSM: Muhutu Social Movement
MTWH: Minister of Tourism Wildlife and Heritage
MWEM: Ministry of Water, Energy, and Mines
NAIP: National Agricultural Investment Plan
NAP: National Agriculture Policy

NAPI: National Agency for the Promotion of Investment
ND: No Date
NDP: National Development Plan
NEC: National Executive Council
NEMA: National Environment Management Authority
NFA: National Forestry Authority
NISR: National Institute of Statistics of Rwanda
NRA: National Resistance Army
NRM: National Resistance Movement
OECD: Organization for Economic Co-operation and
      Development
OECD: Organization for Economic Co-operation and
      Development
ONUC: Opération des Nations Unies au Congo
OUA: Organisation de l'Unité africaine/Organization of
      African Unity
PALIPEHUTU: Parti pour la libération du peuple
      hutu/Revolutionary Party for the Liberation of the
      Hutu People
PDC: Parti Démocrate Chrétien/Christian Democratic
      Party
PDG: Président Directeur Général/President Director
      General
PRA: People's Redemption Army
PSTA: Strategic Plan for Agricultural Transformation
RAD: Rwanda Agriculture Department
RADER: Rwandese Democratic Union
RCEs: Communal Water Authority
RCI-LRA: Regional Cooperation Initiative for the
      Elimination of the Lord's Resistance Army
RDB: Rwanda Development Board

REGIDESO: Regi des Distribution d'Eau et d'Electricite/Agency of Distribution of Water and Electricity

RMTI: Rwanda Ministry of Trade and Industry

RPA: Rwandan Patriotic Army

RPA: Rwandan Patriotic Army

RPF: Rwandan Patriotic Front

RTLM: Radio-Télévision Libre Mille Collines/Free Radio and Television Thousand Hills

SNSA: National Service of Agricultural Statistics/Service National des Statistiques Agricoles

Sq: Square

TSS: Technical Secondary Schools

TVET: Technical and Vocational Education and Training

UBOS: Uganda Bureau of Statistics

UCA: University of Central Arkansas

UDA: Uganda Democratic Army

UFM: Uganda Freedom Movement

UK: United Kingdom

UN: United Nations

UNAMIR: United Nations Assistance Mission for Rwanda

UNAR: Rwandese National Union

UNC: Uganda National Congress

UNDP: United Nations Development Program

UNECA: United Nations Economic Commission for Africa

UNESC: United Nations Economic and Social Council

UNESCO: United Nations Educational, Scientific and Cultural Organization

UNIDO: United Nations Industrial Development

Organization
UNLA: Uganda National Liberation Army
UNLF: Uganda National Liberation Force
UNRF: Uganda National Rescue Front
UPC: Uganda Patriotic Movement
UPC: Uganda People's Congress
UPDF: Uganda People's Defense Force
UPDF: Ugandan People's Defense Force
UPE: Universal Primary Education
UPRONA: Union for National Progress
UPRONA: Union pour le Progrès National/Union for
      National Progress
US: United States
USA: United States of America
USAID: United States Agency for International
      Development
USD: United State Dollar
USGA: United States Geological Survey
USHMM: United States Holocaust Memorial Museum
USIP: United States Institutes of Peace
UWS: Uganda Wildlife Society
VNP: Volcanoes National Park
VTCs: Vocational Training Centers
WNBF: West Nile Bank Front
WSS: Water supply and sanitation
WTTC: World Travel & Tourism Council

Acknowledgments

I am grateful to Almighty God who gives revelations, wisdom, and energy without which this book could not be written. Glory and horror be to Him who wants nations to live in durable peace and prosperity.

I would like to express my gratitude to my lovely supportive wife Francine Nsimire for the patience she showed when I was doing researches. And the contribution of Thomas D. McFarland cannot be ignored; as my university teacher and mentor, he had always been ready to help. And he accepted to preface this work; I wish to thank him for what he has done. I also acknowledge the contribution of Mark Beattie, PhD, professor at Washington State University.

My relatives and friends had also been important to my family and me. Many of them had been helpful in providing encouragements, prayers, and many other kinds of support. People like Fr. David Masikini SJ., Pastor Eugene Shogozabahizi, Flavier Mugalihya, Floribert Hengwa, Matthias Ngandu Yemba, Godefroid Hengwa, Olugasa Kwanzaa Kiza Ombeni, Mery Sorenses, Fisher family, Olson family, Martin family, Criss family, etc. I remain grateful for any help you made.

I am also grateful to the agencies that welcome and support refugees and immigrants worldwide and especially in the USA. They have been doing an excellent job of providing safe settlements to millions of people coming from regions where durable peace and prosperity seem to be considered impossible by many. The Jewish Family Service and the World Relief need to be given special credit together with the US government for their outstanding work of welcoming and supporting refugees and immigrants. Thank you for what you do without which this book could not be published at the right time and the right place.

Br. Paterne Muhaya Bengehya

Preface

I met Paterne Muhaya Bengehya many years ago when I first visited the Dzaleka Camp in Malawi. Throughout the years I have known him, I am always surprised by his resilience and desire to make a difference. The fact that he was able to write this comprehensive book while living for years in the Dzaleka Refugee Camp with limited access to online resources is just one testimony to his desire to contribute to the learning of others.

Although the book does not share how he overcame challenges in his personal life, his accomplishment in writing this scholarly and insightful book demonstrates his resilience and persistence. Just before relocating to the United States, Bengehya shared a draft of *Ten Fundamentals for Durable Peace and Prosperity in the African Great Lakes Region*. Having had traveled to the Great Lakes region to assess the need for access to higher education, I found this book increased my understanding of the African Great Lakes Region in meaningful ways. The history of the region is filled with unimaginable atrocities, incredible natural resources, and people needed by the world. In each chapter I found insights to help me understand what I experienced and felt while in the region.

For the past eight years I have taught university courses for Jesuit Worldwide Learning (JWL) Higher Education at the Margins, previously named Jesuit Commons: Higher Education at the Margins (JC:HEM) online and on-site in a number of refugee camps. My lived experience of the refugee students I met from the African Great Lakes region has led me to be optimistic and hopeful for change. Bengehya, and other students from the region, have demonstrated resilience and an amazing desire to learn so they can address the poverty and lack of education that leads to violence. As these committed leaders gain knowledge and experience, I am filled with hope for the contributions they will make to durable peace and prosperity.

This book provides important ideas and lessons for all who want to better understand the African Great Lakes region. It is a book of possibility. There are implications for the world as the subtitle, *Understanding the True Role of the United States of America, Belgium, France and the United Kingdom* reminds us. We are accountable to understand, or at least be aware of the impact the policies and choices made by governments and businesses outside the region have had on the lives of the people.

Over the last eight years, I have had the opportunity to return to Dzaleka Refugee Camp as well as many of the countries of Africa including DRC, Rwanda, Mozambique, and Kenya. Each time I work on-site, I gain a better understanding of the challenges, and the opportunities if a durable peace could be achieved. Access to higher education is at the heart of transforming the region, and educating eager learners like Bengehya will be the key to achieving peace. I am proud that I have had the opportunity to teach him, and as importantly, to learn from him. This book will prepare people to understand the walk toward peace in the African Great Lakes region.

Thomas D. McFarland, PhD.
Professor Emeritus
International Faculty of Jesuit Worldwide Learning

Chap One
Introduction to the African Great Lakes Region (AGLR): A Region of Atrocious Facts with 'Faith' in the West

"We were ready for massacres and killings on the scale that Burundi had given me the day after I arrived in Rwanda, because they had a coup the day before. I had 300,000 Burundi refugees in the south of Rwanda plus about 50,000 bodies floating in the rivers and so on, all over the place."
(General Roméo Dallaire).

1.1. Overview of Atrocious Facts of the African Great Lakes Region (AGLR) and its 'Faith' in the West

Atrocities and misfortunes that have been manifested in different forms in the African Great Lakes Region (AGLR) such as physical slavery, colonization, wars, murders, genocides, famine, diseases, rape, plunder, and many other forms of social injustices seem to have made millions of concerned people believe that peace and prosperity is impossible. These immoral acts have been negatively affecting several regions of the world repeatedly making many people think that durable peace and prosperity cannot be achieved on earth. Africa is parts of those world regions that have been suffering a lot; and unfortunately, many of its religious leaders have been preaching to Africans fake messages (peace and prosperity belong to heaven only) paralyzing their efforts of discovering the truth to live a free, peaceful, and prosperous life.

However, the earth's lack of eternity does not suppress its capacity to establish durable peace and prosperity for all. God created human beings to dominate other creatures to live peacefully and prosperously on earth but not in heaven as believed by many people. The African Great Lakes Region (AGLR) is located on earth and its people whose image is God are supposed to offer true worship to God and enjoy durable peace and prosperity rather than offering worship to the traditional African gods, to their ethnic group leaders, and to international diplomacy that has considerable influence of the United States of America (USA), the France, the Belgium, and the United Kingdom (UK). We ought to be responsible for our actions and inaction that come out of our belief systems, traditions, and mindsets rather than trying to take somebody else accountable by our ignorance or irresponsibility.

As it is suggested in the next chapters of this book, the AGLR can only be set on the path of durable peace and prosperity for all by the Africans of the region by adequately following a set of principles. The atrocious events that have been characterizing the AGLR are mainly from the minds of the people of the region; that is why they are the main agents of durable peace and prosperity for their respective countries.

Contrariwise, many people in the AGLR and several parts of the world believe that the AGLR will never achieve durable peace and prosperity for all if the US, France, Belgium, and the UK have not decided it for the people of the region. Many other people believe that African as a whole or the AGLR will never be peaceful and prosperous unless it goes back to its traditional way of living that offer worship to its gods. These two popular beliefs in the AGLR are very dangerous and may be considered as a lack of knowledge about fundamental human basic questions tells us 'who am I?', 'where am I coming from?', 'where are we going?', 'who are the gods?', 'who are the people that I put my hope in?', 'who is God'. Failing to have edifying answers to these questions have made many people of the AGLR to consider recovery for better lives for all impossible. That is all about having a way behaving towards oneself and others.

Dangerous unbelief in durable peace and prosperity has led millions of people to become victims of their mindsets nurtured by lamentable ignorance or negligence. Their acts, being mostly the result of their thoughts and beliefs, have been speaking louder that durable peace and prosperity cannot be achieved for the benefit of all without total change of old mindsets that, for example, strongly argue that some ethnic groups, tribes, or races exist to suffer or be used as slaves and some other exist to be leaders and masters for eternity. That is what has been documented and witnessed in the African Great Lakes Region (AGLR) since its discovery by white European colonialists up to nowadays.

Some Western countries like the US, France, Belgium, and the UK have had so many significant interventions in the AGLR since its colonial period, and that tends to make many people unable to critically and logically think about what has been happening in this particular region of Africa. For many, these western countries are mainly responsible for worse that has been happening to the people of the AGLR since its colonization up to now. And some lovers of the AGLR has developed a particular 'hate' against 'Bazungu' (white people) of the US,

France, Belgium, and the UK for their support to some leaders of the region who have been taking part in making the region a worse place to live for all! Are these western countries the masters of the destiny of the people of the AGLR? Are they part of the main fundamentals for durable peace and prosperity for all in the AGLR?

It is known that the roles that have been played by US, France, Belgium, and the UK to influence the political and socio-economic life in the AGLR since the colonial era is huge. Maybe that is why we tend to think that can be considered fundamentals to durable peace and prosperity for all in the AGLR. For example, it is known that the Belgium colonized DRC, Rwanda, and Burundi and did not prepare them for peaceful self-governance or independence. And the USA did not have any colony in the AGLR but was playing an important role behind the scene with its CIA to influence the politics of the region. For example, it was reported that the CIA played a crucial role in the process of assassinating Patrice Lumumba, a prominent post-independent leader and prime minister of the Congo (DRC today).

Moreover, there has been a strong interconnection between the genocides, civil wars, and atrocities that have been happening in the different countries of the AGLR. For example, the Rwandan's after-independence Tutsi discrimination led army Tutsi to take refuge in Uganda; that event opened the door to the invention of FPR in and the 1994 Rwandan Genocide; that event opened doors to the first and second wars of DRC that made millions of victims to lose their lives. It has been argued that mainly the USA and France were playing

behind the scenes. Snow (2005) writes,

> "Critics such as Wayne Madsen, author of
> Genocide and Covert Operations in Africa
> 1993- 1999, assert that Kagame and the RPA
> orchestrated the April 6, 1994, assassination
> of the presidents of Rwanda and Burundi-
> shooting down their plane on its approach to
> Kigali airport with SAM-7 surface-to-air
> missiles taken from Iraq by France in 1991,
> then delivered by the US. military to Uganda,
> the base for RPA guerrilla operations against
> Rwanda prior to 1994."

What many critics and reports are trying to make people

believe is that the problems and causes of the misery and

atrocities of the people of the AGLR are mainly the

interventions of some mighty countries of West

(sometimes powerful western companies). And most of

the critics and reports do not suggest a solution that

sounds plausible to people's problems; instead, they keep

of causing people to fear some Western countries or to

put their total hope and faith in them! When reading this book, it may be surprising for many to learn that many people of the AGLR especially the leaders have been looking for solutions to the problems of their nations in wrong locations.

That has been done since long ago because of the ignorance of the sources and true causes of the problems that the AGLR have been facing since long ago. Snow writes that according to the International Rescue Committee at least 3.5 million people died due to the warfare in the DRC; and Rwandan military and commercial agents had made Rwanda to earn about $240 million in sale of Coltan (columbo-tantalite), used in laptop computers and cell phone, during the period 1999 to 2001; that mineral plundered in DRC moved through criminal syndicates to USA, Swiss, Belgian, and German clients (Snow, 2005).

There are so many facts, critics, and opinions that have been made so far about the international interventions of countries of West in the AGLR. Before the Genocide of 1994 in Rwanda, to put clear the role of France and other western countries in arming Habyarimana regime, it was said that,

> "The Habyarimana regime had at its disposal an arsenal of military equipment, including 83mm missile launchers, French made Blindicide, Belgian and German made light weaponry, and automatic weapons such as Kalashnikovs made in Egypt, China and South Africa [as well as ... armored AML-60 and M3 armored vehicles.23 While part of these purchases had been financed by direct military aid from France, the influx of development loans from the World Bank's soft lending affiliate the International Development Association (IDA), the African Development Fund (ADF), the European Development Fund (EDF) as well as

from Germany, the United States, Belgium and
Canada had been diverted into funding the
military   and   Interahamwe   militia."
(Chossudovsky, 2010).

Chossudovsky also puts that the militarization of Uganda

was an integral part of USA foreign policy. The USA and

Britain had been supporting the build-up of the Ugandan

UPDF Forces and the Rwandan Patriotic Army (RPA).

For instance, the British had provided military training at

the Jinja military base. The USA supported the joint RPF

(Rwandan Patriotic Front) and Ugandan attacks in

Rwanda.

And the British intelligence was used by RFP in August

1990 to prepare invasion into Rwanda (Chossudovsky,

2010). For many, without the USA and the UK, the RPF

could not invade Rwanda and the first and second wars

of DRC could not take place; so, they are to be at first consideration for any initiative for durable peace and prosperity of the AGLR. Do the AGLR people need them as primordial agents of durable peace and prosperity for all?

It may be true that the AGLR need the western countries as they also need the African countries to build strong and safe future together, but many African leaders of the AGLR seem to have too much faith in some of these western countries to main their leadership position. But is what they are doing for their people so sustainable that can lead to durable peace and prosperity for all? What is durable peace and prosperity that is addressed in this book as to be archived in the AGLR when applying the ten fundamental principles explained in the next chapters?

Some might think that the manifested vices to durable peace and prosperity for all in the AGLR such as civil wars, genocides, human rights violation, plunders, pillages, etc. are recent phenomena in the region; but looking back into the history of the region, help us discover that those situations exist there for about 400 hundred years! May we suggest that the AGLR has been experiencing very peace and prosperity destroying period void from true people-serving political visions as it was the case of Israel that for about four centuries, from the last Prophet Malachi sent by God up to the coming of Jesus Christ, experienced a lack of true visionary political leadership that could be used as role model to bring out durable peace and prosperity for all.

The irony of history is that the white colonialists who discovered Africa, in particular, the African Great Lakes Region (AGLR), had claimed to bring 'civilization' to African peoples with evangelization as one of their great tools to achieve their goal! Jesus Christ had been brought to the AGLR for about four centuries now, but the region has been the field of endless destructive conflicts and atrocities from one generation to another and one may say the truth is durable troubles and poverty rather than durable peace and prosperity that people should expect when talking about 'civilization' brought along with 'evangelization'. Was that true 'evangelization' that uses the true 'gospel' or the word of God? Did the people of the AGLR find it relevant to create durable peace and prosperity for all in their communities? Was it not in contradiction to the good human moral virtues that already existed in their tribal cultures?

Likewise, true 'civilization' supported by true 'evangelization' is supposed to be done using true principles for durable peace and prosperity. That is a reality may be ignored by many who never understand well the concepts of 'durable peace' and 'prosperity'; that also stands to be true for those who believe durable peace and prosperity all is impossible for a community, for a nation, for a region, for this aching world.

Ignorance, misinformation, lack of the spirit of understanding, lies, slavery (physical and mental), negligence, lethargy, false patience (waiting for something that will never be realized or for some who will never come or appear) and more other vices have characterized the lives of millions in AGLR since the arrival of the white European colonialists up to now. And that situation has set the foundation of durable troubles and poverty in the region making many believe that their lives are to be like that!

The fact is that the truth about the principles of durable peace and prosperity for all has been hidden for many; others are blocked by negligence and unwillingness to apply what they already know to their daily lives or to teach them to the people of the AGLR. People need to break that ball; they need to cross the river that separates the sphere of ignorance and negligence in which they are living now to the one of truth and willingness to act for the common good.

It may be shocking to argue that the needed true information to unlock better future of the AGLR is within the region itself. It may seem unbelievable to put that what the people of the AGLR need lay in themselves and their land but hidden to the minds to most of them, including to most of the considered most smart people and great leaders of the region.

Besides, it may seem unrealistic to say that the main enemies of durable peace and prosperity in the AGLR are the people of the region. We don't need to waste time accusing God or other nations about what has been happening to us in the AGLR; we have to be honest when taking into consideration what has been taught to us (by our ancestors), what many people have been worshiping, what we believe, think, say, and do. How have we been handling life and its realities (ups and downs)?

Do we blame others for any bad event that happens to us? Do we consider others as important as we are regardless their ethnic, tribe, or race? Don't we still define ourselves using the opinions and definitions of the colonialists? Do we have sound knowledge of principles that bring peace and prosperity as they are supposed to be taught by religions or any other spiritual congregation in the AGLR? There are so many questions to address when looking at how millions of people in the AGLR have been living their lives from one generation to another.

Nevertheless, there is no need to lose hope or to wonder whether true teachings bearing true and powerful principles exist; this book contains some of them that people need to discover or to recall (for those already familiar with some of them) in order to correctly apply to change the lives of many for better in the African Great Lakes Region (AGLR). There is no late time for that. Durable peace and prosperity for 'Self' and 'all' in the AGLR is not impossible; it is the result of successfully using its fundamental principles that empower the human capacity to improve their own lives and those of others without any discrimination and violence; and that is based on true and good knowledge and its correct application to day after day activities enabling people to keep conflicts unable to develop into violent actions, but into actions free from the violation of human rights and dignity that lead to production of goods and services that are needed to secure peace and prosperity. The ten principles suggested in this book cannot suppress conflicts among the people of the AGLR to make it become a paradise-like region, but their accurate knowledge and use will make sure the results are words and actions that build and not those that destroy.

As it is known, reports about the AGLR put it evident that there is a pressing need for durable peace and prosperity in the region. This region has been suffering from the most atrocious acts in Africa since the penetration of European colonialists as we mentioned it in the previous paragraphs; the region has experienced leaders and followers who have been using false stories (unkind talks, wrong words), and acts to paralyze any efforts of the people to set their feet on the path leading to better life for all. Some of the policies and actions authored by both European colonialists and the post-colonial leaders of the AGLR are said to be one of the main reasons for the atrocious, troubling, and uncertain present of people in the region; and some Western countries are the other cause of that! How much veracity can we find in such statement if we dig deep into the matter?

In fact, if three categories of people are the main sources of the problems in the AGLR throughout the history of the region including the European colonialists (including religions or missionaries), some of the post-colonial leaders of the AGLR, and some of the Western countries, then the solutions should come from them. And we know that the European colonialists do not exist anymore in the AGLR; we know that the most of the post-colonial leaders have now 'college education' and work for their countries in 'independence era'; and we know that some Western countries have been trying to intervene to improve people's lives in the AGLR since long ago. But why life has never changed for better in the AGLR? People of the AGLR need to be reminded that the European colonialists are not there anymore spiritually and physically handling colonies in the AGLR and the international community (UN for example) is not acting like past colonialist leaders were acting.

For example, they cannot stop us from discovering and correctly using God's principles that bring durable peace and prosperity for all in a region. And they cannot develop us to the needed level to help us become what we should be to allow better lives for all in the region. We are then the ones to whom all the wrong kinds of stuff have caused harm. We are also the ones that produce them for all the post-colonial leaders accused of committing atrocious actions and injustice are from us (from the population). And we seem to ignore that we have all the power and capacity to make them leave the power non-violently by the use of the principles and laws of durable peace and prosperity. To well address this serious issue in this introductory part of this book before giving more details and facts in its next chapters, let's have a brief historical review on the seeds of conflicts in the AGLR.

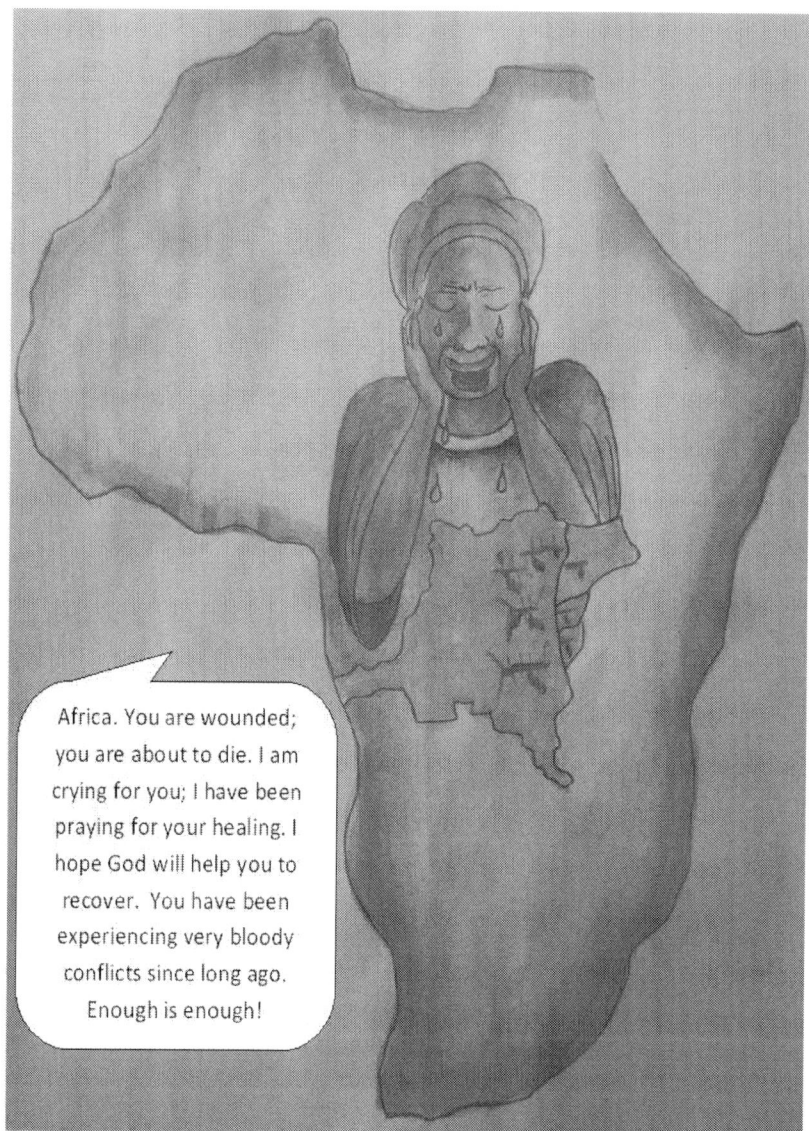

Moreover, the peace and prosperity destructive conflicts of African Great Lakes Region (AGLR) have undoubtedly origins or sources. We need to put is clear that the past periods of the AGLR have more to say about the recent and present critical situations of the region. We are going to discuss it in the next chapters of this book, but let's just have a brief synopsis of the colonial history of Africa. Historically, migrations in Africa since the arrival of Europeans and the Arabs in the continent (which the Europeans called the 'discovery' of African) up to the independence era embody important details that may shed the first light on what can be considered as sources or origins of problems that the people of the AGLR have been facing.

The Post-colonial leadership in the AGLR has the second important part of light to better understand attitudes and acts the helped to produce more seeds of conflicts and nurture them; that was a time where the African people were leading by Africans but failed to avoid peace and prosperity destroying conflicts which have been producing very alarming consequences in the region. It is unfortunate the seeds of conflicts were nurtured to become big trees that have been producing aching fruits for people to consume. And every person who has eaten the fruits of conflict was affected by it; some of the consequences have been psychological such as depression, phobia, trauma, etc.; some have been physical such as death, imprisonment, tortures, injuries, etc.; and some have been socioeconomic for example loss of money, loss of houses, loss of jobs, etc.

Dangerous movements or events of the fruits of conflicts such as genocides, and civil wars, rebel groups (militias) nurtured mainly by ignorance, negligence, hunger and poverty, mismanagement, political irresponsibility and incapacity, regionalism, ethnic discrimination, tribalism, hunger of raw materials by multinational companies, etc. to name just a few have resulted in important losses in the African Great Lakes Region (AGLR). This situation, as mentioned earlier, has persisted for centuries as if the region was created to be a human butchery or a worldly hell forever!

Millions of people have lost their lives there and many still losing it today; the durable atrocities, troubles, and poverty in the AGLR have made millions of people suffer unjustly and others due to the longevity of sufferings and persecutions have lost their hope by thinking and believing that durable peace and prosperity for all (for the population) is non-achievable in the region. How atrociously has the AGLR been suffering since the colonial period? Let us make a brief examination of some of the reported atrocious events of the four countries of the AGLR namely Democratic Republic of the Congo (DRC), Rwanda, Burundi, and Uganda since their colonial era up to nowadays are so awful.

Democratic Republic of the Congo (DRC)

The DRC has been facing terrible events that have devastated its populations since the arrival of the European colonialists. From Leopold II, the King of

Belgian who made Congo his private property up to Joseph Kabila who has been ruling the country for 16 years now, the country has been losing its populations in very huge numbers, its natural resources (minerals, trees, wild animals, etc.) in huge quantities, and its dignity in the eyes of other nations of the world.

During the atrocious exploitation of the country by the King Leopold II, the DR Congo lost about 10 million of its peoples; millions other perished during the administration of the Belgians colonialist to whom the country was sold by Leopold. The work of independence movements of the Congo did not leave the country without mourning; their activities that led to the independence of the country recorded many lost regarding human lives including the death of Patrice

Lumumba, one of the prominent leaders of independence of Congo, declared national hero. And during the despotic reign of the late President Mobutu, many other Congolese were killed although the statistical figures have never been reported; and millions of people were living in lamentable poverty, insecurity, etc. and many other forms of human right violations had been documented (More details will be given in chapter three).

That was the time when the fire has been lit by some African themselves (some post-colonial leaders) to destructively burn in the hearts of many people in the whole AGLR; Burundi, Rwanda, and Uganda had similar political dictatorships that did not care the about the rights of their respective citizens at all. The same fire is still burning today and needs to be put off for people to feel better and become ready to work for durable peace and prosperity for all in the region.

After that, the DRC faced the era of 'the first and the second wars' that resulted in the loss of human lives of about 5.4 million (World Without Genocide, nd). These figures are considered the biggest death toll that the world has never experienced since the Second World War. Can't that be called 'Human Butchery'? Does this country exist to be a human butchery? Was it created for that purpose? According to the War Child Organization report, among the 5.4 million of dead persons 2.7 million were children (War Child UK, 2014). Making a comparison about the United Kingdom (UK) it was also reported about the DRC that,

✓ 1 in 5 children will die before their fifth birthday.

- ✓ Average life expectancy is 47 years (UK average is 79).
- ✓ The government spends an average of USD 2 per person, per year on healthcare for its citizens (in contrast the UK figure is USD 2,939).
- ✓ More children under 5 die every year in Congo (with a population of 63 million) than in China (with a population of 1,325 million).
- ✓ More than 200,000 women and girls have been the victim of rape or sexual violence.
- ✓ More than 1 million people have been forced to flee their homes.
- ● At 20,000 UN troops, DRC is home to the largest peacekeeping mission in the world.
- ● The UN Human Development Index report (2009) ranks DRC as 176th out of 182 countries.

Source: War Child UK, 2014

That is very sad because most of those deaths are provoked by preventable or treatable menaces such as wars, hunger, and diseases like malaria, diarrhea, pneumonia, abortion, etc. Save the Children report of 2014 about the 'state of the world's mothers' shows that only 10 percent of DRC deaths tolls of civil wars happened in combat (Save the Children Federation, Inc.). All the millions of people who died in DRC were not killed by knives, bullets, and bombs of rebels although that were some of the main threatening tools that some people feared when becoming refugees or internally displaced.

Moreover, apart from the death tolls of Leopold II colonial era and that of first and second wars of DRC, many other rebel movements have committed dangerous and atrocious acts to the population of the country. For example, M23 since its start in April 2012 (its founders were old members of National Congress for the Defense of the People - CNDP - after its dissolution as a result of the peace accord of March 23rd, 2009) has made many people lose their lives, families, properties, and peace. Other dangerous movements include but not limited to FDLR (INTERAHAMWE), Lord's Resistance Army (LRA), many factions of Mayi Mayi, and many other groups that have been terrifying some regions of the country regardless the presence of United Nation Organization Stabilization Mission (MONUSCO – Mission de l'Organisation de Nations Unies pour la Stabilisation en RDC). The sad reality with all these groups is that the most victims were and are still the civilians.

According to Armed Conflict Location & Event Dataset (ACLED) Country Report of December 2013, 6 percent of CNDP violence tactically aimed the civilians while

46% of M23 events targeted the civilians (ACLED, December 2013). ACLED also reveals that during the period of the activities of the LRA in the DR Congo, over two-thirds of their operations directly targeted civilians with an average rate of 12 fatalities per event. Mentioning the figures of only M23 and LRA here is just to name a very few of many groups rebels that have been helping the DRC to be transformed into a land of pain and misery regardless its natural potentiality.

And some groups like the INTERAHAMWE are still operating against the civilians up to nowadays making security or temporary stability impossible in some parts of the country. The following map shows how the Mayi Mayi groups have operated in the different region of DRC causing disasters to civilians.

However, durable peace and prosperity of the people of DRC is still awkward even in the regions the country which had few or no activities of atrocious rebel groups. As a matter of fact, the ECHO fact sheet of September 2014 states that about 2 million children under the age of 5 suffer acute malnutrition in the country mostly in the central provinces which do not have civil wars or conflicts. (ECHO Factsheet, DRC, 2014).

This situation shows that the problems that DRC has been facing since Leopold II colonial era are not only due to the civil wars and militias activities: it is clear that both the colonial and post-colonial governments have failed to make life better for the Congolese even in the provinces that have experienced little or no conflict at all.

In the same period of September 2014, it was reported that about 6.7 million people are at crisis or emergency levels of food insecurity in DR Congo. Among a population estimated at 77 million citizens as stated in the ECHO Factsheet of 2014, 2.9 million are internally displaced people, and 445 000 have fled to neighboring countries to find refuge.

Although M23 Rebel Movement has stopped operating in the East of the country, still there are some other rebel groups (about 40) that continue to trouble the peace of the population of the eastern part of DR Congo. Those are reported troubling and revolting situations of the DRC; all the peoples of the AGLR need to be aware of that by taking encouraging decisions to say 'enough is enough'; what has been happening to ourselves and our nearing neighbors should stop.

Nevertheless, the eastern regions of DRC have particularly been the preferred terrains of military and rebel movements' dirty businesses. Maybe because it is the part of the country where the people who support the rebels and militias have easy ways to travel from neighboring countries to supply the necessary logistics and money to their supported destroyers of peace and prosperity for all in the AGLR.

When studying intensely the reports produced by some NGOs about the DRC, some may be tempted to think that the government of the DRC is part of that win-win destructive game that foreign and national sponsors are playing with the rebel and militias groups. What sovereignty can a nation claim to have when its land is easily and quickly invaded by foreign backed militias with severe loss concerning people and wealth?

The ACLED (Armed Conflict Location & Dataset) report of December 2013 mentions that DRC is second most violent country in the ACLED data set when measured by the number of conflict events; also DRC is the third most fatal over the course of ACLED dataset's coverage that is from 1997 up to September 2013, the time this was reported (ACLED, 2013). That is what happens when a 'win-win' politico-military game is being played in a wealthy region like the AGLR for the benefice of some business men and politicians and in detriment of the population, mostly civilians. It is really a pity for a nation to be destroyed by people who are supposed to build it; it is really regrettable to see people being killed by leaders who are supposed to protect them; it is really anger-provoking to see some political leaders sacrifice the lives of millions of people for self-satisfaction or self-interest characterized by hunger for power and money.

The Human Rights Watch Report of 2013 puts that the presidential election of November 28, 2011 in the DRC, that declared Joseph Kabila as winner, was criticized by international and national observers as lacking credibility and transparency with the worst election-related violence in Kinshasa, the capital, where at least 57 opposition party supporters or suspected supporters were killed by security forces – mostly Kabila's Republican Guard –

between November 26 and December 31 (Human Rights Watch World Report, 2013, p.96).

Can we suggest, through what has been reported for the DRC so far, that the enemies of the people's lives are not only the rebel movements or militias? Let's look for example at the following chart showing how some rebel movements in the East of DRC are reported to have been supported by some countries of the African Great Lakes Region (AGLR) as reported by Woman Rights Watch in July 2013.

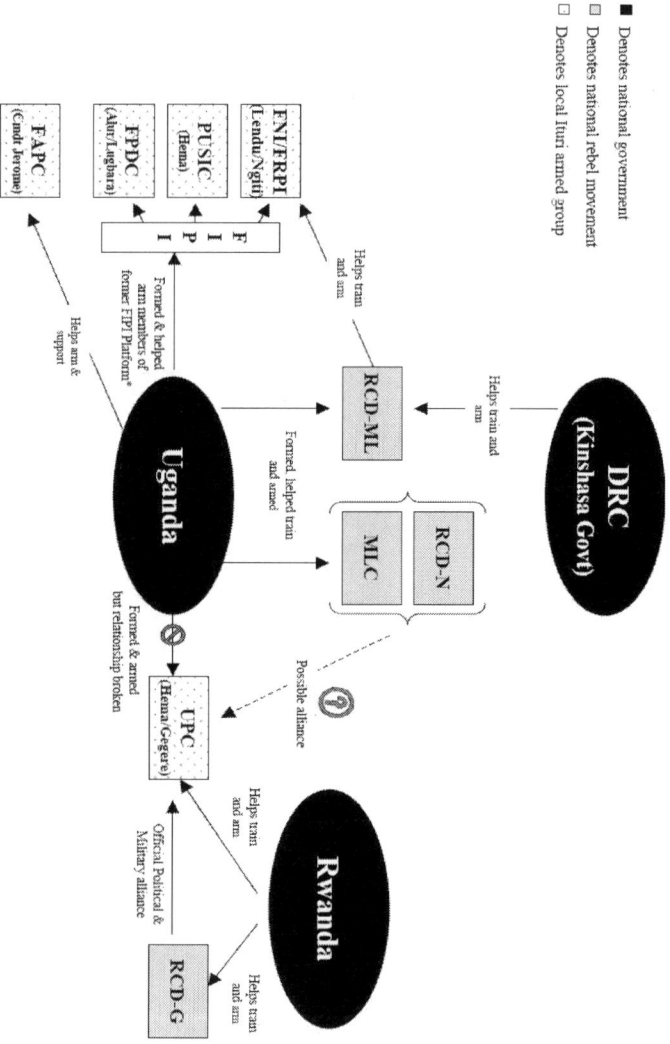

Source: Human Rights Watch (HRW, July 2013).

With regard to the militia activities and political manipulations of the masses in the DRC, it may be assumed that few people in that country are in possession of the true information about what truly is happening in the country; many people are not able to read and other who can read many of them do not have access to the reports of the humanitarian organizations operating in the country.

Also, the media (radio stations for example) fear to broadcast the true information that people need to know to have a clear identification of their real destroyers. So, sometimes what the government officials, army, and the militias do remain a mystery to many for the easily accessible source of information is the radio stations for most people in the DRC. For example, the information in the reports of institutions like 'Human Rights Watch' sometimes remain unknown to the average citizen of DRC or criticized by some politicians and their supporters as untrue to weaken the attention of those who can access and read them in the country.

Many peace and prosperity destroying acts happen in the DRC without people's awareness, and that may be one of the reasons why some people continue to support leaders who cannot help the country to set its feet on the path of durable peace and prosperity for all. It may be amazing for some to learn that many people died during the election period in the DRC. We learn that,

> "Human Rights Watch received credible reports of nearly 150 other people killed in this period, their bodies reportedly dumped in the Congo River, in mass graves on Kinshasa's outskirts, or in morgues

far from the city center. Scores of people accused of opposing Kabila were arbitrarily detained by Republican Guard soldiers and the police. Many were held in illegal detention centers where they were mistreated and some were killed." (Human Rights Watch World Report, 2013, p. 97).

As a matter of fact, a country where politicians own and control the media will never inform people adequately when some or all of them are shady or less honest. In 2012, according to the Ministry of Communications, the country registered 463 radio stations, 445 newspapers, and 134 television stations.

And according to the US Department of State Bureau of Democracy 2013 report on human rights in DRC, the radio station in the country remain the principal medium of public information due to the limited literacy and the high costs newspapers and television. While the government owns three radio stations and three television stations, the majority of the media in the country are owned and managed by government officials, politicians, and the church leaders own some but to a lesser extent. The president Kabila's family owns two television stations. (US Department of State, 2013).

Are those media owners committed to working for the interest of the population or they are just pursuing their interests at all cost? Are they serious with promoting durable peace and prosperity for all without discrimination by using true information that people need in their medias? Do they need a change of mind so that the country may prosper in peace? Or they are just working to enrich themselves by manipulating their journalists! Do they promote the broadcasting of true information and the propagation of the true message of

durable peace and prosperity in the whole country?

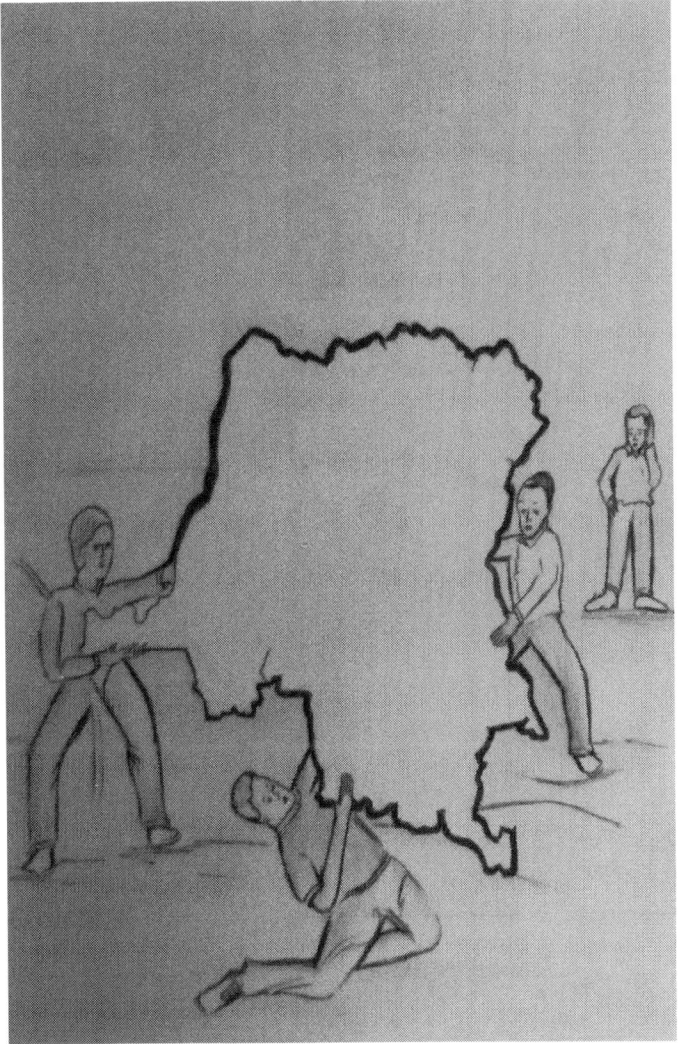

The Democratic Republic of the Congo, which is naturally blessed and able to achieve durable peace and prosperity, has become a terrain of misery. Poverty, torture, killing, rapes, human rights violation, forced labor, plunder of its riches, etc. have been, since the region was discovered by Europeans, the daily 'meals' of the people of DRC! That is a reality of all the countries of the AGLR as well; that situation has made millions of people live on earth as if they were living in hell; that has been so persistent in the DRC, and some may assume that the Congolese people were created to eternally face poverty, injustice, rape, torture, etc.

It is so troubling to notice, when looking at the actual economic situation of the country with a comparison to its colonial period, that the Congolese political leaders of the post-independence era are a failure in their leadership philosophy and approaches to building the nation. During the colonial era, DRC did not experience peace and prosperity due to diverse reasons; the atrocities and brutalities of the colonialists played important role in maintaining Congolese in misery, but amazingly the country was the second more industrialized country in Africa after South Africa! Is it still second today? Is it not the second less industrialized in Africa today?

The post-colonial leaders who have inherited the DRC and the same natural resources and penitential available in the country have failed to maintain the same industrial position that could lead to prosperity and development. For example, while other African countries are making progress in terms of the economy since their independence up to nowadays, DRC is making economic decrease or deterioration. The revenue per habitat was 380 USD at the time of the country's independence, but it was of 119 USD in 1990; that was after 30 years of self-governance.

Moreover, it is astonishing to learn that some experts have estimated the penitential of the cultivable land of the DR Congo to be able to feed the whole population of the world for 50 years and yet the country with millions of people suffering from malnutrition today. The agricultural exploitation contributed to the GDP up to 40 percent in 1960, but its contribution is evaluated at about 10 percent today. And it is reported that about 1.6 million people depend on food aid to sustain their lives (BGR & KfW Entwicklungsbank, April 2007). What are then the true sources of the problems that people are facing in the AGLR and the DRC in particular and how can people do to solve them? This is one of the questions that will find constructive suggestions the next chapters of this book.

Rwanda

Rwanda is also a country that has been losing millions of its people since the colonial period. There had been lamentable human rights violations characterized by ethnic discrimination in Rwanda; that have threatened millions of Rwandans who had decided to leave their country for refuge and are still living in outside their home; and many of those in refuse have much fear to go back home. For example, the genocide of 1994 in Rwanda made the country lose about 800,000 of its citizens who either killed by machetes, by gun bullets, or any other violent means. And many others died outside Rwanda while seeking asylum.

The conflict had many violent incidents up to the extent that up to nowadays many Rwandans are still having bad memories dominated by forgiveness and we have observed and witnessed that some people continue to teach their children to hate people of a different ethnic group. Is not that a nursery of new genocidal killing in the future? Is the future of Rwanda and other countries of AGLR safe without following a particular set of principles that should be used to avoid new massive killings and to establish the county's feet on the path of durable peace and prosperity for all without discrimination?

For people who think better future for all is impossible in Rwanda, the answer to the previous question may be 'yes'; but for the people who know the better future for all is possible and is buried in people hearts and minds and it can be transmitted from one generation to another, the answer is 'no'. The present mindsets of a people and its leaders may accurately predict their future. Is it possible to read the mindsets of Rwanda as a nation and its leaders inside and outside their country?

This country which is today ruled and economically dominated by people of Tutsi ethnic group needs to revisit its ways of thinking and acting. Having a Tutsi at the head of the country has appeared to be a threat to the millions of Hutu people and to some Tutsi people who are still living outside the country as asylum seekers or refugees. As a matter of fact, the Tutsi on the leadership of the country today, although some may deny, considers the Rwandans who seek asylum in foreign countries as a potential menace to the stability of their government. This reality makes it clear that Rwanda is in real need of durable peace and prosperity as other countries of the AGLR.

While it is true that there is a total ceasefire and a seeming security in Rwanda today, that does not guarantee the durable peace and prosperity for all in that country. Both groups (Rwandans in their country and those in exile) regardless their ethnic belongings should think about the true values and principles that can help a nation to live together in harmony after setting the strong

foundations of durable peace and prosperity for all in
their minds (in their country).

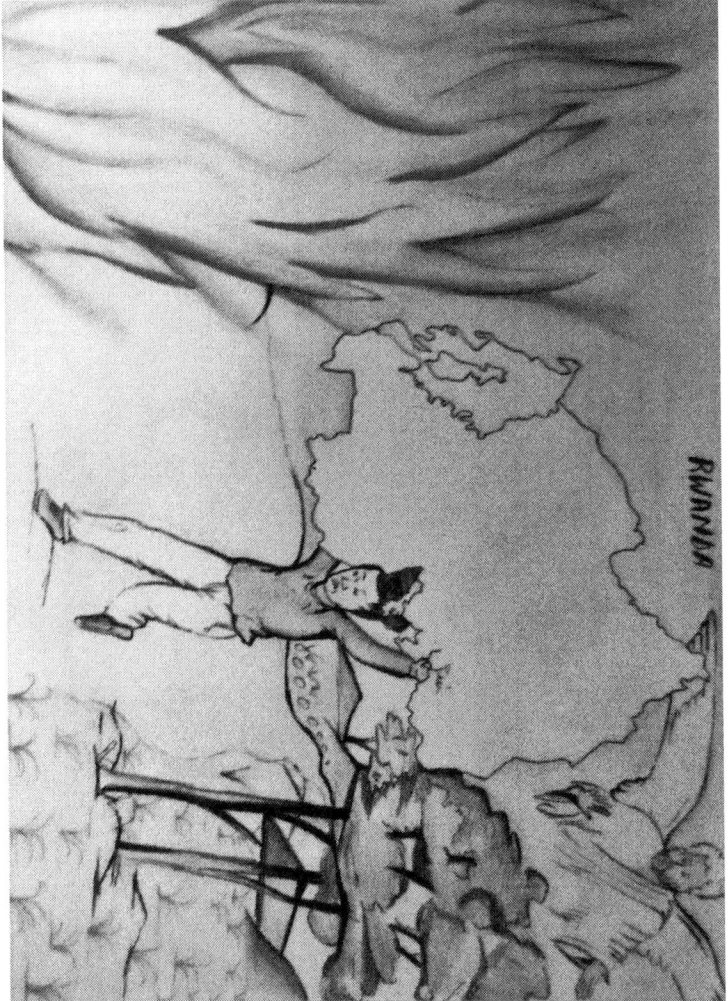

I know some may be saying 'there are peace and development projects in Rwanda now, all Rwandans are to be repatriated to their home country'; but what kind of peace can we talk about in country when in the minds of millions of its citizens there is durable insecurity and troubles? Does durable peace and prosperity for all in a country refer to the cease-fire, nice building, and good roads only? Is it not logical or advisable to start building peace and prosperity for all in people's minds before re-building roads and buildings?

Rwanda has a very bad record of atrocities and killings resulted mainly from colonial activities in the country and ethnic-based conflict that always ends up into violent acts with persistent consequences that are visible up to nowadays. It is known about Rwanda that its colonial rulers helped the Tutsi and Hutu groups to hate each other by the policies they implemented there. And what was created in Rwanda have never left the minds of millions of Rwandans today. From the time of Germany from 1890s colonization, the time of Belgium from the First World War, and up to the after the independence of Rwanda, the country has never experienced a period that comfortably allows all Rwandans to feel free living there without discrimination based on ethnicity.

There were atrocities, killings, and human rights violations when the colonial regimes (Germany and Belgium) reinforced the social position and power of the Tutsi over the Hutu who were the majority of the citizens of Rwanda. There were menaces and murders after independence when the Hutu gained power other the

Tutsi because they represented the majority of the Rwandans in the country. At that time many Tutsi fled to neighboring countries such as Uganda, Democratic Republic of Congo, and Burundi. And there were troubles, killings, and human rights violations in Rwanda, when the Rwanda Patriotic Front (RPF) created in Uganda in 1979 invaded Rwanda in 1990; and from that time up to nowadays, Rwanda has never been a place where all the ethnic group members can feel comfortable to live well.

One of the most dangerous violent events resulting from the historic Rwandan ethnic conflict is the genocide of 1994 that resulted in the killing of about 800,000 Rwandans in the space of 100 days; and most of the reported dead were Tutsi and most of those who perpetrated the violence were Hutu (BBC, 18 December 2008). How the destructive works of some extremists Rwandans have been impacting the lives of millions of people in Rwanda and those of the neighboring countries of the AGLR, from one generation to another, and what can they do to promote better lives for all in the region? This and more other critical questions about the Republic of Rwanda will have edifying suggestions in the next chapters of this book.

Burundi

Burundi has a very tragic history of ethnic conflict like Rwanda. The fact that the conflict is always ethnicized makes it hard to eradicate, and that may lead many people to that the situation will always be the same as long as the ethnic groups exist in the country! But Burundians should not remain unchangeable and inactive if they really need to live in durable peace and prosperity because their country has suffered a lot and still it is today. According to the 2010 UNICEF report, Burundi ranked 166 of 169 in the 2010 human development report. Its population is so poor; it is reported that up to 67 percent of them live on less than USD 1 per day. With a population dominated by youth (51 percent are under 18 and 20 percent under 5), the country faces considerable challenges related to the human basic needs.

Food insecurity, serious health problems, sexual and gender-based violence, corruption, insecurity, impunity, and human rights abuse, etc. are what the majority of people in Burundi have been facing since the historic periods of the country up to nowadays. All those issues bring the country to extreme poverty, low economic growth, high population density (310 inhabitants per Km2) that increase year after year, and high aid dependency and underdevelopment of human capacity.

There are grave problems in Burundi, and more will always be created there if people do not accept to positively change their minds; especially the political leaders. The UNICEF (2010) also reported that in Burundi there are a chronic malnutrition and land issues resulting from overpopulation and repatriation (UNICEF, 2010, Annual Report for Burundi).

So, the millions of orphans, children living on the street, prisoners, HIV/AIDS affected people, and very poor households will continue to suffer and to increase if all the population of the country especially the leaders do not welcome and use new and adequate principles that can bring the country to the new path of durable peace and prosperity all; that should be done by all the leaders regardless their domains or fields of intervention without any possible discrimination based on ethnics, tribes, gender, religion, color, origin, etc..

While Burundi may be experiencing a certain cease-fire in the country, but there is still an important loss in humans due to food insecurity and health problem. According to the UNICEF Humanitarian Action of 2009 in Burundi, malaria is an endemic disease and is the main cause of mortality and morbidity in the country; it is at the base of 50 percent of medical consultations and is the cause of nearly 50 percent of deaths of children aged from 1 to 59 months (UNICEF, 2009, Humanitarian Action Burundi in 2009).

However, as other countries of the African Great Lakes Region (AGLR), Burundi has suffered long-lasting political unrest since her independence of 1962. The history of the country is full of sad events that cost the lives of millions of human beings. Massive killings assimilated to genocide have been registered and resulted in generalized insecurity, poverty, and many other different difficulties that some survivals of the conflicts may be facing today.

Millions of people have been murdered during the genocidal killings that repeatedly occurred at different historical times. From 1959 up to 1962, 50,000 Hutu were murdered by the Tutsi government; in 1972 there was a killing of about 150,000 Hutu by the Tutsi army; in 1993 – 1995, the country lost 50,000 Tutsi and 100,000 Hutu; and from 1996 – 2006, 100,000 peoples died Tutsi and Hutu together (Genocide Watch, 2008).

The statistics of the death toll of people who have been killed in Burundi due to genocides, wars, and ethnic conflicts from 1959 to 2006 are available. Their total reaches 350,000. This number does not include the victims of conflicts who have been dying from 2006 up to nowadays. That is one of the important statistics of killings of the AGLR! If it is not a 'huge human butchery', then it is a 'field of frequent massive killings'!

Can people say that the future of Burundi is safe as there is no civil war or genocide now? Aren't civil wars and genocides in the hearts and minds of many Burundians today, especially those who survived the past menaces of death? How are the mindsets of the leaders in Burundi at the time? Years are passing, but the situation seems to be very slow regarding political and economic improvement. In 2011, the country was ranked the third poorest country in the world according to the United Nations Development Program; it was also reported that Burundi had 80 percent of its population living below that international poverty line of USD 1.25 per day (World Relief, 2014).

And one of the sad realities of the country is that one out of every ten children dies before the age of five years from a disease that can be prevented according to the same source. The mindsets of some political leaders of the Burundi seem not to be safe from durable peace and prosperity destructive conflicts, and that seems to be a reality for many leaders due to egoism, discrimination, and exaggerated hunger for power and money. The same attitude that had made millions of Burundians lost their lives is still alive in many people minds, and real and total positive change is needed.

During the year 2015, while people could say that there were no wars in Burundi, many people lost their lives there, other were persecuted, and other more continue to live in fear and uncertainty. According to the 2014 report of the Amnesty International, the government of Burundi behaved violently vis-a-vis to the citizens to prevent the build-up to the 2015 presidential, legislative, and communal elections. There was an increase of violations of people's rights to freedom of association. The government also robbed people of their right for peaceful assembly; they harassed and intimidated some who were opposed to their will of eternalizing themselves on power.

The Amnesty International (2014) states,

> "Members of the Imbonerakure, the youth wing of the ruling party, the National Council for the Defense of Democracy-Forces for the Defense of Democracy (Conseil National Pour la Défense de la Démocratie–Forces pour la Défense de la Démocratie, CNDD-FDD), are perpetrating human rights abuses under the pretext of maintaining security at local level. The Imbonerakure have intimidated political opposition members, prevented political party meetings from going ahead and attacked members of the political opposition with impunity." (Amnesty International, 2014).

That is one of the challenges many peoples of the African countries have. Some political leaders have not understood yet that they cannot solve the problems of their countries with the behavior that continue to create more destructive problems.

The avarice and the embroidered egoism of political leaders will always create conflicts that are apt to destroy their nations. Unfortunately, the peace and prosperity for all destroying behaviors of many post-colonial political leaders of the countries of the AGLR started since the independence of AGLR countries, and there has never been any true change up to nowadays! And that sometimes begins with a single fake political leader or a small group of leaders who want to live very bigger in detriment of the general population. And later on, the mentality will be contaminated to the masses of ethnic followers. Why? The main reason may lay in the fact that followers mostly become like their leaders. It is just a contamination of attitude, and sometimes the whole community becomes involved negatively. Is that kind of attitude lead to durable peace and prosperity for all the communities of the AGLR as God intended it for all human beings?

Is that still possible in the middle of serious national confusion in which every politician seems to be egoistically running after something? What kind of attitude Burundians and other citizens of AGLR countries need to save their nations from earthly 'hell'? The next chapters of this book provide practical advises as fundamental principles that can bring peoples of AGLR to durable peace and prosperity for all if they are accurately applied to their daily livings in their respective communities.

Uganda

Uganda had been facing some interpersonal and intercultural communications challenges resulting from conflicts among the Ugandans due to their ethnic diversity. Although some conflicts have inter-ethnic aspects that they often hide, most of the conflicts that murder peace there have had dangerous consequences on the people of Uganda. And it can be argued that there are only two big ethnics groups in latent conflict in Uganda as in other countries of AGLR: the Nilotic and the Bantu peoples. Many people judge others by the shape of the noise or by the size (height) of their bodies, etc. That kind of behavior is very antiquated and will never help any leader to establish durable peace and national prosperity. Unfortunately, it has always been the case of all the other countries of AGLR; things that could enrich them are the things that are being used to divide them!

Uganda, as the other above-mentioned countries of the AGLR, also has a critical history of menaces, atrocities, killings, and human rights violation since its colonial era up to nowadays. Many Ugandans have been killed due to civil wars, unrest, and bad political regimes; and other continue to die. This country which accrued its independence in October 1962 and gained the status of Republic with the Kabaka (King) of Buganda (Mutesa II) as first President has never had true presidents or political leaders who can implement true democracy in the country. Almost all the post-independence political regimes (Obote regime, Idi Amin regime, Okello regime, and Museveni regime) have practically failed to lead Uganda towards durable peace and prosperity for all. During the Idi Amin regime, for example, many sources reported an estimate of about 300,000 to 500,000 people were murdered and many other more flee in foreign countries for their safety.

The Lord's Resistance Army (LRA), with its civil war, had also been accused many atrocious and violent acts among them it can be cited,

- ✓ recruiting children by force to serve as soldiers,
- ✓ taking children by force to work as sex slaves (about 30,000 children were taken by force),

✓ the murder of innocent civilians,

✓ mutilation, kidnapping, and death (estimation of more than 100,000 peoples),

✓ and causing loss and displacement of civilians (estimation of about 1.6 million people from the Northern Uganda were displaced).

The northern province of Uganda and the other parts of AGLR (region neighboring Uganda) have suffered more about the LRA activities. Uganda, like Burundi and the other countries of the AGLR, have huge number of children who are suffering from malnutrition, people who are dying from curable illness, hunger, etc. (for more details about this go to chapter 5) while country's resources when managed wisely and honestly by leaders for the interest of all the Ugandan people could lead to the eradication of the main peace and prosperity destroyers and that would benefit all.

There have been many regional initiatives with good and interesting programs, projects, and protocols in the AGLR that seem to have had no positive impact on the durable peace and prosperity of the populations of the AGLR. They have failed to eradicate insecurity and to considerably reduce poverty. The minds of most people seem to remain favorable to the growth of 'seeds of conflicts' were planted in the minds of most people of AGLR since the early African migration and colonization up to genocide eras in the region.

In addition, the grown seeds of conflict in the minds of some peoples in the region have produced harmful and unhealthy fruits among which we may cite the organized and structural massive killing like genocide, construction of false identities and legitimacy, unproductive competitions among the intellectual elites, serious lack of rule of law, impunity, culture of violence, lack of justice, false reconciliation, trauma, poverty, insecurity of persons and their goods, stress and physical isolation, HIV/AIDS, spread of refugees, to just cite a few.

However, each of the four countries of the AGLR had its internal peace agreements that were to put an end to either genocides or civil wars. Here are some of agreements and protocols according to the country.

Rwanda

- ✓ Arusha Accord (Peace Agreement between the Government of the Republic of Rwanda and the Rwandese Patriotic Front) (1993)

Burundi

- ✓ The Pretoria Protocol on Political, Defense and Security Power Sharing in Burundi (10-08-2003)
- ✓ Power-sharing Agreement Between President Buyoya and Hutu parties (July 2001)
- ✓ Arusha Peace and Reconciliation Agreement for Burundi (08-28-2000)

Uganda

- ✓ Agreement between the Governments of Sudan and Uganda (December 1999)

✓ Agreement Between Government of Uganda and the Uganda National Rescue Front (UNRF II) (December 2002)

✓ Agreement Between Government of Uganda and the Uganda People's Democratic Movement (UDPM) (July 1990)

✓ Power-sharing Agreement Between Government and the National Resistance Army (NRA) (August 1986)

✓ Agreement Between the Governments of Uganda and Rwanda (November 2001)

Democratic Republic of the Congo

✓ Inter-Congolese National Dialogue Agreement (April 2003)

✓ Ceasefire Agreement (July – August 1999)

✓ Peace Agreement Between the Governments of the Republic of Rwanda and the Democratic Republic of the Congo on the Withdrawal of the Rwandan Troops from the Territory of the Democratic Republic of the Congo and the Dismantling of the Ex-FAR and Interahamwe Forces in the Democratic Republic of the Congo (DRC) (July 2002)

✓ Program of Implementation of the Peace Agreement Between the Governments of the Republic of Rwanda and the Democratic Republic of the Congo on the Withdrawal of the Rwandan Troops from the Territory of the Democratic Republic of the Congo and the Dismantling of the Ex-FAR and Interahamwe

Forces in the Democratic Republic of the Congo
(DRC) (July 2002)

✓ Agreement Between the Governments of the
Democratic Republic of the Congo and the
Republic of Uganda on Withdrawal of Ugandan
Troops from the Democratic Republic of the
Congo, Cooperation and Normalization of
Relations Between the Two Countries (September
2002)

Did all these agreements, protocols, and programs set the
countries of AGLR on the path of durable peace and
prosperity for all in the AGLR? Or they were just made
so that the parties in conflict may 'eat together' and
forget the future of their respective counties? Who is
blamed when political actors and militia leaders fail to

understand that they should work hand in hand to build the AGLR?

1.2. Overview of the Role Played by the USA, the UK, the France, and the Belgium in Some of the AGLR Atrocious Conflicts

"The ones I hold accountable for not understanding
and not rising above self-interest to a level of humanity
where every human counts and we're all the same are:
the British, the French, and the Americans. Self-interest,
political posturing, image dominated their decision
processes in regard to Rwanda."
(General Roméo Dallaire)

The role of some Western countries such as USA, UK, France, and Belgium has been understood and interpreted differently by different authors, ONGs, agencies, commentators, the political actors, peoples of the AGLR, etc. It may appear curious to find out that most of what is said about the role of these western countries in the AGLR, as argued by different category of people, seem to converge toward the same view point that the West had and has the capacity to solve the problems of the African Great Lakes Region (AGLR) have been facing since the colonial era up to nowadays. They seem to mean that the USA, UK, France, and Belgium had the ease to stop or prevent the 1972 genocide in Burundi, the LRA Rebel movement in Uganda, the post-independence ethnic discrimination in the countries of the AGLR, the 1994 genocide in Rwanda, the first and second 'liberation wars' in DRC, and many other atrocious acts committed in these four countries of the AGLR. And by doing that, those western countries can lead the region towards durable peace and prosperity for all.

The following authors may serve as example among the many other researchers about the atrocious events of the

AGLR who show proofs or evidence of USA, UK, France, and Belgium involvement or inaction in DRC, Rwanda, Burundi, and Uganda. They all seem to put that the responsibility of these western countries is huge mainly in the genocidal killings of Rwanda that touched the whole AGLR. Jacques Morel (2017) shows, his book, 'La France au cœur du génocide des Tutsi', that before the 1994 Rwandan genocide the Rwandan Army was almost led by France and operated thanks to their aids.

L'Association Survie (2007) also shows in their book 'La complicité de la France dans le génocide des Tutsi au Rwanda : 15 ans après, 15 questions pour comprend' that the genocide of Tustis in Africa was not African only by the fact that the international community bears the responsibility of inaction and France is responsible of by the fact that country was supporting the regime that organized the genocidal killings in Rwanda.

The same reality is inscribed by Collombat & Servenay (2014) in their book "'Au nom de la France". Guerres Secrètes' ; they show that the French soldiers had been at war in Rwanda since August 5th, 1990, fighting on behalf of the late Habyarimana regime against a group of about 3,000 soldiers who attacked from Uganda and led by Fred Rwigyema.

In his article about the role of Britain in the 1994 Rwandan genocide, Martis (2017) summarize it showing that the Britain used its diplomatic weight to severely reduce the UN force by the fact that their ambassador to the UN, Sir David Hannay, proposed that and the US agreed on the proposition; he shows that the Britain also helped to ensure the delay of other plans for intervention which allowed the Rwandans to continue killing each other; he also engraves that the Britain made sure the word 'genocide' is not used to prevent any UN international pressure from helping put an end to the killings in Rwanda.

Many people in the AGLR believe that their political leaders have strong support from Western countries that make them behave the way they do; thus the supporters can influence the mentalities and characters of the so called political leaders to bring durable peace and prosperity for all in their respective countries! About the 1994 genocidal killings in Rwanda, Point (2011) puts,

"May 25th, President Clinton, in a speech about American policy on humanitarian action, says: "Whether we get involved... in the end must depend on the cumulative weight of the American interests at stake." ... "As the killings continued, the French government continued to supply weapons through eastern Zaire (DR Congo). President Francois Mitterrand said, "In such countries, genocide is not too important." (reported in the newspaper Le Figaro)" (Point, 2011).

It seems that many people in the AGLR have been expecting so much from some Western countries to build a better future for their countries. They also have been blaming some countries of the West for their failure to intervene in different atrocious situations in the AGLR to stop possible disasters. The reality here is that even some leaders with important responsibilities in the AGLR seem to manifest the same mentality as if some countries like USA, UK, France, and Belgium have the very first word to say about the countries of the AGLR (DRC, Rwanda, Burundi, Uganda).

Are the USA, UK, France, and Belgium the deciders of the fate of the AGLR? Are they the main root cause of the genocides, civil wars, rapes, famines, etc. in the AGLR? Are they aids and interventions in the AGLR to be considered as one of the fundamentals for durable peace and prosperity in the region? Should they be considered as 'gods' or worshiped by some political leaders and/or many people of the AGLR instead of worshiping the Only and True God the Creator of the universe as believed by about 95 percent of the populations of in Christian, Muslim, and African Traditional regions of the region? How should the people of the AGLR consider the countries of the West such as

USA, UK, France, and Belgium? What role have they been playing in the AGLR? What role can they play in the process of durable peace and prosperity in the AGLR? Are they one of the fundamentals for durable peace and prosperity for all in the AGLR?

The examination of some of the main historical interventions of the USA, UK, France, and Belgium in some of the major atrocious events and difficult situations of the AGLR seem crucial at this point. In fact, it has been reported by diverse sources that during the main atrocious events of the AGLR have always been backed by some westerners or western countries giving them a kind of responsibility for has been happening so far in the region.

And so many people construct their beliefs on reports, comments, and assumptions that are made about the relationship between USA, UK, France, and Belgium without deep discernment. Some historic facts about the 1994 Rwanda genocide maybe shed light on what we wanna suggest here. When the airplane of the late Rwandan President Habyarimana was shot down near Kigali Airport killing him and the late Burundian President Cyprien Ntaryamira on April, 6th 1994, the Rwandan Armed Forces (FAR) and the Hutu militia (the Interahamwe) began the killing of Tutsi and moderate Hutu politicians the following day as if 'plane shooting' was equivalent to 'civilian killing'!

And how such killings could just happen without being planned ahead? To the open eyes of the world as witness of that event, no USA, UK, French, and Belgium took a fire-gun or machete to take part in the killings; otherwise, ten Belgian soldiers of UNAMIR who were guarding the moderate Hutu Prime Minister Agata were tortured and murdered after being tricked into giving up their weapons (Point, 2011). April, 8th 1994, General Romeo Dallaire, head of the UN peace-keeping, made an urgent request to the UN Security Council to double force to 5,000 people; unfortunately, he was told to make no intervention in the conflict. As a matter of fact, French, Belgium, and the USA sent troops in Rwanda to rescue their citizens. No African is rescued including the civilian Rwandans! That is what amazed of the 1994 Rwandan genocide survivors, Innocent Rwililiza, who put,

> "The French knew that a genocide was in preparation, since they advised our army. They supposedly just did not believe it... One day, in

Nyamata, armored cars finally came to collect the white Fathers. In the main street, the interahamwe believed that they had come to punish them and they fled, yelling at one another that the Whites were here to kill them. The tanks did not even stop for a Primus break to have a laugh about the misunderstanding. Also, a few weeks later, the Whites sent professional photographers to show the world how we had been massacred. So you may understand that into the survivors' hearts there slipped a feeling of abandonment that shall never go away, but I do not want to anger you with this." (Cited by Point, V. (2011) – From *The Survivors Speak*, by Jean Hatzfeld).

What happened in Rwanda during the Rwandan genocide of 1994 is that after seven days of killing on April 15th in Rwanda, the Belgium withdrew its soldiers from the UN force; and after eleven days of killing on April 19th, the USA and the UN Security Council decided to withdraw 90 percent of the UN peacekeepers in Rwanda.

So, on April 21st the UN peacekeepers in Rwanda were reduced to 270 soldiers; only the New Zealand, Nigeria, and the Czech Republic soldiers stayed in Rwanda to support the work of trying to stop violence in the country. And it was reported that "General Anyidoho, a Ghanaian, refuses to leave Rwanda, disobeying Ghanaian law and UN central command, but supporting UNAMIR and Dallaire and ordinary Rwandans." (Point, 2011).

Moreover, there are several historic events that many people consider when trying to responsibilize or to show how much the UN and some western countries are responsible for the worst that has been happening to people of the AGLR. Some of them are mentioned in the following points.

✓ The King Leopold II of Belgium was reported in July 1890 for mass violation of human rights by George Washington Williams, an American Civil War soldier, Christian minister, politician, lawyer, journalist, and writer on African-American history, who came to the Congo (DRC) to establish a program that could enable the African-Americans to work in Africa. He was surprised by what King Leopold's agents were doing to Congolese and that disappointed him; he wrote a report about that to the US President in October 1890 and letter on an open letter to Leopold II. Can that be considered that as the first denouncement of the Belgium peace and prosperity destroying interventions in the AGLR?

✓ The Belgium and the USA through its CIA were said to be the main planners and perpetrators of the first prime minister of Congo (DRC), Patrice Lumumba, in whom many people hoped could lead the country to durable peace and prosperity. Many authors have written about that fact showing that there are enough evidence to prove it. For example, Whitelaw puts,

> "Today, new evidence suggests Belgium, Congo's former colonialist ruler, was the mastermind. According to The Assassination of Lumumba, a book published recently in Belgium by sociologist Ludo de Witte, Belgian operatives directed and carried out the murder, and even helped dispose of the body. Belgian authorities are investigating, but officials admit de Witte's account appears accurate."

✓ In Rwanda, the Belgian colonialists introduced an ethnic identification system by giving to Rwandans identity cards (ID) according to their ethnics; that was done to be able to distinguish the superior ethnic group members from the interior ones. And General Roméo Dallaire witnessed genocidal killings in Rwanda based on

ID cards introduced by Belgians. He puts, "You had to have an ID card and on it was written either Hutu or Tutsi. If you were a Tutsi they took you aside and slaughtered you right there. Ditches were full of bodies wriggling of all ages as these drunken guys kept it up and so if you didn't have a card it was a 50-50 chance." (United States Holocaust Memorial Museum – USHMM – 2002).

✓   During the Mobutu regime in Zaire (DRC), the USA knew very well that Mobutu was not leading his country democratically; the USA knew Mobutu's atrocious dictatorial acts and mismanagement of the country's wealth, but continued to support him. Are not they responsible for what Mobutu did for his country for not stopping to support him? "12.32. The US has long been involved in central Africa and the Great Lakes Region, its unstinting support for Zaire's Mobutu and (together with apartheid South Africa) UNITA, the rebel movement that is the sworn enemy of the Angolan government, being the best-known examples." (IPEP, nd).

•   General Dellaire asked the on May 5th, 1994 to jam the hate radio that was broadcasting to incite people for genocide in Rwanda; the UN asked the USA, but his demand was rejected saying it was too expensive adding that any act of silencing the RTLM might violate government of Rwanda's sovereignty to control the radio broadcasts in its territory.

- The UN asked the USA to supply 50 armored personnel carriers in May 17th; an argument on who will pay for them made a delay and these arrived in July.

- The 3,000 French soldiers who went to Rwanda in June 22nd 1994, after a UN Security Council approval of their 60 day mission, set up the 'Turquoise Zone' in North-East Rwanda used as a safety zone for the Hutu; so, the French the Hutu soldiers and the Interahamwe to keep their weapons and the transmitter for RTLM continued broadcasting from the Turquoise Zone! The sad fact is that is that the Hutu soldiers and the Interahamwe were allowed to keep their weapons when crossing the boarder to enter the eastern part of DRC fleeing the FPR force that was getting more control of the Rwanda Territory.

It maybe important to mention here that I have eye witnessed this situation in the East of DRC in the town of Bukavu where one of our neighbors lost his life for giving rent to a Hutu family that fled from Rwandan Turquoise Zone. That Rwandan family left a landmine in the rented house when they ran away from the first war of Congo of 1997 led by the late Laurent Kabila with the support of the Tutsi; So, when the son of the owner of the house tried to get in the room, the landmine tore him into pieces! Many other people of DRC have been reported dying by the weapons that the French allowed the Hutu soldiers and the Interahamwe to keep in the Turquoise Zone.

● Just after the 100 days of genocidal killings in Rwanda, people could see airplanes loaded, armored vehicles, water tankers,... carrying humanitarian to the refugee camps on Rwanda's borders; in the camps, among the people who were concerned about the aid were thousands of innocent people, thousands of genocide perpetrators, and many other who were still armed and who continued to cause fear and brutality. Is the rescuing aid more important than the preventing one? Did some of the Western countries and the UN rescue the genocide perpetrators so that they may organize new killings, rapes, and sounders in the DRC? Where they rescued so that the post-genocide regime in Rwanda and its allies may find a pretext to get in the DRC militarily?

●   The International Criminal Tribunal for Rwanda (ICTR) is set up in November 1994 in Arusha, Tanzania, after a vote by the UN Security Council; for the killings that happened in 100 days in Rwanda with a population of, the ICTR had 5,800 days of proceedings, 93 people indicted, 61 sentenced, 14 acquitted, more than 3,000 witness accounts, and a cost of around USD 2 billions (Leithead, 2015 – BBC News, Africa Correspondent). Why such large sum of money wasn't spent by donors in Rwanda prior to the 1994 genocide to prevent it from happening? Do they really have much responsibility for the killings that happened in Rwanda that can be considered as one of opened doors that helped to create a multitudes of rebel groups and militias in DRC killing millions of Congolese?

- There were critics about the International Criminal Court in 2014 of having spent about USD 1 billion in 12 years and only with two convictions; and that concerned only Congolese warlords (Davenport, 2014). What about the other warlords that have been acting to make the AGLR a 'hell'? What about the bosses and partners of those warlords that were reported to work in partnership with them in a systematically organized plunder in the AGLR on cost of the blood of millions innocent people? The following are the lists of names of persons and companies cited in the 'Final report of the Panel of Experts on the Illegal Exploitation of Natural Resources and Other Forms of Wealth of the Democratic Republic of the Congo' in 2002.

- Persons for whom the Panel recommends a travel ban and financial restrictions (including their date of birth and designations)

1 AHMAD Ali Said 01.03.1959 Businessman

2 AHMAD Ahmad Ali 01.01.1929

3 AHMAD Imad Businessman

4 AHMAD Said Ali 09.04.1935 Businessman

5 AHMAD Hassan 21.05.1957 Businessman

6 AHMAD Moussa Ahmad

7 AHMAD Nazem 05.01.1965 Businessman

8 AKHIMANZA Steven K. Businessman

9 AL-SHANFARI Thamer Said Ahmed 03.01.1968 00000999 (Oman) Chairman & Managing Director ORYX Group and ORYX Natural Resources

10 BOUT Victor Anatoljevitch BUTT, BONT, BUTTE, BOUTOV, SERGITOV Vitali 13.01.1967 or ??? 21N0532664 29N0006765 21N0532664 21N0557148 44N3570350 Dealer and transporter of weapons and minerals

11 BREDENKAMP John Arnold 11.08.1940 Businessman

12 BURUNDI Colonel UPDF

13 DAURAMANZI Charles Shareholder MBC

14 ENGOLA Sam Businessman

15 FORREST George A. Businessman

16 GATETE Edward Officer RPA; Operation Congo Desk

17 HORN Heckie Manager Saracen Uganda Ltd

18 KABANDA Emmanuel Officer RPA; Operation Congo Desk

19 KABAREBE James Chief of Staff RPA; Former Chief of Staff DRC; in charge of Congo Desk

20 KABASELE TSHINEU Frédéric Manager COMIEX, representative of COSLEG

21 KALUME NUMBI Denis General, shareholder SENGA SENGA

22 KARIM Peter Officer UPDF

23 KATUMBA MWANKE Augustin Minister of Presidency, DRC

24 KAZADI NYEMBWE Didier Director Agence National de Renseignements DRC

25 KAZINI James Chief of Staff, Maj. General UPDF

26 KHANAFER Nahim Businessman

27 KIBASSA MALIBA Politician, former Minister of Mines, shareholder SENGA SENGA

28 KITEMBO Gertrude Businesswoman

29 KONGOLO Mwenze Minister DRC, shareholder SENGA SENGA

30 MANASE SIMBA Businessman

31 MAWAPANGA Mwana Nanga, Ambassador DRC in Harare

32 MAYOMBO Nobel Chief Military Intelligence (CMI) in Uganda

33 MNANGAGWA DAMBUDZO Emmerson Speaker of Parliament ZIMBABWE

34 MOYO Mike Wing Commander ZDF

35 MOYO Sibusio Bd-Gen (Rtd) ZDF

36 MUAMBA NOZI Richard MWAMBA NOZY Congolese diamond trader; Counterfeiter

37 MUNYUZA Dan Colonel RPA; In charge of security DRC (96-98)

38 MWENZE KONGOLO Minister National Security, DRC

39 NUMBI KALUME Denis Minister of Planning and Reconstruction DRC

40 NZIZA Jack Officer RPA

41 OKOTO LOLAKOMBE Jean-Charles PDG MIBA

42 OMARI HADJI Businessman

43 OTAFIRE KAHINDA Colonel UPDF

44 MARINUS Anthony Manager Eagle Wings

45 PISKUNOV Anatol Businessman

46 PISKUNOVA Valentina Businesswoman

47 RUCHACHA BIKUMU Felicien Businessman

48 RUPRAH Sanjivan Samir Nasr Medhi Khan Businessman

49 RWIGEMA Alfred Manager Eagle Wings

50 SALIM SALEH AKANDWA NAHO Caleb Lt General (Ret.) UPDF

51 SHEFER Niko Nico 25.12.1950 7616225 (Israel) 6651101 (Israel) Businessman

52 SMIERCIAK Ronald S. Manager Eagle Wings

53 YUMBA MONGA Manager GECAMINES

54 ZVINAVASHE GAVA MUSUNGWA Vitali

- **Business enterprises considered by the Panel to be in violation of the OECD Guidelines for Multinational Enterprises (with their type of business and country)**

1 AFRICAN TRADING CORPORATION Sarl Trading of natural resources from DRC SOUTH AFRICA

2 AFRIMEX Coltan trading UK

3 AHMAD DIAMOND CORPORATION Diamond trading BELGIUM

4 A.H. PONG & Sons Import-Export SOUTH AFRICA

5 A. KNIGHT INTERNATIONAL Ltd Assaying UK

6 A & M MINERALS and METALS Ltd Trading minerals UK

7 ALEX STEWART (Assayers) Ltd Assaying UK

8 AMALGAMATED METAL CORPORATION Plc Trading coltan UK

9 AMERICA MINERAL FIELDS (AMFI) Mining USA

10 ANGLO AMERICAN Plc Mining UK

11 ANGLOVAAL MINING Ltd Mining SOUTH AFRICA

12 ARCTIC INVESTMENT Investment UK

13 ASA DIAM Diamond trading BELGIUM

14 ASA INTERNATIONAL BELGIUM

15 ASHANTI GOLDFIELDS Mining GHANA

16 AVIENT AIR Private military company ZIMBABWE

17 BANRO CORPORATION Mining SOUTH AFRICA

18 BARCLAYS BANK Banking UK

19 BAYER A.G. Chemical industry GERMANY

20 B.B.L. Banking BELGIUM

21 BELGOLAISE Banking BELGIUM

22 CABOT CORPORATION Tantalum processing USA

23 CARSON PRODUCTS Commercialization of resources of the DRC SOUTH AFRICA

24 CHEMIE PHARMACIE HOLLAND Financial and logistical support to EWRI NETHERLANDS

25 COGECOM Coltan trading BELGIUM

26 C. STEINWEG NV Freight Forwarders BELGIUM

27 DARA FOREST Timber exploitation THAILAND

28 DAS AIR Airline company UK

29 DE BEERS Diamond mining and trading UK

30 DIAGEM BVBA Diamond trading BELGIUM

31 EAGLE WINGS RESOURCES INTERNATIONAL Exploitation coltan from the DRC USA

32 ECHOGEM Diamond trading BELGIUM

33 EGIMEX BELGIUM

34 ENTREPRISE GENERALE MALTA FORREST Construction, Mining, Trading DRC

35 EUROMET Coltan trading UK

36 FINCONCORD SA Coltan trading from DRC SWITZERLAND

37 FINMINING Coltan trading from DRC SAINT KITTS

38 FIRST QUANTUM MINERALS Mining CANADA

39 FLASHES OF COLOR Diamond trading USA

40 FORTIS Banking BELGIUM

41 GEORGE FORREST INTERNATIONAL AFRIQUE Management DRC

42 HARAMBEE MINING CORPORATION Mining CANADA

43 H.C. STARCK GmbH & Co KG Processing coltan GERMANY

44 IBRYV AND ASSOCIATES LLC Diamond trading SWITZERLAND

45 INTERNATIONAL PANORAMA RESOURCES Corp Mining CANADA

46 ISCOR Mining SOUTH AFRICA

47 JEWEL IMPEX Bvba Diamond trading BELGIUM

48 KABABANKOLA MINING COMPANY Mining ZIMBABWE

49 KEMET ELECTRONICS CORPORATION Capacitor manufacture USA

50 KHA International AG Minerals trading and exploitation GERMANY

51 KINROSS GOLD CORPORATION Mining USA

52 K & N Project development BELGIUM

53 KOMAL GEMS NV Diamond trading BELGIUM

54 LUNDIN GROUP Mining BERMUDA

55 MALAYSIAN SMELTING CORPORATION Coltan processing MALAYSIA

56 MASINGIRO GmbH Minerals trading GERMANY

57 MELKIOR RESOURCES Inc Mining CANADA

58 MERCANTILLE CC Trading in natural resources from DRC SOUTH AFRICA

59 MINERAL AFRIKA Limited Trading in natural resources from DRC UK

60 NAC KAZATOMPROM Tantalum processing KAZAKHSTAN

61 NAMI GEMS Diamond trader BELGIUM

62 NINGXIA NON-FERROUS METALS SMELTER Tantalum processing CHINA

63 OM GROUP Inc Mining USA FINLAND

64 OPERATION SOVEREIGN LEGITIMACY (OSLEG) Pvt Ltd Commercial interests ZIMBABWE in the DRC ZIMBABWE

65 ORION MINING Inc Mining SOUTH AFRICA

66 PACIFIC ORES METALS AND CHEMICALS Ltd Coltan trading HONG KONG

67 RAREMET Ltd Coltan trading from DRC SAINT KITTS

68 SARACEN Security company SOUTH AFRICA

69 SDV TRANSINTRA Transport FRANCE

70 SIERRA GEM DIAMONDS Diamond trading BELGIUM

71 SLC GERMANY GmbH Coltan transport GERMANY

72 SOGEM Coltan trading BELGIUM

73 SPECIALITY METALS COMPANY SA Coltan trading BELGIUM

74 STANDARD CHARTERED BANK Banking U.A.E.

75 SWANEPOEL Construction SOUTH AFRICA

76 TENKE MINING CORPORATION Mining CANADA

77 THORNTREE INDUSTRIES (Pvt) Ltd Provides capital to MBC ZIMBABWE

78 TRACK STAR TRADING 151 (Pty) Ltd Exploitation and trading minerals DRC SOUTH AFRICA

79 TRADEMET SA Coltan trading BELGIUM

80 TREMALT Ltd Mining British Virgin Islands

81 TRINITECH INTERNATIONAL Inc Coltan trading and exploitation USA

82 TRIPLE A DIAMONDS Diamond trading BELGIUM

83 UMICORE International Metals and Materials Group BELGIUM

84 VISHAY SPRAGUE Capacitor manufacture USA and ISRAEL

85 ZINCOR Mining SOUTH AFRICA

- **Companies on which the Panel recommends the placing of financial restrictions (including their addresses, type of business, and principal officers).**

1 AHMAD DIAMOND CORPORATION

ANTWERP BELGIUM Diamond trading Mr.

AHMAD Imad

2 ASA DIAM ANTWERP BELGIUM Diamond

trading Mr. AHMAD Ali Said

3 BUKAVU AVIATION TRANSPORT DRC Airline

company Mr. BOUT Victor

4 BUSINESS AIR SERVICE DRC Airline company

Mr. BOUT Victor

5 COMIEX-CONGO KINSHASA DRC Mr.

KABASELE TSHINEU Frederic

6 CONGO HOLDING DEVELOPMENT

COMPANY DRC Trading and exploitation of natural

resources DRC Mr. Félicien RUCHACHA BIKUMU

Mrs. Gertrude KITEMBO

7 CONMET UGANDA and DRC Coltan trading Mr.

Salim Saleh Mr. and Mrs. PISKUNOV

8 COSLEG ZIM and DRC Joint-venture COMIEX
and OSLEG Mr. KABASELE TSHINEU Frédéric
ZVINAVASHE Gava MUSUNGWA Vitalis

9 EAGLE WINGS RESOURCES
INTERNATIONAL PO BOX 6355 Kigali, Rwanda
Exploitation coltan from the DRC Mr. Alfred
RWIGEMA Mr. Anthony MARINUS Mr. Ronald S.
SMIERCIAK Tel: +250.51.17.25

10 ENTERPRISE GENERAL MALTA FORREST
Exploitation Cobalt, Copper in DRC Mr. George
FORREST

11 EXACO Exploitation Cobalt, Copper in the DRC

12 GREAT LAKES GENERAL TRADE BP 3737
KIGALI, RWANDA Mineral trading Maj Dan
MUNYUZA Mr. E. GATETE Mr. Steven K.
AKHIMANZI Tel/Fax: +250.78.792

13 GREAT LAKES METALS Kigali, Rwanda
Mineral trading

14 GROUP GEORGE FORREST Exploitation Cobalt
and Copper Mr. George FORREST

15 MINERALS BUSINESS COMPANY Boulevard Du 30 Juin, Immeuble exSCIBE, Kinshasa, DRC Mineral trading Mr. KABASELE TSHINEU Frederic Lt General ZVINAVASHE Gava Musungwa Vitalis Mr. Charles DAURAMANZI

16 OKAPI AIR ODESSA AIR Uganda Airline company Mr. BOUT Victor

17 OPERATION SOVEREIGN LEGITIMACY (OSLEG) Pvt Ltd Harare, Zimbabwe Commercial interests ZIM in DRC Lt General ZVINAVASHE Gava Musungwa Vitalis

18 ORYX NATURAL RESOURCES DRC Diamond exploitation in the DRC Mr. AL-SHANFARI Thamer Said Ahmed

19 RWANDA ALLIED PARTNERS Kigali, Rwanda Mineral trading Mr. Hadji OMARI Mr. Simba MANASE

20 RWANDA METALS Kigali, Rwanda Mineral trading

21 SARACEN UGANDA Ltd Uganda Security Company Lt General (Rtd) Salim Saleh Mr. Heckie

22 SIERRA GEM DIAMONDS ANTWERP BELGIUM Diamond trading Mr. AHMAD Said Ali Mr. AHMAD Hassan Mr. AHMAD Nazem

23 TANDAN GROUP SOUTH AFRICA Holding Mr. Niko SHEFER

24 THORNTREE INDUSTRIES (Pvt) Ltd Provides capital to MBC Mr. Niko SHEFER

25 TREMALT Ltd Exploitation cobalt and copper Mr. John Arnold BREDENKAMP

26 TRINITY INVESTMENT GROUP DRC and UGANDA Exploitation resources and tax fraud Mr. NGOLA Sam General KAZINI

27 TRIPLE A DIAMONDS ANTWERP BELGIUM Diamond trading Mr. AHMAD Moussa Ahmad Mr. AHMAD Ahmad Ali

28 TRISTAR Kigali, Rwanda Holding FPR

29 VICTORIA GROUP DRC and UGANDA Exploitation resources and tax fraud Lt General (Rtd) Salim Saleh Mr. KHANAFER Nahim

136

- France was reported to protect the interests of 'francophone' nations by supporting the Habyarimana Regime against the RPF invasion from Uganda that had support from 'anglophone' block. "12.15. Immediately upon the RPF invasion from Uganda into Rwanda in October 1990, the French government committed itself to defend and support the Habyarimana regime. Among the usual variety of French motives, francophonie unquestionably played a key role." (International Panel of Eminent Personalities – IPEP, nd).

- "Two days after that French aircraft started to land in Kigali. I had 45 minutes notice that they were coming in. Belgian aircraft landed the next day. Italians landed four days later and there were 300 US forces in Bujumbura and there was a ship of Marines off of Dar-es-Salaam about 800 to 1,000. They came in to evacuate the white men and the odd Rwandan who was politically well suited to what they want. As an example the French evacuated the bulk of the president's family who were not necessarily the nicest people on earth. And so all the expatriates within five days picked up what they had, left the Rwandans who had served them for years, decades, who raised their kids, left them to be slaughtered behind and went back to Brussels and Paris and all these other places."

- In his article about the respectability of USA in the atrocities committed in the AGLR, Yaa-Lengi puts,

> "Let me introduce you to the HORRORS that are seldom spoken about and are never mentioned during the "State of the Union" addresses of US presidents since Bill Clinton; horrors that the American government under Bill Clinton was part

of triggering them; horrors that have claimed more human lives since World War II with estimates going from 8 to over 10 million lives; horrors that started in Rwanda (1990-1995) then have continued unabated in the huge Congo-Zaire (DRC) from 1996 until now. Every American MUST become acquainted with these horrors, because, as we claim God and country, God sees and knows about them, so we, "country", should know about them for ourselves" (Yaa-Lengi, 2015).

Yaa-Lengi is an American who appears to be among many peoples of the West and Africa who strongly that the USA as a superpower on planet earth can lead the AGLR towards durable peace and prosperity for all. The USA claims God to be their trust! Who the countries of the AGLR should claim? The USA? The UK? The France? The Belgium? From chapter 10 to 15 of this book, there are specific detailed messages that give clear suggested answers to these questions with a deep understanding of people's problems in the AGLR.

1.3. Leaders of the AGLR Should Rethink 'Durable Peace and Prosperity' in a New Way

Leaders in the African Great Lakes Region, regardless their areas of work, need to reflect on how well they should behave in their day to day interactions with the populations to make sure that what they say and do is not teaching people conflicts. As it will be shown in this book, some leaders in the region have helped people to organize civil wars and genocides to happen particularly the religious political leaders.

For example, it can be amazing to learn that religious leaders had much responsibility in the genocide that happened in Rwanda in 1994 the result of which is still affecting the whole AGLR today; it is also the same in DRC where some religious leaders have been playing important role in secret to nurture conflicts or civil wars. In North Kivu, province of DR Congo, a chief rebel leader said to be a pastor was using the Bible to justify their civil war. And in Uganda, there was a civil war said to be fighting the holy war using the Bible to justify its killings, rapes, and other kinds of atrocities made in North Uganda. This situation that started long ago with the colonization of African countries continues up to nowadays.

The early Christian missionaries used the Bible to teach poverty, ignorance, and blind obedience to people in the African Great Lakes Region to maintain the power of the colonial regime. That situation inherited by some false leaders in Christian churches, in political parties, in governments, and in rebel movements as a 'precious colonial legacy' to enrich themselves doesn't make any initiative for durable peace for the region possible.

That is why all religions in the AGLR need to re-teach their members the true message of their sacred books about durable peace and prosperity for all. By the way, some of the chapters of this book will strongly emphasis on religious teachings on durable peace and property as stated in the sacred books of Christianity and Islam. Some passages concerning durable peace and prosperity in Quran (the sacred book of Islam) and Bible (sacred book of Christianity) will be quoted to show how these two books strongly recommend people to prosper and to live in harmony and peace in their communities.

We mostly consider these two books by the fact that Islam and Christianity represent an important fraction of the total population of the AGLR. That is why we are going to put more emphasis on Christianity which has more followers than Islam; about 80% in the AGLR follow Christianity as their religion, and about 10% follow the teachings of Islam (The World Fact Book). All Christians of the AGLR ought to have the same understanding of the teaching of the Bible on peace and prosperity by putting them into practice and by teaching them to others.

The Bible puts "Take the teachings that you heard me proclaim in the presence of many witnesses, and entrust them to reliable people, who will be able to teach others also." (2 Timothy 2:2). Thus, the ten fundamentals for durable peace and prosperity for all in the AGLR suggested in this book may be summarized in the following then principles.

- Everybody in AGLR should have accurate 'self-awareness' and 'true knowledge' of their own land and its people.
- There should be a positive change of negative mentality for every single individual of the AGLR starting from the political leaders.
- The study and application of laws related to peace and prosperity is a must for the countries of the AGLR.
- The promotion of a social justice free from impunity should be a reality for the people of the AGLR.

- There should be healing of inner wounds created by chronic lies, permanent fear, feeling guilt, hatred, and long-lasting anger against people.

- The accurate study and use of religious teachings about peace and prosperity (Christianity, Islam, and African Traditional Religion) are crucial in the AGLR.

- The AGLR need a constructive family education and proficient formal education that are to be used as real tools for community and national peace and prosperity for all.

- The promotion of intercultural communications for all the communities of the AGLR is necessary.

- A good management of external aids (Foreign or international Aids) should be operational in the AGLR. People should not consider foreign resources as main contributors to durable peace and prosperity for all in the AGLR.

- There should be a true reverence to God followed by hard and smart work in the AGLR.

We hope that lovers of durable peace and prosperity in the AGLR will carefully examine these ten principles for durable peace and prosperity. We need to revisit our beliefs and hopes. Is it going to be 'save us Jesus' or 'save us West'?

However, the fact that the USA, France, Belgium, and the UK have been involved in many of the historic events of the AGLR, as it was shown in the previous paragraphs, tends to make many people in the World, and mainly the AGLR believe that durable peace and prosperity for has much to do with these Western countries than the concerned countries of the region. In this book, it is shown that no Western country is part of the fundamentals for durable peace and prosperity for all in the AGLR. And the West doesn't hold the destiny of the people of the AGLR in their hands. Now, are the USA,

UK, France, Belgium one of the causes of the atrocities and troubles that made millions of people suffer and other lost their lives in the AGLR?

More light in answer to this question is provided in the next chapters of this book with a non-affirmative argumentation. Leaders and followers, teachers and students, bosses and servants, soldiers and civilians, young and old persons, women and men, of all the races, ethnics, and tribes, etc. all are called to deeply think about the reality of the principles inscribed in this book. When correctly applied to people daily lives, due to the power they bear, these principles can change the political and socioeconomic disastrous situations that have been ravaging the African Great Lake Region (AGLR) since their assistance as States.

Chapter Two
Overview of the Republic of Rwanda

2.1. Country Profile

● **Location and Population**

Rwanda is a small country of African Great Lakes Region (AGLR) covering an area of 26,338 sq km (10,169 sq miles). The Rwandan census of 15 August 1991 enumerated the population at 7,142,755 (Gourou, 2009). These are figures of this country before the 1994 genocide; although thousands of people lost their lives in Rwanda during the genocide area, the after-genocide estimation of the population (of mid-2008 by the United Nations) was 10,009,000. This makes a density of 380.0 inhabitants per sq km.

● Official languages are French and English.

- National language: Kinyerwanda.

- Climate of the country: tropical.

- Neighboring countries: Uganda at the north, Democratic Republic of Congo to the west, Burundi to the south, and Tanzania to the East.

Rwanda called 'a country of thousand hills' due to its numerous hills that provide an outstanding beauty to the land.

- **Population of Rwanda**

Population by 5-year Age Groups and Sex, 2010

Age	2010		
	Male	Female	Total
0 - 4	916,676	901,476	1,818,152
5 - 9	694,199	695,436	1,389,635
10 - 14	593,297	605,760	1,199,057
15 - 19	542,911	561,139	1,104,050
20 - 24	532,937	558,779	1,091,716
25 - 29	468,261	506,372	974,633
30 - 34	313,166	365,495	678,661
35 - 39	220,162	263,401	483,563
40 - 44	186,410	214,896	401,306
45 - 49	165,034	192,708	357,742
50 - 54	141,541	168,134	309,675
55 - 59	96,042	118,855	214,897
60 - 64	60,359	80,944	141,303
65 - 69	36,208	56,981	93,189
70 - 74	28,692	44,238	72,930
75 - 79	18,530	27,305	45,835
80+	15,028	21,454	36,482
Total	5,029,453	5,383,373	10,412,826

Source : Rwanda, National Population Projections update 2009

● Map of the Republic of Rwanda

Source: United Nations – Department of peacekeeping operations –
Cartographic section, January 2014

2.2. Natural Resources

✓ **Land and Agriculture**

The land of Rwanda is naturally blessed with high hills and mountains with an altitude varying between 900 m and 4.507 m. The country has an abundance of rainfall. Its climate is tropical temperate with an average annual temperature that varies between 16°C and 20°C. The variation of temperature is not significant. Rwanda does not have enough land for agricultural activities for its population. The average arable land is about 0.60 ha per household use (Twagiramungu, 2006).

The consequences of the scarcity of arable land in Rwanda are many. They include but not limited to over-exploitation of the available land and degradation of the natural environment that have a strong link with soil erosion. Because of the soil erosion, the soil that was initially insufficient for the population is losing it fertility and there is a risk of destruction of crops. That erosion constitutes a dangerous threat to the future of the country. It is assumed that the hydrous erosion reduces the capacity to feed 40,000 people per year and causes annual loss of about 15,000,000 tons of soil estimated at 945,200 tons of organic materials, 41,210 tons of nitrogen, 280 tons of phosphorus, and 3,055 tons of potassium for the whole country (Twagiramungu, 2006).

In Rwanda, agriculture is the most important sector that gives jobs to about 87 percent of the active population of the country. It contributes the economy of the country up to 46 percent of the GDP, and produces about 80 percent of the foreign exchanges (forex). (Kanyarukiga, 2004).

The total surface where agriculture is practiced covers 52 percent of the total surface area of the country and is cultivated permanently. The main produced crops are sorghum, beans, eleusine, maize, rice, wheat, barley, peas, soja-bean, peanut, sweet potato, potato, cassava, and banana. The cash crops are coffee, tea, and pyrethrum.

According to the Rwanda Skill Survey of 2012, efforts have been made by the government to boost the production in the agricultural sector of the country. A National Agricultural Policy (NAP) was formulated in 2004 and a Strategic Plan for Agricultural Transformation (PSTA) was established and updated in 2009. The content of the two documents was made effective by some programs like Crop Intensification Program (CIP), One

Cow per Poor Family (GIRINKA Program), and LWH Program (Land Husbandry, Water Harvesting and Hillside Irrigation). Regardless the strides made by the government of Rwanda to improve the agricultural sector, it is still exposed to serious challenges that that threaten its future. Some of those challenges include but not limited to over-cultivation of soil due to over-population relying on agriculture, soil erosion mainly in areas where 80 percent of arable land located, and large need of irrigation during the time of drought – irregular rains – landslides – and climate change.

The insufficient access to finance, the insufficient investment capital for farming, aggro-processing, and export development are other major challenges addressed in Rwanda Skill Survey 2012 on agriculture sector (RDB,

2012). So, to achieve more improvement in its agricultural sector, Rwanda is still having more to do in this crucial sector that constitutes the cornerstone of its national economy.

For example, to just mention a few of the many suggestions made by the Rwanda Skill Survey of 2012 we can cite the urgent need of trained technicians and artisans in the agricultural sector of the country. The suggested areas of training involved

- ✓ Agriculture Education & Extension,
- ✓ Horticulture,
- ✓ Food Safety and Security,
- ✓ Irrigation & Water Engineering,
- ✓ Plant Pathology,
- ✓ Veterinary Public Health & Meet Technology,
- ✓ Comprehensive Veterinary Medicine,

- ✓ Fisheries and Aquaculture Management,

- ✓ Leather Science & Technology,

- ✓ Agricultural Resource Management,

- ✓ Animal Nutrition & Feed Sciences,

- ✓ Poultry Science,

- ✓ Clinical Pathology & Laboratory Diagnostics,

- ✓ Veterinary Surgery,

- ✓ Animal Genetics & Breeding,

- ✓ Applied Veterinary Parasitology,

- ✓ Dry-land Resource Management,

- ✓ Agricultural Information & Technology and Management,

- ✓ Marketing and business management,

- ✓ and Agro-processing and packaging.

These suggestions that were made about Rwanda may also be relevant to other countries of AGLR.

In fact, the countries of the AGLR, instead of consecrating their strengths on sectors where the economies of their countries lay foundations, most of their political leaders focus on domains that are not really the cornerstones of durable peace and prosperity of a country. For instance, among the three traditional economic sectors (primary sector, secondary sector, and tertiary sector) only the tertiary economic sector attracts a huge number of people in the AGLR and most the leaders who focus much on primary sector do that for dishonest purpose like dig and sell the minerals for important sum of money that does not really benefit the general population.

That is why the degree of dependency to the foreign intervention of the countries of the AGLR will always be high and they will always be importing more than exporting if their people (in particular most of their leaders) are not ready for urgent positive change of mentality as we will discuss about it in chapter seven of this book.

✓ **Forests**

Rwanda has a diverse and abundant forestry reserve. It comprises ombrophile forests, gallery forests, and savannah. The fauna and the flora of the country are also rich and are mainly found in the three national parks of the country – Volcanoes National Park that gives home to the mountain gorillas, gorilla beringei, and other variety of plants and animal species – Nyungwe National Park with more than 1,200 species of flora and 275 species of birds – Akagera National Park with 900 species of plants and 90 mammals. These three national parks are among protected areas that generate revenues Rwanda thanks to the arrivals of tourists. More than 500 bird species are reported to exist in the country (Rufford, 2009). However, the relict and gallery forests of Rwanda are located in Gishwati forest that covers 600 ha, Mukura natural forest with 800 ha, relict forests and savannahs of the eastern province, etc.

But with the activities of human beings, the natural protected areas of the country have been reduced. They have lost about 50 percent of their original surface area during the last 40 years. For example, the Akagera National Part had a surface area of 250,000 ha at the time of its creation in 1934, but today its surface area is of 108,500 ha. The Volcanoes National Park had 34,000 ha at the time of its creation in 1925, but nowadays its surface area is 16,000 ha. The Nyungwe National Park that was created in 2005 with a surface area of 103,000 is also at risk of losing its surface area as other national parks.

How will the ecosystem of this country and that of the whole AGLR be in the next 50 years if more protective efforts are not made? Protecting human lives that depend on a good ecosystem in the AGLR also means protecting the rare species of the AGLR that exist nowhere else.

> "The presence of forest dependent birds' species and some plant species which are not found anywhere else in the country i.e. new species for Rwanda like Platylepis glandulosa and Malaxis weberbaneriana, Orchidaceae which are only known to exist in Congo and Uganda, explains well the importance of conserving these only remaining gallery forests in Rwanda." (Rufford, 2009).

The generations of people who survived the genocide in Rwanda are running the risk of a progressive silent-death that takes place every day with the deterioration of the ecology of the country. While the average population may not see the direct impact of such situation on future durable peace and prosperity of the nation, the informed population needs to raise awareness of the general population in to avoid the disastrous consequences of breaking laws that govern people's relationship with the environment. Otherwise, the country's natural capacity to support the life will be fading away progressively like a smoldering charcoal – the smock is not seen, but the fire is there – that nobody is putting off.

✓ **Fisheries**

Rwanda Ministry of Agriculture acknowledges that the Fishing industry and the Animal Feed Production sector are still at their infancy stage. The companies that are doing fish business in the country are the following Rwanda Fish Industry, Lakeside Fish Farm, Sopicaki Ltd, any many other cooperatives. The business of fish farming exists in Rwanda, but it is done on small area – on only 218 Ha and 718 cages operating in over 186 cooperatives with a membership of up to 6,269 people among them 2,551 females and 3,718 males (RAD & RDB, nd).

So, Rwanda is in need of a high Feed fish factory because the fish are in high demand in the country. The production of fish in Rwanda is not meeting the national

163

demand of its population. For example, the local market
estimated of having 12.5 million people have demands
that consist of almost 90 percent of Tilapia, 5 percent of
Sambaza, and 5 percent other types of fishes. Based on
FAO statistics in 200981, Rwanda's total catch was at
4,250 tons.

However, the number of people involved was estimated
at 35,700. 25,000 were fish farmers; 8,700 were
fishermen; and 3,000 were traders. Rwanda's 2008
survey shows that in 2008, total catch was at 3,119 MT.
10,612 households were engaged in the fishing industry.
Only 2,957 households had their own fish farms."
(Promar Consulting, 2012).

✓ **Livestock**

In Rwanda, there is a rearing of animals but it is dominated by domestic or family initiatives. Households have very small number of heads of animals. The Rwandan ministry of Agriculture data of 2006 showed that the country had increased the number of cows up to 60 percent from the year 2000 to 2005, the goats by 67 percent, the sheep by 195 percent, the porch 93 percent, the poultry 44 percent, and the rabbits by 67 percent. Regardless the effort made by the government of Rwanda to reduce poverty of its people through farming, there is a considerable environmental challenge. An important area of pastoral land exists, but it is exposed to bush-fire and trampling.

Also, the demographic pressure that hits the county does not also allow the farmers to extend far their farming activities. So, framing is practically difficult but farmers work hard to make sure their animals are having what is necessary to produce profits. The government of Rwanda in its Vision 2020 has several policies that aim the reduction of poverty; among the policies, the country has a vision of transforming the sector from subsistence to productive and market-oriented agriculture.

By the way, the Ministry of Agriculture has put in place an agricultural policy that has four main areas of intervention which are,

- the modernization and transformation of Agriculture,
- the development of important commodities,

- competitiveness of the products on the market,

- high entrepreneurship capacity of the farmers.

All the efforts of the government of Rwanda in the agricultural sector are contributing to the alleviation of poverty by stepping towards food security for the general population and income generating activities for farmers.

The contribution of the agricultural sector to the GDP in Rwanda is high; it is about 40 percent. The livestock also contributes to the GDP in terms of 8.8 percent. According to the Ministry of Agriculture's strategic plan of transformation of Agriculture in Rwanda of October 2004, the livestock population in Rwanda consisted of 991.697 cattle, 1.270.903 goats, 371.766 sheep, 211.918 pigs, 2.482.124 chicken and 498.401 rabbits and the level of animal products in tons is as follows; milk

97.981, meat 39.126, eggs 2.432, fish 7.612 and hides and skins 1.499. (Butera & Rutagwenda, 2004).

✓ **Mining**

Rwanda is a country naturally poor in terms of minerals. However, the Rwandan Ministry of Trade and Industry reports some export revenues in the mining sector which was recently privatized. The figures of different years show that there was an increase of revenue. From US$32M in 2004 to US$93M in 2008, to US$56M in 2009. "Still, mining has been the largest revenue earner in terms of export products, for the past six years (2004 – 2009). In 2010, mining sector export revenues increased to US$68M." (MTI, 2011). It is reported that Rwanda exact the following minerals

- cassiterite (a tin ore);

- Colombo – tantalite (commonly called coltan – an ore that is the source of niobium and tantalum);
- and wolfram (a tungsten ore).
- amphibolites,
- granites and quartzites,
- volcanic rocks,
- dolomites,
- clay,
- kaolin, etc.

The sector currently employs 35,000 people (MTI, 2011).

✓ Tourism

The tourism in Rwanda is mostly attractive because of the presence of the maintain gorillas there. It is considered, by the Rwanda government, as a priority sector that will aid in the fulfillment of the goals set in their Vision 2020. And this sector is developing possibly year after year because the data of 2007 mention that about 826,000 foreign visitors were recorded by the sector of tourism while in the following year in 2008 there was a considerable increase and the number was about to reach one million of visitors (MTI, 2009). In 2008, only the Volcanoes National Park (VNP) in Rwanda about had about 17,000 people who went to see the gorillas.

This statistic showed that Rwanda is progressively recovering from a serious shortage of tourists in the previous years. The country had only 417 tourists in 1999 (Nielsen & Spenceley, 2010). And some estimations indicate that tourism revenues significantly increased between 2007 and 2008, from $138 million to $209 million (MTI - Rwanda Ministry of Trade and Industry - November 2009). Apart from gorillas, Rwanda has other wildlife and biodiversity that attract tourists in the other two national parks.

Although the country has revised the former tourism policy and created a sound sustainable tourism master plan, the sector is still facing some serious challenges. The Rwanda Ministry of Trade and Industry 'Report of 2009' mentions some of the challenges by citing:

✓ over-reliance on a single tourism product,

✓ international awareness and perceptions of Rwanda not widely based on tourism,

✓ low capacity and under-skilled human resources,

- ✓ little involvement of communities and micro, small and medium enterprises (MSMEs) in the sector,

- ✓ expensive and difficult to access from key tourism source markets as a destination,

- ✓ under-developed regulatory framework for the tourism sector,

- ✓ constraints due to quality and quantity of infrastructure,

- ✓ difficulty of accessing land for tourism investments,

- ✓ little focus on the environment and sustainability,

- ✓ low availability of finance and partnership for private sector investment in the sector.

✓ **Energy**

There is a shortage in energy production in Rwanda. The country produced a total of 55 MW energy in 2008. That was insignificant taking into consideration the national demand energy from other basic economic sectors of the country such as Mining, Agriculture, Manufacturing, ICT, Finance, and Construction. In the vision 2020 of Rwanda, the target for energy production is put at 1,000 MW. However, about 60 percent of the energy produced by ELECTROGAZ is consumed by the industry and the public and private services of the country. To supplement the national need of energy, the country utilizes about 75 percent of the imported petroleum products in the sector of transport.

The Rwanda skill survey of 2012 done by RDB states that analysis of supply and demand of energy in Rwanda indicates that about 86 percent of primary energy is still coming from biomass. By the way, 57 percent represents the energy used in form of wood, 23 percent energy from charcoal, and peat and smaller amounts of crop residues produce 6 percent. And the electricity supply of the country only produces about 3 percent of the total primary energy source while the petroleum products account for 11 percent; that makes a total of 14 percent of non-biomass primary energy that is consumed in the entire country.

The following figure shows the consumption of the primary energy source in Rwanda in 2012:

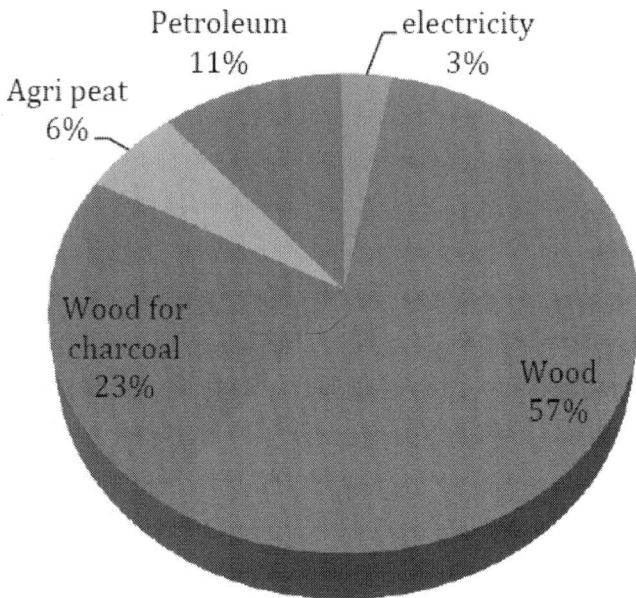

Source: Rwanda Development Board (RDB). Rwanda Skills
Survey 2012. Energy Sector Report. Kigali: RDB

The environmental conditions of a country are the mother

of all activities that sustain human life. Rwanda is also a

country that will not make the exception of that natural

reality. If this country continues to use about 94 percent

of the total energy from the biomass – especially wood

and charcoal – its environmental conditions will

progressively continue to deteriorate, and the result is that the durable peace and prosperity of its nation will remain impossible.

As the country has the natural possibility of constructing hydro-electrical projects, that can be one of the best ways of sparing trees that protect the environment. However, Twagiramungu (2006) mentions that recently Rwanda produced at Jabana and Gatsata electricity from diesel thermic sources. Other hydro-electric projects like at Nyabarongo river in Bulinga that will be able to produce 28 MW, the shared project with tree countries at Akagera at Rusumo with 60 MW, Rusizi II, Mukungwa III, Rukarara and more other micro hydro-electric projects. Are all these projects working healthy towards reducing the negative impact of the biomass energy on the environment of the country? Are they going to adequately sustain the economy of the country making the lives of the general population better?

✓ **Water**

As in almost all the countries of AGLR, Rwanda has too much water. There is abundant water on surface and in underground. Lakes and rivers occupy a surface area of about 211,000 ha. That makes about 8 percent of the national territory area. The outflow of the water underground that is renewable is estimated at 66 m^3/s; among that 9 m^3/s is estimated to be produced by 22,000 known sources. The country has a number of rivers namely Sebeya, Koko, Rusizi, Rubyiro, as effluents of Lake Kivu (102800 ha on the Rwandan side, 473 m of maximum depth), Ruhwa and many other small rivers. 67

percent of the national territory of Rwanda is part of the Nile basin taking 90 percent of the waters of the country by its two main rivers Nyabarongo and Akagera. Small lakes like Bulera, Ruhondo, Cyohoha South, Mugesera, Muhazi, Rwampanga, Mihindi, Mirayi, etc. are part of the basin of Nile River in Rwanda.

- **Transportation in Rwanda**

The transport sector is generally dominated by road transport that totals to 14,000 Km of roads and tracks (Rwandan Ministry of Infrastructure, 2013).

- **Education**

The education in Rwanda is under the responsibility of the Ministry of Education (MINEDUC). It is structured into five educational levels that include pre-primary

Education, primary education, secondary education (lower and upper), technical and vocational education and training (TVET), tertiary education, and adult literacy. The pre-primary education concerns the nursery schools of the country. It lasts for a period of three years. The ages of its attendants vary from three to six years. The primary education is done in primary schools and lasts for six years. It registers children aged of seven up to twelve years. It ends with a national exam that determines the qualified pupils that will be admitted in the lower secondary education. The primary education in Rwanda is compulsory.

The secondary education is organized for a duration of six years. It is divided into two categories. The lower secondary in which students enter at the age of 13 and finish at the age of 15; and the upper secondary in which students are admitted at the age of 16 and finish at the age of 18. Both programs end with national examinations. In Rwanda, the lower secondary education is also compulsory as the primary education; they are commonly known as 'nine years basis education' (9YBE). After completing successfully the 9YBE, students have the option of starting the upper secondary education taking different courses by entering different fields of study such as teacher training, languages, humanities, technical studies, or sciences.

The other kind of education that provides the youth the opportunity to acquire knowledge is the Technical and Vocation Education and Training (TVET). This kind of education is available in Rwanda; it gives people knowledge and skills that make them able to earn a living by being employed after the training. It is also an opportunity for the people who are already employed or working for themselves to upgrade their skills. This type of education in Rwanda takes place in the Technical Secondary Schools (TSS), Vocational Training Centers (VTCs), and Colleges of Technology. The Tertiary Education functions on the basis of credit accumulation and modular scheme (CAMS) system. There are about seven different tertiary education levels.

The Rwandan Higher Education Qualifications Framework informs about the kind of qualification awarded for each tertiary education level. The level 1 is about the Certificate of education; the level 2, Diploma in higher education; level 3, Advanced Diploma in higher education; level 4, Ordinary Degree; level 5, Bachelors Degree with Honors; level 6, Masters Degree; and level 7, Doctorate (Ministry of Education, 2014). Finally, there is Adult Literacy Education in Rwanda that gives the unlearned adult population the opportunity to learn the basic writing and reading skills.

● **Religions**

In Rwanda, the dominant religion is Christianity. According to the National Institute of Statistics of Rwanda (NISR), 95 percent of the population of Rwanda confess Christianity as their religion. The NISR statistics gives us the following information.

- The dominant religious group in Rwanda is the Catholics, who represent 44% of the resident population of the country;

- the second most prevalent religious group are the Protestants with 38%;

- the Adventists represent 12% of the population;

- the Muslims 2%;

- and the Jehovah's Witnesses (1%).

"While those with no religious affiliation represent 2.5%, adherents of the traditionalist/animists and of other religions each represent less than 1% of the population." (NISR, 2014).

However, the Constitution of Rwanda protects the religious freedom of people. And the government of Rwanda works to enforce the law; and there seems to be no report denouncing abuses or discrimination based on religious affiliation or belief. So, in Rwanda, every person is free to choose or to change religion based on their own will. The law of Rwanda regulates public meetings by establishing fines or imprisonment for people who meet in public without prior authorization from the government. All NGOs including churches and religious congregations or organizations are required to seed legal status from the Ministry of Local Government and the Ministry of Justice before starting their activities.

In Rwanda, there is a requirement imposed by the government to all students in primary schools and in the first three years of secondary education in public schools to be taught some lessons of religions as an extracurricular subject. And no political party is allowed to base its ideology on religious beliefs; the constitution prohibits the creation of political parties based on race, ethnic group, tribe, clan, region, sex, and religion or on any other aspect of life that may push people to discrimination or division. In addition, there are a number of religious holidays (for Muslims and Christians) that are established as national holidays by the government of Rwanda. Those days include Good Friday, Easter, Assumption, Eid al-Fitr, and Christmas. This shows the power of the Christianity and Islam over the government institutions of the country.

2.2. Brief Political History and Conflict Analysis

- **Historical Settlements**

The history of Rwanda notifies that the first people to reach the region were the pygmies called the 'Twa' or 'Batwa'. These people arrived there around 700BC. They are physically short in size and very skilled in pottery. The second group of people to settle in the country was the 'Bantu' – Hutu – people. They are presumed to have settled in Rwanda between 5th and 11th centuries AD (Twagilimana, 2016).

They came to the region with iron-age tools and were recognized by their farming techniques. The third category of people to settle in Rwanda was the Tutsi. Physically tall, these people migrated there about 14th century AD and were recognized as cattle raisers. They were powerful and good, and raising cattle.

The history shows clearly that all the three ethnic groups of the country came from somewhere else. Any discrimination based on the fact that some are not the original owner of the land is fake and illogical. If all the ethnic groups are to be sent where their historical ancestors were living, then the country will become empty of the population; and animals, trees, and any other natural creatures there will say "thank you human race for leaving us alone; thank you for making our land free". And if these creatures existing naturally in the land could have the ability to make the human race to pay for rent, the people who came early will have more to pay than the ones who came later.

So, the people of Rwanda should understand this reality and stop believe that people of a different ethnic group is not supposed to own cattle, land, or any other possession. It can be learned, through the history, that there were two social classes in Rwanda before the colonial era. The 'Tutsi' represented a higher social class and the 'Hutu' the lower one. And the belonging to a social class had nothing to do with the ethnic group although their names are used for that sake today. The number of cattle was used to determine a person's social class; if a person acquires a certain number of cattle could be accepted to belong to the Tutsi group regardless his/her ethnic group. And a very poor Tutsi would be assimilated into the Hutu group.

It seems that there were no damaging ethnic conflicts based on ethnic group belonging, but the social classes were determined by the possession of a person. How then the 'Tutsi' and 'Hutu' have become conflicting ethnic groups? Was it because most of the people in each social class had almost similar physical traits? Were the Tutsi rich because of exploiting others or using them in forced labor as colonialists did? The history of Rwanda that does have important information that tries to answer these questions. The leadership mentality of the leaders of the people (especially the kings and the colonialists) has more to say about that. At the end of this chapter, you may have a clear view that ignorance and manipulation might have created what have been happening in Rwanda, and in the whole region of African Great Lakes.

But taking into consideration the skills of the last group that immigrated to Rwanda and who later were mainly identified as 'Tutsi', it can be assumed that they settled to Rwanda with something that was very needed and wanted and which was very scare in the land (cattle raising). Maybe that was one of the reasons why the Tutsi were economically powerful than other groups they met in Rwanda. However, social mobility was possible; for example, a Hutu who acquired a large number of cattle or other wealth could be assimilated into the Tutsi group and impoverished Tutsi would be regarded as Hutu.

Durable peace and prosperity for Rwanda cannot be achieved without the deep and clear understanding of the origin of some people's mentality that is impeding their own well-being and that of their neighbors. Where does, most of what people believe today, come from? How did that get developed through people across time? How has that been destroying the well-being of the country for centuries now? How can that be a danger in the future if most mentally affected people do not change their minds? These are some of the questions we shall be thinking about when looking at some of the historical events that have some light to shed to understand why people have been manipulated to destroy themselves, their relatives, and their neighbors.

- **Historic Kingdoms of Rwanda**

The first kingdom of Rwanda was established in the 15th century. One Tutsi Chief managed to conquer several other chiefdoms and built the Kingdom of Rwanda. From the first King up to the last King Mwami Rwabugiri, all the kings (Mwami) of Rwanda were generally Tutsi. During the kingdoms era, there was a belief that the Hutu had a gift of healing and agriculture and the gifts of Tutsi was military and the power to leader. That is why some Hutu (Abiiru) served as members of the council of advisers to the King. They had a significant authority, but were marginalized during the 18th century.

Between the periods of 1860 and 1895, the King Rwabugiri made a decentralization of the land by redistributing it to the Tutsi chiefs. They became lords of the land and the Hutu were paying manual labors for the right of using them. So, the Tutsi become the federal masters of the Hutu. So, the Hutu who were members of the Council of advisers (Abiiru) together with other notable Hutu lost power because the land was not redistributed following heredity principle.

The following is the list of kings of Rwanda (Fortune of Africa, 2016).

- Gihanga (1081 – 1114)
- Kanyarwanda I Gahima I (1114 – 1147)
- Yuhi I Musindi (1147 – 1180)
- Ndahiro I Ruyange (1180 – 1213)
- Ndahiro Ndoba (1213 – 1246)
- Ndahiro Samembe (1246 – 1279)

- Nsoro I Samukondo (1279 – 1312)
- Ruganzu I Bwimba (1312 – 1345)
- Cyilima Rugwe (1345 – 1378)
- Kigeli I Mukobanya (1378 – 1418)
- Mibambwe I Sekarongoro I Mutabazi (1418 – 1444)
- Yuhi wa II Gahima II (1444 – 1477)
- Ndahiro wa II Cyamatare (1477 – 1510)
- Ruganzu wa II Ndoli (1510 – 1543)
- Mutara I Nsoro II Semugeshi (1543 – 1576)
- Kigeli II Nyamuheshera (1576 – 1609)
- Mibamwe II Sekarongoro II Gisanura (1609 – 1642)
- Yuhi III Mazimpaka (1642 – 1675)
- Cyilima II Rujugira (1675 – 1708)
- Kigeli wa III Ndabarasa (1708 – 1741)
- Mibambwe III Mutabazi II Sentabyo (1741 – 1746)
- Yuhi IV Gahindiro (1746 – 1802)
- Mutara II Rwogera (1802 – 1853)
- Kigeli IV Gahindiro Rwabugiri (1853 – 1895)
- Mibambwe IV Rutarindwa (1895-1896)
- Yuhi wa V Musinga (1896 – 1931)
- Mutara III Rudahigwa (1931 – 1959)
- Kigeli V Ndahindurwa (1959 – 1962)

● Colonial Era and Ethnic Division

As mentioned in the above paragraphs, the country of Rwanda existed as a kingdom before the arrival of European colonizers. From that reality, it can be accepted that the country known today as Rwanda, although colonized by Germans first and Belgians second, its borders were not fixed by the colonizers as it is the case of others African countries. For many centuries, foreigners were not allowed to enter and settle this country for the Rwandan people believed that their kingdom was at the center of the world. "Even as a boy, before I had traveled more than a few miles from home, I knew that I lived in one of the most beautiful places on earth. Our ancestors knew it, too. Before the European colonizers arrived in Rwanda at the turn of the twentieth century, Rwandans thought their country was at the center of the world. They thought their kingdom was the most civilized and their monarchy the most powerful." (Sebarenzi & Mullane, 2009, p.10 – 11).

Believing of having built a most powerful kingdom in a most beautiful country of the African Great Lakes Region might have had created a kind of proud in the minds of rulers of Rwanda until they discovered that some other people (colonialists) appeared to be smarter than themselves during the colonial era! How proud were the Rwandans and their ancestors about their country when were unable to best govern it by preventing from ethnic killings and genocides? Had they never think that one day they will turn it into a terrain of conflicts and human blood-shed?

The irony of the history is that the 'beloved land of Rwanda' was not protected by the Rwandans and yet it is agreeable that the more people are proud of what belongs to them, the more they are willing to protect it! And it is amazing to learn that today some extremists Rwandans educators are teaching their children that their country extended its borders all over the whole vast region of Kivu in the DRC – covering the North-Kivu Province, South-Kivu Province, and Maniema Province – with the aim of preparing school children to future aggressions that will never allow durable peace and development of the AGLR.

However, when the Germans entered the country, they did not dissolve the established social system in the kingdom of Rwanda which had a Tutsi Monarch. They joined with the existing kingdom power of Tutsi to subjugate the Rwandans particularly the Hutu who were naturally known as farmers. That reality may tempt people to have the impression that although the whole Rwandan population was colonized, the most targeted population for subjugation by the colonialists was the less powerful Rwandan (mostly Hutu and Twas). Nevertheless, after the First World War Germany lost it control of Rwanda and the Belgium invaders officially took the country in 1916.

During this period, a latent conflict already existed among the ethnic groups of Tutsi and Hutu. The German colonizers just gave more power to people who were already in power. The Belgians did nothing to change the existing political and socioeconomic situation of the country. Instead, they continued to give more favor to the minority Tutsi who already were in position of power by intensifying the existing situation. This reality was based on the racist viewpoint of Belgian colonialists. Barnett writes "Belgium's sponsorship of Tutsi mastery was legitimated by its racist ideas about who was fit to rule." (Barnett, 2002, p. 50).

In 1933, to make the Hutu fill more embarrassed and inferior than the Tutsi, the Belgians authorities officially gave to Rwandans identity cards according to social class they belonged to and that was considered as their ethnic groups. Belgians used the physical morphology of Rwandans to better determine whether they belong to Hutu, Tutsi, or Twa ethnic group. Although ethnicity was not necessarily determined by the physical appearance of people in Rwanda during the time of Kingdoms, that situation was made alive during the time of colonization. "Subsequently, all Rwandans at birth would be registered as Hutu, Tutsi or Twa and adults were obliged to carry their identity cards." (Nzioka, 2011, p.4).

So, the Hutu became underestimated and discriminated by Belgians in all aspects of life. The divisions were very shocking to Hutu and were highlighted by the introduction of Christianity and education in Rwanda. Nzioka (2011, p. 4) stress on it by putting "The mission schools and seminaries were mainly for the Tutsi elite. While trained Tutsi became doctors, teachers and agronomists, the few educated Hutu took up lower administrative jobs or became shopkeepers or tradesmen."

In fact, the seeds of ethnic conflicts that were put in the minds of people of Rwanda were increased and watered by Belgians so that they may produce roots of conflict that have been growing to bear 'fruits' which are the destructive consequences of most of what has been happening in the AGLR since independence of Rwanda and Burundi. There was probably a growth of resentment in the minds of unfavored people and a growth of complex of superiority in the minds of favored ones.

During the movements of decolonization in 1950, a Hutu political movement was gaining the majority rule while the Tutsi was trying to resist the democratization for fear of losing their per-colonial domination and their acquired privileges from the colonizers. But being minority, they failed and lost their 'Tutsi feudalism'; it is what the Hutu fought against as the "BaHutu Manifesto" in 1957 states: "The problem is basically that of the political monopoly of one race. (…) this political monopoly is turned into an economic and social monopoly (…) turned into a cultural monopoly which condemns the desperate Hutu to be forever subaltern workers (…)" (Sida, 2004).

Although the Hutu movements were becoming more and more powerful because of the majority, they were less educated than the Tutsi. During the colonial era, the Tutsi had many opportunities of education and professional training than the Hutu as it is clearly shown in the following drawing.

However, there was a quick formation of ethnic-based political parties. The "Mouvement Social Muhutu; Muhutu Social Movement" (MSM) was the first to be created in 1951 by Gregoire Kayibanda. APROSOMA (Association for the Social Promotion of Masses) was also created by Gitera. In 1959, the UNAR (Rwandese National Union) was established by the Tutsi and immediately demanded independence. They just wanted to maintain the monarchy that already existed in the country.

To make UNAR less influential, the Belgians supported another created party of Tutsi RADER (Rwandese Democratic Union) which was not in cooperation with the members of UNAR considering it as a creation of Belgians. Being minority and divided, the Tutsi opinions could not prevail. That was exactly the satanic strategy of colonialists in Africa, especially the Belgian; 'divide to reign, to dominate' that was what they knew to do very well in their colonies in Africa.

The creation of divisions in Rwanda was worse than any other country of African Great Lakes Region because the other countries AGLR, mostly DRC, are still suffering the result of that destructive Belgian initiative. Was it reasonable to consider colonialists as 'civilizers' while they appeared to be like excellent agents of division in their colonies? Is it not correct to say that some people are playing the same or similar role to illegally get what they want in Africa? When and how most African political elites will cease being deceived to create divisions among themselves?

What knowledge or principles can be so powerful to stop unhealthy conflicts and divisions in Rwanda and its neighboring countries if they are not inspired by God's Word? It is alarming, as we shall address it in the eleventh chapter of this book, to learn that some religious leaders have been supporting peace troubling and divisive political parties and some movements; and are the ones who are supposed to preach the truth of the Word of God to people.

If some religious leaders in Rwanda had supported Gregoire Kahibanda whose regime discriminated against the Tutsi minority as it has been reported, how then can they preach peace, unity, and inclusive leadership to Rwandans? How can the informed people trust them?

Instead of being 'role model', they have always been after money and power. And that have led many people in the AGLR to be discouraged and to lose faith in the Word of God.

On the eyes of some people, things seem to be different in Rwanda today comparing to its past; but deeply looking on how some of its citizens fear to live in the country and how some other are busy propagating and teaching conflicts, we may be tempted to believe that nothing has changed at all in the inner deep heart of many Rwandans. The millions of Rwandan refugees and asylum seekers may have something to say about this reality.

However, the history of Rwanda informs that during the year 1959, MSM was transformed by Kayibanda into MDR-PARMEHUTU (Rwandan Democratic Movement/Party of the Movement and of Hutu Emancipation) having its regional base Gitarama Ruhengeri, a place where the colonialists helped the Tutsi to establish their dominance base. And APROSOMA was based in Butare. The first massive killing in Rwanda occurred in November 1959 when Hutu killed hundreds of Tutsi and thousands of them displaced and fled to neighboring countries. Even the children were not put aside; the killing was based on ethnics regardless the age of the individual. This was the beginning of what was called "Hutu Peasant Revolution" that lasted from 1959 to 1961.

As shown in this drawing, in the African Great Lakes Region, many children have lost their lives because of their suspected-belonging to different ethnic group from militias'. Some were shockingly hit to the walls repeatedly until their death... and some were severely tortured to death.

Die for only this one wall-hit. Help me to economize my physical energy; I know I still have many other babies like you to kill. Follow your parents in the world of dead. They are waiting for you. By that way, we will avoid any revenge from your ethnic group in the future. So, we shall live safe and in peace.

Moreover, in early 1960, there were many replacements of Tutsi chiefs in their jobs by Hutu chiefs that resulted in empowering more and more Hutu who made many organized massive killing of Tutsi. The history of conflict inscribes that at least 500 people were killed, most of them Tutsi (Sida, 2014). And 22,000 Tutsi were internally displaced and 130,000 became refugees among them 50,000 fled to Burundi.

The consequence of those movements and killings was the end of Tutsi domination and the very beginning of the manifestations of the fruits of a latent ethnic conflict in Rwanda. January 28, 1961, Rwanda became a republic; and September 1961, PARMEHUTU won a victory in a UN-supervised referendum. In July 1962, Rwanda was granted independence with Grégoire Kayibanda the first president of the country. And by 1962, with the Hutu movement coming to power, 120,000 people mainly of Tutsi ethnic group took refuge in neighboring states for fear of violence and persecution.

● **Post-colonial era (Independence period)**

The post-colonial era in Rwanda has very tragic events than other historical periods. After the independence, Tutsi refugees in Tanzania, Uganda, Burundi, and Zaire, with high desire to regain their former positions in Rwanda, started to organize themselves by trying to attack the Hutu government that was governing the country. This was a new cycle of ethnic conflict and violence that continued up to nowadays going even beyond the borders of Rwanda.

The following illustration depicts the scene that sometimes makes the headline or the object of some lessons of geography and history to school children by some so-called educators, the enemies of peace.

It's like the people in refuge were thinking day and night about ways to defeat the people leading their country. Refuge sounds to be a bad solution for durable peace of a country; instead of making people think of a peaceful way of coming back to their country, it gives them the occasion of putting more 'manure' to the seeds and roots of their trees of conflict to produce more harmful fruits in the future. This is general to all the Great Lakes Region where refugees teach even to their children conflict; they teach them to hate people of different ethnic group. We have witnessed some of these teachings of conflict in some refugee concentration camps in Africa.

Likewise, the military Tutsi attacks against Kigali started early before the independence. The first incursion of Tutsi refugees against Rwanda was recorded in 1960. Between the periods of 1962 and 1967, ten other such attacks occurred; each provoking retaliations killing large numbers of Tutsi civilians in the country. And after each attack, the number of internal displaced people and refugees increased.

For example, the attack of December 1963, organized by Tutsi refugees from Burundian camps and supported by Burundi, resulted in a massive killing of an estimated 10,000 Tutsi including all the rest of the Tutsi politicians. From December 1963 to January 1964, the period of which the killing happened, the number of refugees increased to 336,000 which was an estimation of 75% of the Tutsi population during that time. 200,000 fled to Burundi and 78,000 to Uganda (Sida, 2004).

By the end of the 1980s, some 480,000 Rwandans had become refugees, primarily in Burundi, Uganda, Zaire, and Tanzania. They continued to call for the fulfillment of their international legal right to return to Rwanda. However, Juvenal Habyarimana, then president of Rwanda, took the position that population pressures were already too great, and economic opportunities too few to accommodate large numbers of Tutsi refugees. To understand well how some of the people of Rwanda were very motivated to kill, it is good to know that the hate propaganda and the genocidal ideologies were promoted among the population on a daily basis. Money, time, and energy were spent to mobilize the population of one ethnic group to hate the other ethnic group and to prepare for future killing!

Both the First and the Second Republics of Rwanda developed a high degree of authoritarian control similar to the one that the Tutsi had before independence. The rule of the Hutu presidents was characterized by remoteness, authoritarianism, secretiveness, balance of power between lineages and regions, corruption, favoritism. There was a development of hatred and negative stereotypes against Tutsi; these were mentioned in the textbooks in schools, in the media, and in popular songs in the country. This being the case, it could be assumed that negative stereotypes and hatred became part of the national culture of the country.

I wonder at the attitude and the behavior of Hutu who were born during that ugly historical period of their country. Taking into consideration the teachings and propaganda of the State, what represented the Tutsi ethnic group in the eyes of the young Hutu of that period? I also wonder about the Tutsi who were born during the same historical period in exile or in Rwanda. What were their parents teaching them about the Hutu? Obviously, the young Tutsi could just see what was happening in the Rwandan society against them and take it at the deep of their hearts. Unfortunately, that is how problems are being passed from one generation to another in the AGLR.

Some parents are still using bad stories and words to nurture the spirits of their offspring up to nowadays; even the very bad staffs that belong to their progenitors that are supposed to remain dead are being brought to life! The problem that is impeaching durable peace and prosperity of the general population is very grave and needs to be addressed decisively. And Rwanda can be considered as the historical center of the problem.

In fact, in 1973 the Major General Juvenal Habyarimana, made a coup and took power. It was a non-violent coup that marked the beginning of the Second Republic in Rwanda reinforcing the state ideology of Hutu power. In 1975, there was establishment National Revolutionary Movement for Development (MRND) as a one-party state by Habyarimana after abolishing all other parties in the country.

In 1978, the President Habyarimana was elected in a restricted national election. His rule was, in reality, a military dictatorship. In 1983 and 1988, he was reelected. During his reign, there was a certain stop of violence against Tutsi. They were allowed to work in public sector and in government posts, but were banned from having political and military posts. Their access to education was also limited as it was the case of Hutu during the colonial era.

2.3. The Genocide of 1994

✓ **The Pre-Genocidal Period (1980 – 1990)**

It seems that many countries have been playing behind the scene to destabilize the peace of the African Great Lakes Region. While it might be true that some western sponsors were implicated in the Genocide in Rwanda; but historically, its roots of were already set in the minds of some Rwandan people and are to be considered the sole responsible of what happened in their country. The teaching of hate and conflict to the youth, the prior ethnic killings, the fight power and riches, the social discrimination based on ethnic belong made the country a ruin; millions of Rwandan to flee the country for their safety. Rwandan people were repeatedly warned by the spiritual and supernatural personalities that appeared to some children in the country.

During the period of 1980 – 1990, there were so many apparitions in Rwanda that some people thought were related to psychological or medical problems of the seers. In fact, God sent messages in Rwanda so that people may repent, stop planning evil, and turn back to Him. The messages predicted the killings (the genocide) that could happen in the country if people do not repent. But people could not believe the messages of the seers and were considering them of being mentally sick or having madness. Do millions of Christians in the AGLR know how God speaks on a regular basis? Do they believe in spiritual communication? Can a person who does not believe in frequent spiritual communication believe in the Bible? For the Bible itself was written by people who had spiritual connections that allowed them to have spiritual messages that were inscribed in different books that were assembled to make what is called today the written 'Word of God'. Mary mother of Jesus Christ appeared to some kids in Rwanda, but it sounds like people did not believe in the message they were given.

The place where the apparitions were first recorded in Rwanda during the period of 1980 to 1990 is called Kibeho. A place located in the south-western of the country. At Kibeho College, adolescent schools girls have experienced the presence of God's messengers who were bearing messages that could eradicate the tensions

between the Tutsi and Hutu if believed.

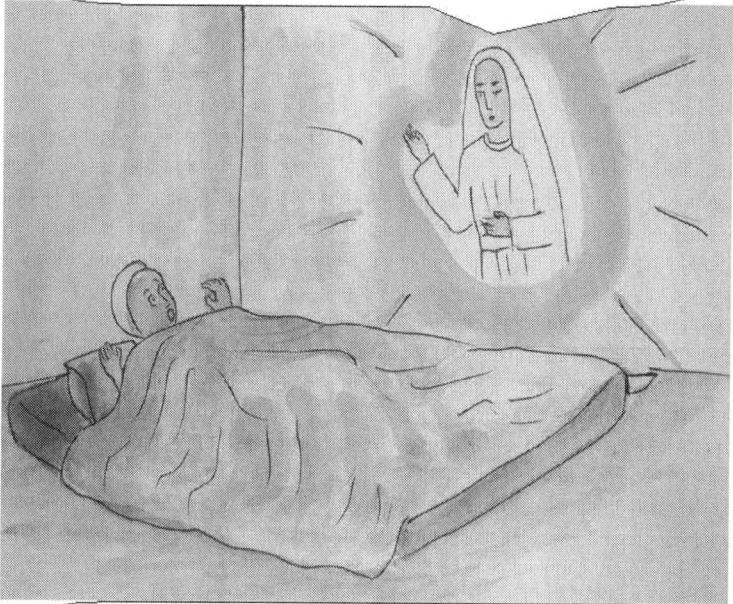

Peace be with you. I am Merry, Mother of the Word. I have come to you with a message that shouldn't be neglected. There is no much time remaining for my son to come; the day of the last judgment is near. Tell the people of your country to repent and turn to Jesus Christ. Otherwise, there will be millions of people who will lose their lives. I have come to show you my children the way so that you may not be lost forever. There will be a river of blood in Rwanda if people don't come back to God. There will be too much pain... this is the time to stop planning evil...

Many people in Rwanda experienced visions or sudden apparitions about 10 years before the killings of 1994 as a sign of warning. But people didn't repent or stop planning to organize ethnic massive killings or genocide.

Human beings have conscience that helps them to differentiate what is right from what is wrong. But how many of them are always ready to sacrifice self-interest in order to follow what is right. It means that what they were planning was not right. God also warned them repeatedly, but could not submit and change their minds. Are the survival Rwandans and their children ready today to listen to God's communications for a future of durable peace and prosperity?

God always warns people, but mostly they do not want to understand. And if they understand, they do not believe. And if they believe they do not submit to His instructions; as if to say 'We know it is God, but He must consider our wants and wills.' Many stories of Jesus

Christ appearing to people had been told. But how many

people believe and submit to his orders?

You men of this country, this message is for you. Your daily night meetings are will kill the peace and prosperity of your nation. Stop what you are planning if you want to live. Repent and turn to me. I am the Word of God, the Son of God who died so that you may live. Stop, please. If you don't stop, your ax which is cutting trees will be used to cut human beings, and you will regret that forever. You should know that you are one people regardless your ethnic differences! Give this message to all the men of your country. Tell them to stop what they are planning in their hearts.

I see Jesus Christ. I hear what he is saying. It seems to be very serious!!! We should stop and repent to live in durable peace and prosperity.

The apparitions that started with Alphonsine Mumureke on November 28, 1981, a 16 years old girl at the time, were experienced by many other adolescents and adults. Mary, when appearing to Alponsine, told her that she was the 'Nyina wi Ijambo' meaning the 'Mother of the Word.' On January 12, 1982, Anathalie (Nathalie) Mukamazimpaka reported having experienced the apparition of Mary too. Marie Claire Mukangango also had the same on March 2, 1982.

Many other students in Kibeho, about 33, had experienced apparitions of the Virgin Mary and Jesus Christ at different times and periods. That pushed the Catholic Church to create two commissions with the aim of determining whether the apparitions were valid or not. One commission had scientific and medical mandate, and the other one had to make theological investigations. The two commissions observed that the seers had no health or psychological problem during the periods of apparitions. They also noticed that there was mystical power during the time of apparitions very difficult to explain or understand by science or human capacity.

The two commissions did not investigate all the seers, but only eight first ones were targeted (those who had visions during the first year of apparitions). The task of the commissions took many years and it's only after 20 years that they concluded that only three of the investigated apparitions were valid with reference to the 'Norms for Judging Alleged Apparitions and Revelations' published by the Congregation of Doctrine of Faith in Rome in 1978.

And in Rwanda, the local Bishop of Gikongoro, Augustin Misago, during a mass on June 29th, 2001, publicly said that the apparitions of Mary and Jesus to Alphonsine Mumureka, Nathalie Mukarazimpaka, and Marie Claire Mukangango were authentic. And that declaration was approved by the Catholic Church (Rome) on July 2, 2001. (Tardif, 2001).

The approval by the Church came very later when millions of people had become victims of the genocide of 1994 in Rwanda. People are to be paying too much attention to the apparition because the history of genocide in Rwanda puts it clear that what was seen by the Seers had come to pass in the country. For example, in August, 1982, the Seers had experienced a terrible vision lasting 8 hours in which the rivers of the country were bloody. They had seen mass murders, headless corpse, and fire; and all these sad scenes happened in Rwanda.

What is this in the river today? Is the water muddy or bloody? Can we use this water? This is human blood in this water. The water in this river is full of blood!!! It is all red.

Yes, it is blood. But what are we going to do. We will use it as it is; otherwise, we will not survive. This shows that many people in this country have lost their lives. And now, I believe in the prophecies of the school children who were told my Mary and Jesus Christ that there will be a river of blood in Rwanda. That happed about 10 years ago.

Catholic Church Approved Apparitions/Seers:

Name	Quick Facts	Notes
AlphonsineMumureke	AlphonsineMumureke Born: 1965 Dates of Apparitions: 11/28/1981 – 11/28/1989 (8 years)	Alphonsine was the first of the students to be visited by Mary. She was ridiculed and called a fool. During her apparitions, the students hurt her and even burned her, to no avail and thus many students began to believe the apparitions. Alphonsine asked Mary if she would appear to her schoolmates as well, which Mary eventually did. Alphonsine fled Kibeho during the 1994 Rwandan Genocide and eventually studied theology with a specialization in catechesis. She later entered the monastery Sainte Claire in Abidjan.

 Nathalie Mukamazimp aka	Nathalie Mukamazimpa ka Born: 1964 Dates of Apparitions: 01/12/1982 – 12/03/1983 (6 months)	Remains in Kibeho near the Marian shrine and has committed to welcoming and praying with the pilgrims.
 Marie Claire Mukangango	Marie Claire Mukangango Born: 1961 Dates of Apparitions: 03/02/1982 – 09/15/1983 (18 months)	Marie Claire at first mocked her schoolmate, Alphonsine when she began reporting that she had been visited by Mary. But in March 1982 she began having apparitions as well. It was Marie Claire that Mary taught the 'Rosary of the Seven Sorrow', giving her the mission of teaching this new Rosary to others. Marie Claire was married to ElieNtabadahiga in 1987. Marie Claire and her husband were captured and killed in 1994 during the Rwandan Genocide.

Unapproved Apparitions/Seers by the Catholic Church

Name	Quick Facts	Notes
	Valentine Nyiramukiza Dates of Apparitions: 05/15/1982 – present	Apparitions take place on May 15th of each year.
	Stephanie Mukamurenzi Born in 1968 Dates of Apparitions: 25/05/1982 -15/09/1982	Stephanie's apparitions lasted from May 25, 1982 until September 15, 1982. The messages that Mary passed to her were to repent, convert and pray, with hope and from the heart. Mary told this Seer: "God loves you already. It is the devil who wants to ruin you. You must refuse all means that he is using to catch you."
	Emanuel	Emanuel was a pagan

	Segatashya Dates of Apparitions: 02/07/1982 – 01/08/1983	shepherd boy who never attended school. In 1982 he began seeing visions of Jesus Christ. He claimed that Jesus himself taught him how to make the sign of the cross and pray the Lord's Prayer and the Rosary. The pagan boy was baptized in 1983 and choose the name that he claims Jesus requested, "Emanuel."
	Agnes Kamagaju Dates of Apparitions: 04/08/1982 -29/08/1983	Agnes claims that she first saw Jesus on 08/22/1983 and still receives visits from Him on most Fridays. You may be interested in watching this 6 part video interview of Agnes
	VestineSalima Born: 1960 Dates of Apparitions: 09/15/1982 – 12/24/1983	Vestine claimed that Mary appeared to her at her home, beginning in July 1980 and initially told only her parents and sister. September 15, 1982 was her first public apparition, at school. In her diary, she recorded that Jesus visited her at first, and later the Virgin Mary. Bishop

		Gahamany helped Vestine to spread the messages of the apparitions throughout Rwanda.

Sources: http://www.catholicrevelations.org/PR/emmanuel %20segatashya.htm

The fact of not approving these 5 apparitions by the Catholic Church does not cancel their impact on the people who experienced them. Some other churches in Rwanda might have agreed on their veracity or authenticity.

So, many Rwandan people did not believe the divine messages and God's written laws, and that can be considered as one of the reasons why they killed each other. They did not also believe God's commands through the many apparitions they had. During that period, millions of Tutsi people were scattered in the countries of AGLR seeking asylum. Those who fled to

Uganda found a 'golden occasion' to gain and develop military skills.

In fact, during the year 1986, the Tutsi who were refugees in Uganda were used in the military troops of Yoweri Museveni to fight against the dictatorship of Milton Obote. The military movement of Museveni, the National Resistance Army (NRA), became victorious by taking power in Uganda. The Rwandan refugees in Uganda, those who helped Museveni in the battle for power, formed their own movement called Rwandan Patriotic Front (RPF) dominated by Tutsi.

During the year 1989, there was a severe economic crisis in Rwanda. It was caused by the collapse of the prices of coffee, an agricultural product on which the economy of the country depended. The power of the President Habyarimana was weakened by that crisis; this man who was opposed to the multi-party political system could not continue to lead the country. He was obliged to allow multi-party democracy due to the pressure of western donors in July 1990. Unfortunately, democracy was not given change to prevail in Rwanda because of the sudden attack of the RPF troops that invaded the country in October 1990. Instead, he found another way of dealing with the situation.

In fact, the literature of Rwandan genocide teaches that the Habyarimana regime initiated and patronized the strategy of ethnic division in Rwanda as a way of fighting against the RPF and making his power more and more durable.

On October 1, 1990, the popularity of the President Habyarimana was being diminished due to the attacks of the RPF in the country. About 20 years on power and still hungry for it, Habyarimana and his close collaborators decided to create fear and hatred in the general populations against all the Tutsi including those who had no link or collaboration with the RPF. To achieve their goals, they used the RPF led by Tutsi to victimize all the Tutsi inside the country. They said that the Tutsi inside the country were collaborators of RPF; a strategy of turning the Hutu against them by propaganda or campaigns.

More other strategies were used by leading elites of Rwanda as Forges, A. D. (1999) explains,

> "For three and a half years, this elite worked to redefine the population of Rwanda into

'Rwandans', meaning those who backed the president, and the 'ibyitso' or 'accomplices of the enemy', meaning the Tutsi minority and Hutu opposed to him. In the campaign to create hatred and fear of the Tutsi, the Habyarimana circle played upon memories of past domination by the minority and on the legacy of the revolution that overthrew their rule and drove many into exile in 1959. Singling out most Tutsi was easy: the law required that all Rwandans be registered according to ethnic group. Residents of the countryside, where most Rwandans lived, generally knew who was Tutsi even without such documentation. In addition, many Tutsi were recognizable from their physical appearance." (Alison Des Forges, 1999, p. 3).

The government of Rwanda in that period called for assistance from Zaire (DRC) and France; they fought against the RPF, but March 29, 1991 a cease-fire was signed to avoid the killing of civilians. But the propaganda of Habyarimana and colleagues continued all over the country.

✓ **The Four Years Period of Genocide (1991 – 1994)**

In Rwandan, during the period of 1990 to 1991, some civilians were trained to become militias known as INTERAHAMWE ("Those who stand together") to help the Rwandan Army to fight against the RPF troops, the politicians in opposition, and any other person opposing to Habyarimana regime and its political ideology based on dictatorship and discrimination of Tutsi. For the period from 1990 to 1993, many people lost their lives in Rwanda as a result of the atrocities and violence committed by the Interahamwe; most of the victims were Tutsi and some moderate Hutu. Some newspapers agencies were also persecuted by the Habyarimana regime through its Interahamwe Militias.

The situation was very dangerous because of the propaganda of some Hutu Leaders. In November 1992 for example, the Hutu people were mobilized to bring the Tutsi back to Ethiopia via the rivers (by the Prominent Hutu activist Dr. Leon Mugusera appeals to Hutu to send the Tutsi "back to Ethiopia" via the rivers).

And many Tutsi were thrown into the rivers by the extremist Hutu who told them to use the free transportation back to their original home land. The stories of some Rwandan people who escaped the killings tell that the Interahamwe had no pity or exception; children, young or old persons, women, and men belonging to a different ethnic group were strongly targeted to be finished.

While the Interahamwe continued their murderous operation, in February 1993 another offensive attack was launched by the RPF and progressed to reach the capital Kigali. Again the government of Rwanda called the French forces to help them fight against the RPF; the fight was decisive that it lasted for several months. Many people lost their properties, their relatives, their lives.

The Habyarimana regime and the RPF, after negotiations, were called to sing a peace accord in August 1993. It stressed mainly on the return of Rwandan refugees in their country and the formation of a government of coalition between the Hutu who were leading the government and the Tutsi who were fighting in the RPF. To make sure the peace accord was implemented, the United Nations sent 2,500 troops to Kigali for oversee.

Unfortunately, the Habyarimana regime refused to share power with the RPF. The extremist Hutu who were opposed to the implementation of the Arusha accords seemed to fear that the exiled Tutsi could be very dangerous to their future security because of what they had done to them in the previous years. Hutu in the government seemed not to be sure the former victims

Tutsi were ready to excuse their past wrongs. David Newbury, cited by Nzioka B., mentions "Because the accords did not grant past killers amnesty for their past transgressions, the Hutu extremists "were afraid that the Tutsi, who had long been persecuted, would respond in kind if given the chance again to govern." (Nzioka, 2011 p. 6 – 7). From that fear, there was a development of new strategies to fight hard against the civilian Tutsi who were present in the country and the RPF militias who were fighting for power-sharing in the country.

So, the late president Habyarimana made sure his power could not be shared. "To craft solidarity and stay in power, Habyarimana and his government turned to the politics of blame, they labeled the Tutsi minority as traitors and accused them of supporting the RPF attackers who wanted to overthrow the Rwandan government—the classification of us-versus them mentality was invoked" (Nzioka, 2011, p.7). They intensified the training of more civilians to become militias and integrate the Interahamwe group. From September 1993 to March 1994, many civilians had become members of Interahamwe group. And the extremist media began to broadcasting propaganda to attack the Tutsi without excuse.

For example, exhortations for attack could be heard from the extremist radio like the Radio-Télévision Libre Mille Collines (RTLM) that mobilized Hutu to kill Tutsi. This station was a semi-private station launched in 1993 by some political actors with ties with the ruling regime considered to be among the organizers of the genocide.

Some people argue that the media had few or small impact on incitement of people to kill, but there is no such small thing – bad is bad regardless its size or frequency. For example, Scott Strauss inscribes that a survey conducted to know whether the media had many contributions to the genocide in Rwanda resulted in a low percentage. He puts "The most direct question about radio media effects put to respondents was: "Did the radio lead you to take part in the attacks?" About 85% of respondents said "no;" 15% said "yes" (N=176). About 52% of respondents said they owned a radio (N=157)." (Straus, nd, p.9).

In contrast, the majority viewpoint says that the media had much negative impact on genocidal actions in Rwanda. For example, Roméo Dallaire who was the force commander of the UN mission in Rwanda during the genocide wrote that "In Rwanda the radio was akin to the voice of God, and if the radio called for violence, many Rwandans would respond, believing they were being sanctioned to commit these actions." (Strauss, p.3 – 4).

And Linda Melvern cited by Scott Strauss (p. 4) argued that the RTLM radio in Rwanda was 'a propaganda weapon unlike any other' in the country. Small or big, like or unlike, the truth is that RTLM had broadcasted some message of ethnical hate; if they were not the seeds of conflicts, they might pray the role of water or other important substance that helped in the process of making them germinate and grow to produce harms.

However, the genocidal propaganda did not only negatively affect men; women were also incited to hate each other. The propaganda was so powerful that it created divisions between Hutu and Tutsi women. In her article 'Women's participation in the Rwandan genocide: mothers or monsters?' Hogg (2010) conducted interviews with some detained genocide female suspects in Rwanda to collect their viewpoints on the participation of women on the 1994 killings in the country. She inscribes,

> "The propaganda also sowed divisions between women in Rwanda, by claiming that Tutsi women were 'working for the interest of their Tutsi ethnic group' and threatened to steal the jobs and husbands of Hutu women. One female detainee in the Kigali Central Prison thus explained: 'Women believed in the need to kill Tutsi for 3 reasons:
> 1. Tutsi were perceived to be associated with the RPF. Women, like men, believed the propaganda. Most women had confidence in what they heard.
> 2. Hutu women hated and were jealous of Tutsi women.
> 3. Hutu women were jealous of Tutsi' wealth. Women wanted their goods.'

> This woman had personally believed the propaganda at first but after the genocide started, changed her mind: 'When I saw so many children, women and old people killed, who could not have been part of the RPF, I began to understand that it was not a war, but a genocide that was planned in advance. I think the genocide was possible because of pre-existing hatred between Tutsi and Hutu, but that the politicians used these sentiments to achieve their goals." (Hogg, 2010, p. 86 – 88).

That is why the negative mass propaganda will always lead some Africans to violence because of their power over millions of people who have not yet developed their 'logical analysis and critical thinking capacity'. A positive change of mind is among the top requirements for durable peace in Rwanda as it is in the entire African continent. When dangerous conflicts infiltrated the minds and hearts of millions of women in a country, the consequence will surely negatively affect all the generations that are to be educated or prepared by contaminated women. It is the future of the country that is put in danger.

People say 'Educating a woman is to educate the whole world.' So, the power of the anti-Tutsi propaganda penetrated many households in Rwanda. That is why some women strongly took part in the killings during the genocide. And some who succeeded to flee the country continued to teach conflict to their children for future violence against the Tutsi. That is very dangerous because some Tutsi women and men also do the same to their children! Is the future of Rwanda safe with such teaching in the minds of some parents and children? Does that kind of mindsets allow durable peace and prosperity?

That was what leaders in Rwanda wanted for their countries by making 'genocidal propaganda'. Leaders who strongly seek their self-interests in detriment to others' are always a danger for the community peace; because their power and wealth come from insecurity. They hate peace because it does not give them occasion to steal, to kill, to dominate, to dictate, to be worshiped. If they are so powerful, you can only escape them by God's power which is the most Superpower,

People who focus on serving themselves with the gifts and power that God give them will always be ready to torture or to kill others in order to eternalize their self-serving actions. This kind of attitude in leadership is able to destroy the whole nation. It was observed in the mentality of the leaders in Rwanda during the genocide era as Forges mentions,

> "From the start, those in power were prepared use physical attacks as well as verbal abuse to achieve their ends. They directed massacres of hundreds of Tutsi in mid-October 1990 and in five other episodes before the 1994 genocide. In some incidents, Habyarimana's supporters killed Hutu opponents – their principal political challengers – as well as Tutsi, their declared ideological target." (Forges, 1999, p. 4).

"Both on the radio and through public meetings, authorities worked to make the long-decried threat of RPF infiltration concrete and immediate." (Forges, 1999, p. 10). The political leaders created false information that was used to make the Hutu in Rwanda think that their neighbors Tutsi are very dangerous for their security for are working hand in hand with the RPF. For example, they were told that the Tutsi had hidden firearms in the bushes behind Kibungo cathedral; that they had elaborated maps that showed fields to be taken from Hutu in Butare.

Not only political leaders were campaigning for genocide but also the community leaders and even the churches. Forges (1999, p.10 – 11) inscribes,

> "Community leaders and even clergy assured Hutu that they were justified in attacking Tutsi as

a measure of self-defense. Authorities offered tangible incentives to participants. They delivered food, drink, and other intoxicants, parts of military uniforms and small payments in cash to hungry, jobless young men. They encouraged cultivators to pillage farm animals, crops, and such building materials as doors, windows and roofs. Even more important in this land-hungry society, they promised cultivators the fields left vacant by Tutsi victims. ... Many poor young men responded readily to the promise of rewards. Of the nearly 60 percent of Rwandans under the age of twenty, tens of thousands had little hope of obtaining the land needed to establish their own households or the jobs necessary to provide for a family. Such young men, including many displaced by the war and living in camps near the capital provided many of the early recruits to the Interahamwe, trained in the months before and in the days immediately after the genocide began. Refugees from Burundi, in flight from the Tutsi-dominated army of Burundi, had also received military training in their camps and readily attacked Rwandan Tutsi after April 6."

Consequently, the national security became more and more fragile in Rwanda; and the international community was warned by the Human Rights Organizations but there were no effective interventions. During the month of March 1994, some workers of international organizations started to evacuate their families from Kigali fearing the consequences of the killings that they believed to happen soon.

April 6, 1994, a plan in which the President Habyarimana and the President Cyprien Ntaryamira of Burundi was shot near the Airport of Kigali in Rwanda. They two presidents were killed by that sad event. Some people believed that they were killed by the FPF soldiers for the sake of power; some other believe that they were killed by some Extremist Hutu who suspected the President Habyarimana of being ready to accept the implementation of Arusha Peace Accord... So, they killed him to avoid any possible power-sharing with the

Tutsi. But the killings did not wait for the verification of the fact to start; the same night people started slaughtering each other.

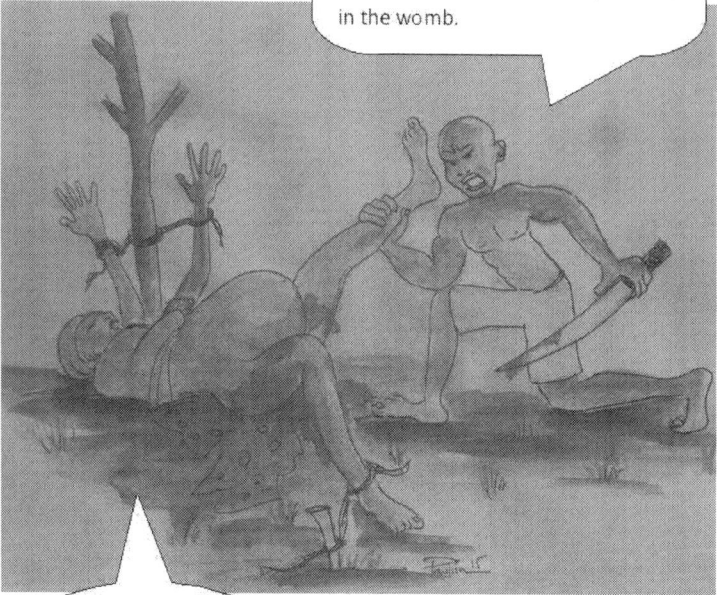

The killings were very intense because only for the first day on April 7, 1994, there were thousands of deaths; the victims were mainly the Tutsi and moderate Hutu politicians. The Rwandan Armed Forces (FAR) and the Interahamwe were so organized that they were going house to house to achieve their purpose after setting up roadblocks. In a house, every member of a family was killed without exception; this included even children.

Surprisingly, the UN troops stayed watching what was happening. They did not intervene saying they did not have the mandate to do so. They were mere observers! It was during that mass killing that the RPF took the advantage of attacking offensively on April 8, 1994, to end the genocide and to rescue 600 soldiers of its troops that were already based in Kigali waiting for the Arusha

Peace Accords to be implemented. While the RPF was

fighting the genocide continued.

On April 21, 1994, Agathe Uwiliyingimana, a moderate Hutu Prime Minister, was killed together with the ten Belgian soldiers who were guarding her. Other UN troops were violently tortured and disarmed; they did not retaliate because they were instructed by their Commander not to violate their mandate. Due to that event, the UN reduced its forces from 2,500 to 250.

At the UN Security Council on April 30, 1994, a discussion about the crisis of Rwanda took about eight hours; and the word 'genocide' was not mentioned in the resolution that condemned the killings. While the international community remained reluctant to adequately intervene to protect civilians, thousands of people flee into the neighboring countries namely Tanzania, Burundi, and Zaire (DRC) to escape massacres.

Most of these people were Hutu and feared the advancement of RPF movement.

On May 17, 1994, the UN accepted to send 6,800 troops to Rwanda to stop the killings of civilians in the country. But the application of the decision delayed because of the discussion on the question of the cost of the operation. Finally, the Security Council sent, on June 22, 1994, the French forces in South-West Rwanda in a territory controlled by the government. Although the French forces were present there and had created a 'safe region' where people could find refuge, the killings continued in that territory. So, the word 'genocide' was used by the United States to mention what was happening in Rwanda during the killings of 1994. The RPF took control of Kigali in July 1994 and the Hutu government took refuge with a huge number of Hutu seeking asylum in Zaire (DRC).

The French troops left Rwanda and the Ethiopian UN troops replace them. Upon capturing the Capital of the country, the RPF put in place an interim government of national unity. During a period of 100 days, the death toll of killings in Rwanda was estimated at 800,000. It was just the Rwandan citizens killing Rwandan citizens! Some people believe the UN with the powers of its famous Security Council was behind the Rwandan genocide because they did not intervene to stop the killing as they were able to do so. While this statement may be true, but they could not be behind and be in front at the same time.

If there are always some people behind the civil wars and conflicts in Africa, there is also always people who stand in the front to fulfill the hidden agenda of the powers in sponsorship. And the people in front are always the citizen or the neighbors. So, can the people behind appear at the front at the same time? Not normal, I think. Do they force the local populations to discriminate, to hate, to rob, to rape, and to kill? No, I believe. Why then can some people strongly believe that the western powers are the main cause of conflict in the AGLR? If they are considered to be the main cause of conflict, they will also be the main source of peace and development in the region! Can they achieve that for Africans?

The report of the independent commission for the investigation of the actions of the UN during the

Rwandan genocide of 1994 clearly mentions that the Security Council did not answer officially to the project of engagement of the UN Mission in Rwanda sent to them by the General Dallaire which stated that the UN Peacekeepers could intervene using force against the violators of human right and the perpetrators of crimes against humanity in order to protect the civilians. Dallaire had good will to protect civilians but could not do that without the authorization or the order from the Secretary General of the UN (Nation Unies - Conseil de Sécurité, 1999, p. 9).

Can we affirm that the United Nations Security Council knew it was good to protect civilians but they did not do that? The situation in Rwanda was so disastrous that many of eyes witnesses suffered the memories of what

they saw. For example, Dallaire explains how terrible the
genocidal events of Rwanda were and how they affected
his brain. He puts,

> "I did try to write this story soon after I came
> back from Rwanda in September 1994, hoping to
> find some respite for myself in sorting out how
> my own role as Force Commander of UNAMIR
> interconnected with the international apathy, the
> complex political maneuvers, the deep well of
> hatred and barbarity that resulted in a genocide in
> which over 800,000 people lost their lives.
> Instead, I plunged into a disastrous mental health
> spiral that led me to suicide attempts, a medical
> release from the Armed Forces, the diagnosis of
> post-traumatic stress disorder, and dozens upon
> dozens of therapy sessions and extensive
> medication, which still have a place in my daily
> life." (Dallaire, 2003, p. 5).

All Rwandan people are to understand that they are the
best solutions to their problems. The lessons learned from
Rwanda genocide that have negative impact on almost all
the people of the African Great Lakes Region are
eloquent, and should be taken into consideration by any

wise nation in need of durable peace and prosperity. Not willing to help people in dangerous situations is not so different from being pleased by the danger they are facing. Reviewing the book 'The French Betrayal of Rwanda', written by Daniela Kroslak, Berny Sèbe mentions the main points about Rwandan genocide that always attract the attention of researchers or scholars when studying the background of the sad events of 1994 in Rwanda. He writes,

> "Several aspects of the event have generated intense scrutiny from a variety of scholars in various disciplines: the speed and scale of the massacres (about 10% of the entire Rwandan population was massacred); the ethnicization of political life under Belgian colonial rule (which 'constructed' ethnicity around the Hutu and Tutsi poles); the inability or unwillingness of the international community to stop the cycle of violence once it had started; and, France's responsibility in supporting the Hutu-dominated regime which ultimately orchestrated the genocide of part of the country's population (Tutsi and moderate Hutu)". (Sèbe, 2008, p.1)

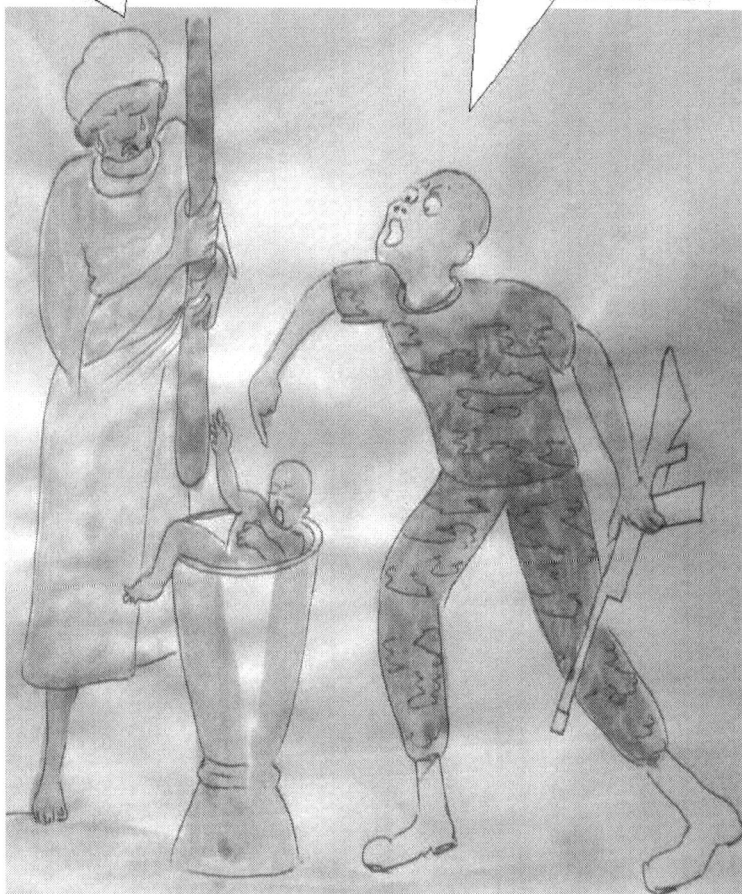

During the period of August to November 1994, an international tribunal was established by the UN Security Council to oversee the trials of suspected persons who were involved in the genocide in Rwanda.

✓ **The Period After the 1994 Genocide**

The UN started the process of bringing back Hutu exiled neighboring countries in January 1995. That was done in partnership with Tanzania and Zaire (DRC) where many Hutu took refuge during the genocide. The process that aimed to make return about a half million Hutu to Rwanda in five months failed to be successful due to the UN Security Council refusal to send an international force to scrutinize the refugee camps of the AGLR where the Rwandan refugees were living. But the Rwanda was left in a grave poverty and suffered from financial problem. The people who lost their relatives for example parents were among the most vulnerable in the country.

The Tutsi dominated government of Rwanda started to attract the attention and support of international of western powers. On February 19, 1995, the US (60 million) and other western governments promised to give 600 million US dollars of aid to Rwanda. Besides that, the UN Security Council mobilized all the states to take into custody the people suspected of having taken part in the Rwandan genocide. But during the year 1995, the government of Rwanda was in a high need of financial aid waiting for the promises to be realized by western donors.

On June 10, 1995, they made a request to the UN to withdraw its forces from the territory of Rwanda; the UN responded to the request by considerably reducing the number of its troops. The Rwanda refugees who were scattered in the African Great Lakes Region by genocide refused to return to Rwanda when asked by the Rwandan government and the UN. These people who feared persecution a huge number of them remained in foreign countries up to nowadays.

After the genocide of 1994 in Rwanda, the killings did not stop; there was a cease-fire which was not synonymous to a cease-murder. In September 20, 1995, when Pope John Paul II visited Nairobi, during a mass celebration, he asked Rwandans and Burundian people to stop killing each other.

Bones of my parents!

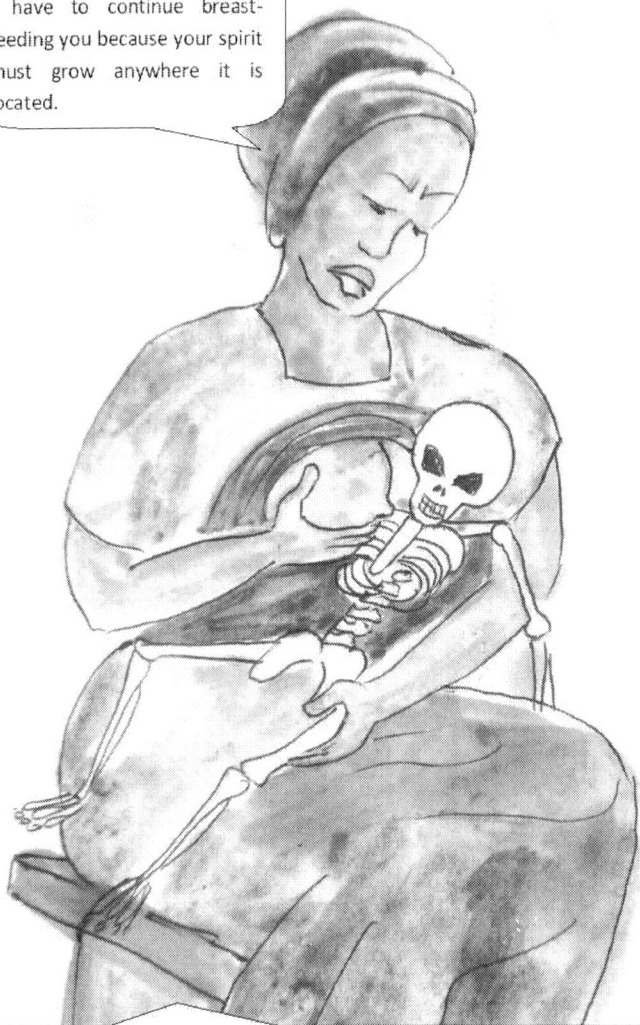

On December 12, 1994, the United Nations Tribunal for Rwanda announced that eight suspects were charged with genocide and crimes against humanity. The next day of the same month the mission of the UN peacekeepers was extended for more three months by the Security Council, and it was ready to reduce the number of its troops in Rwanda. Some of the people who stayed in Rwanda were in serious trauma and depression.

In fact, in November 1996, the mass repatriation of the Rwandan Refugees who were living in Zaire (DR Congo) began. Some were not willing to go back to Rwanda left the refugee camps to go in deeply in the interior of the DRC. The government of Rwanda ordered suspension on arrests of the suspected genocide perpetrators. Was it their strategy of encouraging many Hutu refugees to go back home in order to deal with them seriously upon their arrival? Maybe it was because the trials for Hutu involved in the genocide began in the following month in December 1996. In Mid-December 1996, the refugee camps in Tanzania were closed and all Rwandans were repatriated to their country.

However, in Arusha, the first genocide trials came to the International Criminal Tribunal on January 10, 1997. Jean-Paul Akayesu who was a government official was accused of giving order to start mass killings in his administrative area. The same month and year on 17, Francois Bizimutima became the third Hutu condemned to death by the court in Rwanda for his role in the genocide in the country. While some were being put to death by the jurisdiction of the country, others were being killed by civilians.

For example, on January 13 – 17, 1997, some Hutu extremists killed a woman who testified against Jean-Paul Akayesu together with her seven children and husband. And on January 22, more than 300 people were killed when the Rwandan army wanted to capture some Hutu insurgents responsible for killings in Northwestern Rwanda in which three Spanish aid workers also died. On that occasion, the UN officials mentioned that most of the victims were returned refugees who knew what happened during the 1994 genocide and were ready to be trial witnesses.

My lovely Father,

I am holding the bone of your head in my hands. Listen to me where you are. Every morning and evening I call you for help, but you never answer. Now answer my call.

It seems that another genocide is being prepared in the minds and hearts of people. This time around, join with all the spirits of our ancestors to give us victory. The people who came from the Horn of Africa will never lead the country any more. Give us the power we need to finish this race of snake!

Another documented murder took place in February 1997; Guy Pinard, a witness to the 1994 genocide, was killed by Hutu terrorists while saying mass. And five human rights observers are killed in an ambush in the territory of Cyangugu. That can be considered among a few of the after-genocide killings that were known and recorded by the media.

The government of Rwanda accused Zaire (DRC) of providing arms to the Rwandan Hutu refugees in the refugee concentration camps. In February 14, 1997, Kofi Annan who was the Secretary-General of the United Nations at the time asked the Security Council to look into the matter. Today millions of Rwandans are living in foreign countries not because they love to but because of fear of persecution once back in their home country.

We had many occasions talking to some Rwandans who are in exile; it easy to read the feeling of fear when considering the future of their country. And many people in Rwanda may be living with much fear of tomorrow too. The fear of those who are not willing to go back home.

How then can people of Rwanda get out of the setting of the paralyzing fear of tomorrow, the uncertainty of today, and the bad memories of the past to welcome durable peace and prosperity for all in their country and the whole AGLR? That one of the questions that this book will try to answer; important inputs about that can be explored from the sixth to the fifteenth chapter.

Chapter Three
Overview of Democratic Republic of Congo

3.1.Country Profile

● **Location and Population**

The Democratic Republic of Congo (DRC), formerly called Zaire, is located at the center of Africa with an area of 2,344,885 sq km (905,365 sq miles). Its population was 64,704,000 according to the estimation of UN in mid-2008. The density of the population was 27.6 per sq km at mid-2008.

✓ The capital: Kinshasa

✓ National languages: Kiswahili, Lingala, Kikongo, Chiluba

✓ Official language: French

✓ Neighboring countries of DRC:

✓ Sudan and Central African Republic to the north,

✓ Republic of Congo to the west,

✓ Angola and Zambia to the south,

✓ Burundi, Uganda, Tanzania, and Rwanda to the east.

This country is huge; it is about eighty times bigger the European country that canonized it (Belgium).

Population Density of DR Congo, 1960 – 2016

Index	1960	1985	1995	2005	2015	2016
Population (Millions)	15,248,246	29,985,665	42,183,620	56,089,535	77,266,814	79,722,624
Population density (Persons per sq km)	6	13	18	24	34	35

Source: World Population Review, DRC, 2016

The Democratic Republic of the Congo is highly populated by a numerous variety of ethnic groups. Some of its ethnic groups go beyond its national territory; so, the Bakongo (Kongo people) are divided between the DRC, the Republic of the Congo, and Angola; the Zande ethnic group is shared between the DRC and Sudan; the Chokwe between the DRC and Angola; the Bemba between the DRC and Zambia; the Alur between the DRC and Uganda; and the Tutsi between the DRC and Rwanda – Burundi.

Map of DRC

Source: United Nations – Department of Field Support -
Cartography Section, July 2011

3.2. Natural Resources

- **Land and Agriculture**

While the country's total area is of 2,345,410 km² the land occupies a surface of 2,267,600 km², and the water of 77,810 km². With 9 neighboring countries, DR Congo has total land boundaries of 10,744 km with the following border countries. Republic of the Congo 2,410 km, Angola 2,511 km, Zambia 1,930 km, Tanzania 473 km, Burundi 233 km, Rwanda 217 km, Uganda 765 km, Central African Republic 1,577 km, and Southern Sudan 628 km. And the country has a coastline of 37 km (CIA - World Factbook, 2016).

The Terrain and the climate are very favorable to agriculture. The sol is rich and able to produce food to feed 2 billion people (ANAPI, 2016). That means the

DRC can feed all the populations of the African continent who are about 1.2 billion, and still have more left over. Some other estimates have shown that the country can feed the world's population for a period of 50 years! In equatorial river basin, the climate is tropically hot and humid; in the southern highlands, it is cool and dry; in the eastern highlands and Ruwenzori Range, it is cool, cold, and wet; in the north of the Equator, there is a wet season from April to October and a dry season from December to February; and in the south of the Equator, the season is wet from November to March and dry from April to October.

The following estimations shows how the land in the Democratic Republic of the Congo is used:

- arable land: 2.96% (1998 est.), 3% (1993 est.)

- permanent crops: 0.52% (1998 est.), 0% (1993 est.)

- permanent pastures: 7% (1993 est.)

- forests and woodland: 77% (1993 est.)

- other: 96.52 (1998 est.), 13% (1993 est.)

- Irrigated land: 110 km^2 (1998 est.), 100 km^2 (1993 est.)

However, the main grown crops that provide revenue to the country include,

  o Coffee

  o Cotton

  o Horticulture

  o Tobacco

  o Raw sugar

o Cocoa

DRC has a National Agricultural Investment Plan (NAIP) which plays the role of national planning framework for national and external funds for the sector. This plan considers the needs, the achievements, and the gaps in agricultural sector of the country for a period of eight years (2013-2020). It combines all the programs and the projects of the sector and its outlook. NAIP is organized into five programs that include,

- Program 1: Promotion of Agricultural Value Chains and Agribusiness
- Program 2: Managing Food and Nutrition Security and Strategic Agricultural Reserves
- Program 3: Research, Extension and Agricultural Education

- Program 4: Agricultural Governance, Gender and Strengthening Human and Institutional Capacities

- Program 5: Adaptation to Climate Change

The Ministry of Agriculture and Rural Development (MINAGRIDER) is in charge of the supervision of the structure of the NAIP.

- **Food Produced in DRC (Food Crops production by type by province).**
- **Rice:**
  - Equateur (territory of Bumba),
  - Eastern Province,
  - South Kivu (Fizi highlands), and
  - Maniema.
- **Soya-beans:**
  - ✓ Eastern Kasai (Kabinda)
  - ✓ Equateur.
- **Sugarcane:**
  - ✓ Bas-Congo (Kwilu-Ngongo) ;
  - ✓ South Kivu (Kiliba) ;
  - ✓ Eastern Province (Lotokila, Yanonge) and
  - ✓ Bandundu (Mushie pentane).
- **Cassava:**

✓ Bandundu (Kwango districts, Kwilu, Plateau and Mai-Ndombe)

✓ Bas-Congo.

- Domestic production in 2007: 15,004,430 tons

• **Corn:**

✓ Eastern Province, Katanga and both Kasaï.

- Domestic production in 2007 : 1,155,720 tons

• **Rice:**

✓ Rice is produced in different provinces. Its distribution goes through many territories and areas of the country. For example, in the Eastern Province – Yahuma, Banalia, Opala, Bafuasende, Aketi and Buta. The territory of Bumba in Equateur Province is also favorable for the cultivation of rice.

- Domestic production in 2007: 316,180 tons

• **Bean:**

✓ North Kivu, South Kivu, Kasai Occidental Eastern Province, Katanga, Bas-Congo and Bandundu;

- Domestic production in 2007 : 112,250 tons

- **Peanut:**
  - ✓ Bandundu (in the territories of Idiofa, Bulungu, Masimanimba, Bagata, Gungu and Mushi) ;
  - ✓ Katanga (Tanganyika District and Haut-Lomami)
    - Domestic production in 2007 : 369,370 tons
- **Plantains:**
  - ✓ North Kivu and South Kivu (in the territories of Beni, Rutshuru, Masisi, Walikale, Kabare, Fizi and Mwenga). The soil in North Kivu is very fertile because of its volcanic origin.
    - o Domestic production in 2007: 488,810 tons
- **Potato:**
  - ✓ North Kivu Province (Masisi, Rutshuru, Walikale, Lubero, ..)
  - ✓ South Kivu (Uvira, Kabare, Bukavu, ...)
    - o Domestic production in 2007: 93,560 tons
- **Wheat:**
  - ✓ North Kivu (Masisi and Lubero)
  - ✓ Katanga (Moba Lubudi and Mitwaba).
    - Domestic production in 2007: 8,690 tons

- **Forests of DRC**

The forests DRC are very rich; if they are exploited adequately, they can generate too much money for the economy of the country. Forests in the country cover a vast area of 2 million square kilometers; and about half of that area is in high rain-forests and closed; the other half is mainly open forest and woody savannah. The country has about 18 million hectares of parks and conservation areas which makes 8 percent of the national territory.

There is an estimation of about 10,000 species of plant; 400 species of fish, 409 species of mammal, and 1 117 species of bird. With such a rich diversity of species, the country ranks the 5th richest in terms of biodiversity on the planet earth. Although the rate of deforestation is thought to be law of about 0.4 percent per year, the country suffers a loss of 400,000 – 500,000 hectares of its closed forest each year. (FERN, March 2006).

In the 2013-2017 Country Strategy Paper, the African Development Bank mentions that DRC's forest management remains a challenge although the country has terminated the illegal forest concessions and adopted a new Forest Code that puts emphasis on sustainable development. (AfDB, June 2013).

- **Fisheries**

The fishing potential of DR Congo is of 707,000 tons per annum, but the country's annual fish production is estimated at 250,000 tons per year making it only 35 percent of the total potential. There is much more to be done in this sector to improve the economy of the nation making a considerable contribution to the prosperity of the nation. It is unreasonable for a country to be importing things that its peoples can produce when they are empowered to do so.

In the fisheries sector, the country imports about 100,000 tons of fish per year while it can provide the modern fishing tools to the sector to produce more 457,000 tons. Doing that the country could be able to satisfy the national need of fish and it will be able to export about 357,000 tons to other nations. Three types of fishing are taking place in the country presently; there are Customary fishing (using dugout canoes that can bear a load of two tons), Artisan fishing (using canoes equipped with outboard motors that can bear a load of 1.5 tons per fisherman), and Semi-industrial fishing (using seiner fishing boats which allows about 30 to 300 tons/year).

The key fishing zones in the country as identified (by the DRC Ministry of Agriculture and promoted by ANAPI)

NO.	Waterways	Potential (Tons)	Halieutic Species
01	Lake Tanzania –Tanganyika	450 000	214 species of fish, Stolothrissa tanganicae, Limnothrisa miodan, Latest and Luciolates, etc.
02	Lake Kivu	12 000	Baremore, Hyd'ocynus porskaili, lates niloticuls albertinus, Tilapia, hydocyon Goliath ubangersis Bagi, etc.
03	Lake Albert	13 300	Baremore, Hyd'ocynus porskaili, lates niloticuls albertinus, Tilapia, hydocyon Goliath ubangersis Bagi, etc.

04	Lake Moero	28 000	Tilapia macrochir, Clarus, Synodontis, Barbus attirelis, Momyridae
05	Lake Tshangalele	4 400	Tilapia, Serrono Chromis, Clarias
06	Lake Nzilo	2 500	Lalex, Barbus, Clarias, Tilapia
07	Kamalondo Depression	25 000	Lates niloticus
08	Congo River	137 000	Tilapia, Haplochromis Melander, Athiopius Protopterus, Protopterus Senegalus
09	Atlantic Coast	27 700	Captain, Ray, Conger, Perch, Soles, Bream, Daradas, Catfish (Arius), Sardinella (mackerel), etc.
	Total	**707 000**	

Source: ANAPI, 2013

- **Livestock**

The natural state of the land in the DRC is favorable for pastoral activities with more than 87 million hectares on which livestock can be exploited successfully. Vast plains and vast grassy and wooded grassland cover the hectares. Regardless its enormous pastoral potential, the country imports livestock from foreign countries to meet the national needs of the general populations.

- **Minerals**

Mineral resources of the DRC constitute its main exports. The minerals contribute to the GDP of the country of about 15 percent and 11 percent of State revenues; they earn about 30 percent of the country's foreign currencies. The country produces cobalt, copper, cadmium, petroleum, industrial and gem diamonds, gold, silver, zinc, manganese, tin, germanium, uranium, radium, bauxite, iron ore, coal, hydro-power, timber, etc.

The DRC possesses more than 1,000 mineral substances but only a few are exploited. It has the second biggest reserves of copper in the world, 80 percent of the world's cobalt and coltan, 25 percent of its gold reserves, and 30 percent of its diamonds reserves. It had been reported that,

> "The most important minerals for the DRC are cobalt, copper, and diamonds. The country also produces some gold, tin, iron, nickel, and tantalum, amongst others. According to the USGS, in 2010, the country's share of the world's cobalt production amounted to 51%; industrial diamonds, 25%; tantalum, 14%; gem-quality diamonds, 5%; and copper and tin 3% each. The DRC has some of the largest deposits of non-ferrous metals in the world. It has about 3% of the global copper reserves and 45% of global cobalt reserves, about 25% of the global diamond reserves, and reserves

of some precious metals such as gold and tantalum. In relative terms, the DRC is the largest cobalt producer globally, it boasts the 10th highest gold reserves globally, and the country has the largest diamond reserves in Africa. The country's vast mineral resources will attract significant international interest." (KPMG Global Mining Institute, 2014).

The following chart gives the estimation of the main deposits of minerals in the DR Congo.

Ore	Reserves (tones)
Copper	75 million
Lethium	31 million
Niobium	30 million
Manganese	7 million
Zinc	7 million
Cobalt	6.7 million
Iron (over 60%)	1 million
Cassiterite	450,000
Gold	1,500
Diamonds (carats)	206 million

Source: Investing DRC 2013, Africa Report

- **Energy**

DRC has also a huge potential of energy which is estimated at 100,000 MW. But what is amazing is that the political leaders of the country never exploit even the half of the total potentiality that naturally exists there. Only 2,400 MW is exploited making almost 2.5 percent of the total estimated potential of the country. The sad reality is that most of that electrical production is exported to foreign countries while in the country fewer than 10 percent of households have access to electricity (AfDB, June 2013). That is one of the lowest rates in sub-Saharan Africa where the average is 30 percent.

- **Water**

There is abundant water in the DRC. This country is reported to have over half of Africa's water reserves, but an estimated 51 million people – or three-quarters of the population – have no access to safe drinking water (United Nations Environment Program – UNEP, 2011). The water is mainly located in the lakes, the Congo River and its effluents. Naturally, the network of the water-ways that is navigable is of 12,700 km making it very useful to the easy circulation of people and goods from one place to another.

DRC has the second largest volume of water in the river which is about 40,000 cu m per second. The water resource potential is of 19,967 m^3/yr./inhabitant – situation of 2008 (AfDB, June 2013); but there is a serious shortage of potable water in the country. There is a very low access to water of 39 percent in the urban areas and of 20 percent in the rural. Low quality of service, low recovery rates, and weak management characterize the sector.

- **Transport in the DRC**

The sector of transport is also affected negatively by lack of good leadership as other sectors of the country. In DRC, only 2 percent of the national road network is paved, and 11 percent of rural feeder road net is in practicable condition. The rail network is scarcely operational; being essentially the legacy of colonialists, the Congolese political leaders have failed to modernize it or to keep it in good condition. The Congo River and lakes offer a nice possibility of transport, but still, there is a shortage of safe and modern ships for transportation.

The following map shows the lines of the common means of transportation in the DRC

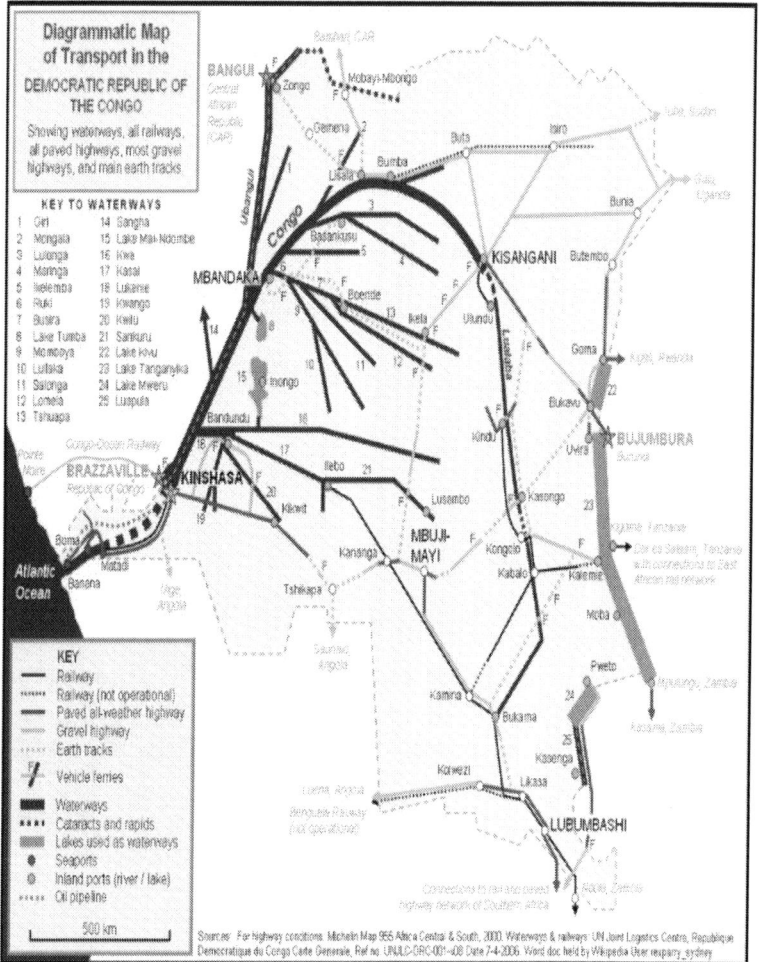

Source: (CAADP, 2013)

- **Formal Education (Schooling)**

Education in the DRC is managed by the Ministry of Primary, Secondary and Vocational Education (EPSP), the Ministry of Social Affairs (MAS), and the Ministry of Higher and University Education (ESU). These three ministries are in charge of the education system of the country. But there are other ministerial departments of the country in charge of social welfare, health, scientific research, youth and sports, employment, etc. sometimes organize some activities that support the education system of the country.

Regardless the sharing of responsibility in this sector, education is still far from reaching the acceptable national standard for a country in need of durable peace and prosperity. There are in the country four categories of schools such as,

- Schools directly controlled by the Government,

- Schools run by churches in partnership with the Government (they are regulated by the Government),

- Schools which are private but accredited by the Government, and

- Schools which are private but not accredited by the Government.

So, public schools are the schools directly controlled by the Government and the schools run by churches in partnership with the Government; other schools are considered private ones. The capital city, Kinshasa, centralizes the management of the education by Ministers appointed by the President of the country. There are provincial Ministers appointed by the Governs of the provinces who manage the education at the provincial level. The General Secretariat (SG) is in charge of all administrative and pedagogical services. He makes sure the Government's policy is implemented in all the schools of the country.

The EPSP controls 30 educational provinces all over the country. Provincial divisions (PROVED) and sub-provincial divisions (Sous-PROVED) represent the ministry in the provinces. The heads of Provincial Divisions are presented in the sub-provincial divisions by other heads at that level. DRC has three educational levels in charge of the ministry of EPSP. The pre-primary level (ISCED 02) which is optional and run for three-year cycle; the primary (ISCED 1) which takes 6-11 year-old children and last for six years; and the secondary level (ISCED 2 and 3) that includes the following four levels

- ✓ the long cycle (humanities) for a period of six years, which gives access to higher and university education, is subdivided into two sub-cycles, the first cycle of two years for 12-13 year-old children (ISCED 2) and the second cycle for 14-17 year-old children (ISCED 3),

- ✓ the for Vocational Specialization Cycle (CSP), which lasts one or two years,

- ✓ the Arts and Crafts Cycle lasting one to two years, and

- ✓ the Vocational Cycle lasting four to five years (DRC, 2010).

Source: MPSVE & ISSP/OU, 2013

Other educational programs such as literacy for young people and adults, vocational learning, remedial education, etc. are the responsibility of the Ministry of Social Affairs (MAS). On papers, the education sector of DRC seems to be well organized but practically it is observed that there is still more to do to make sure the Congolese people are receiving an adequate education that may contribute effectively to national durable peace and prosperity. This is one of the Congolese sectors that suffer from the management of people who seem to speak and write well, but fail to work well! It is all about a serious shortage of the use of moral virtues and the love of the nation.

In fact, the education in DRC is a very heavy burden on the heads of parents and guardians of children. They play major responsibly in the educational sector of the country by paying fees to their children even for those who are still at pre-primary and primary levels. The government has adopted the UN-Human rights stating free primary education to citizens but never fulfill that. Millions of children are not going to school to the lack of school fees. The government supplements the money paid by parents by giving to teachers a minimal amount but both combined do not allow teachers to satisfy basic needs for the whole month. And most of the time, teachers do not get their meager salaries from the State at all. That situation puts some educators at risk of accepting bribes from lazy students in exchange of good school reports, transcripts, certificates, and even diplomas for which they did not work. So, ineffective leaning or training sometimes result in granting undeserved certificates or degrees in DRC.

● **Religions**

DRC is a country dominated by Christian religion. The country is populated by 50 percent of Roman Catholic Christians, 20 percent of Protestants, 10 percent of Kimbanguists (this is a Christian religion which has its inspiration from RDC), and about 2 percent of Muslims. And among the Christian population in the DRC, about 90 percent of them attend the Roman Catholic Church (Nationsencyclopedia.com, 2016). There are other religions like Latter-day Saints (Mormons), Orthodox Christians, Jews, Jehovah's Witnesses, animist indigenous religions, etc. that are represented in smaller number in the country. People seem to be very committed to religious activities in DRC where about 90 percent of its population attends religious services each week.

There is religious freedom in the country as it is stated in the constitution and other laws and policies. Religions in DRC have built strong and powerful institutions that have a remarkable impact on the population of the country. Apart from church communications, some religions in the country have organized themselves to be more and more able to communicate to people by creating and managing some media. For example, the Catholic religion owns and controls Radio Maria that operates mainly in Bukavu; they also have Radio Amani in Kisangani. The Islamic religion owns and manages 'The Voice of Africa' that broadcast in Kinshasa and Kikwit. Many other private and religious radio stations broadcast in DRC conveying messages from several Christian groups.

3.2. Brief Political History and Conflict Analysis

- **Early settlements and arrival of Europeans in Congo (Precolonial Congo)**

The early history of the Congo (Democratic Republic of Congo - DRC) informs that the early settlers in this were hunter-gatherers. Where they came from is not clearly mentioned, but it is said that they were nomads (people who often move from place to another for temporary settlement to find fresh pasture for livestock). These early populations of DRC are considered the ancestors of 'pygmy' peoples assumed by historians to be the first inhabitants of the country.

Around 1,000 BC, Bantu migrants from the Northern of Africa entered Congo region. "Around 1000 BC, Bantu migrants had reached the Great Lakes of East Africa. Halfway through that millennium, the Bantu had also settled as far south as the countries of what are now Angola and the Democratic Republic of the Congo." (Forum on Chine-Africa Cooperation, 2009). And by 1100 AD they formed kingdoms (for example Loango in the north and Kongo in the south).

During the 1300s the Kongo Empire became highly structured and developed. Its territory extended up to a region that today covers parts of the south-west of Congo, the north of Angola and a portion of the Republic of Congo (Brazzaville). This kingdom lasted for some 500 years. The first European explorers to reach the

Congo were Portuguese. They arrived at the mouth of the Congo River in 1482 (Diego Cao was the first European Navigator to visit Congo). They made the first contact with the Kongo Kingdom and Europe (Jeal, 2013).

Among the diverse benefits the Europeans had from Kongo Kingdom was the slave trade that had negative impacts on the populations of Congo as it had on all Africans. The slave trade produced to the Congolese a feeling that they were 'less human beings' by the fact that they were sold like goods. That was one of the most dangerous activities of colonialists that contributed to the creation of the feeling of 'complex of inferiority' in people's minds not only in Congo but in all colonized African countries. It paralyzed – and still in some people's minds today – any effort to positively cope with today's aching and changing world. That was the manure if not the water which made the seeds of conflict able to find a favorable soil to grow on the 'outraged and discouraged minds' of black African peoples.

- **Congo as a Free State (private property of Leopold II)**

During the 1870s, the king of Belgians Leopold II started his colonial program in central Africa. His ambition to have a colony in Africa was made effective by a British explorer Henry Stanley in 1871 when navigating Congo River to the Atlantic Ocean as a first European to do so. The information brought back to Europe stimulated Leopold II's interest, and that was the beginning of his colonial project in Africa. It was the beginning of a very dangerous and difficult period for peoples of Congo where his colony was established. That was the time when the culture of massive atrocities such as murder, rape, humiliation, corruption, intimidation (causing fear), misappropriation of properties, etc. was introduced in Congo.

Leopold II brought hail to peoples who were still living on earth to become more and more rich and powerful. I consider this period as the time where black Congolese were infected by a disease that was trying to paralyze their self-esteem, self-confidence, self-motivation, and self-awareness; a disease that was transmitted to many in the next generations up to nowadays. Leopold II and his agents planted the first worst seeds of conflict in the minds and souls of millions of peoples of Congo during the period of 'Congo Free State'; those 'ancient parents' and 'role model' of many Congolese of today might have transmitted their infectious state of mind (attitude towards white people) to their descendants up to the very recent generation. For example, the Congolese of Leopold II era learned from the colonialists that leaders use force, discrimination, torture, killing, stilling, lying, corruption, putting villages on fire, cutting hands, etc. to maintain the power and to produce riches for personal interest.

Most of the post-colonial Congolese political leaders have used the same strategies in their leadership; that was and still is a very wrong role model that puts in danger the durable peace and prosperity of the general population of the country. As Leopold II agents used torture and hand cutting to enforce forced labor, many insurgents have used the similar atrocious methods to get minerals and other types of riches in the DRC.

In fact, the history informs that in 1885 Leopold II proclaimed Congo a free State under his direct rule. The foreigners invaded the land and all the kingdoms by force using guns to stop all forms of resistance. Some people like the Kuba fought against the enforcement of Leopold's authority by his agents but they failed. They enforced the forced-labor for a voracious search for rubber. Women, men, and children were all forced to work to reach a given amount of rubber a day; failing to do that resulted in hand-cut, severe torture, and killing.

The atrocities of Leopold II in the Congo resulted in death of 10 million people. That was a very bad beginning of a so-called 'civilization'. What happened during that historic time of Congo was as worse as the 1994 Rwandan genocide because no humanitarian or international organization was aware of what was happening in DRC until Morel denounced it. People were forced to work; they were dispossessed from their belongings; and then, they were killed! And Morel was not the only man who denounced that but appeared to be in good position to be heard. People like George Washington Williams and William Sheppard had attracted the attention of the world about what was happening in the Congo.

Hochschild writes "Although it was Edmund Dene Morel who had ignited a movement, he was not the first outsider to see King Leopold's Congo for what it was and to try hard to draw the world's attention to it. That role was played by George Washington Williams, a black American journalist and historian, who, unlike anyone before him, interviewed Africans about their experience of their white conquerors." (Hochschild, 1999, p.4). Some of what Leopold's agents did in the Congo can be found in the open letter wrote to Leopold II by George W. W. What is revealed in the letter is so amazing that it seems good to put the whole letter here. The letter puts,

"Good and Great Friend,

I have the honor to submit for your Majesty's consideration some reflections respecting the Independent State of Congo, based upon a careful study and inspection of the country and character of the personal Government you have established upon the African Continent.

It afforded me great pleasure to avail myself of the opportunity afforded me last year, of visiting your State in Africa; and how thoroughly I have been disenchanted, disappointed and disheartened, it is now my painful duty to make known to your Majesty in plain but respectful language. Every charge which I am about to bring against your Majesty's personal Government in the Congo has been carefully investigated; a list of competent and veracious witnesses, documents, letters, official records and data has been faithfully prepared, which will be deposited with Her Britannic Majesty's Secretary of State for Foreign Affairs, until such time as an International Commission can be created with power to send for persons and papers, to administer oaths, and attest the truth or falsity of these charges.

There were instances in which Mr. HENRY M. STANLEY sent one white man, with four or five Zanzibar soldiers, to make treaties with native chiefs. The staple argument was that the white man's heart had grown sick of the wars and rumors of war between one chief and another, between one village and another; that the white man was at peace with his black brother, and desired to "confederate all African tribes" for the general defense and public welfare. All the sleight-of- hand tricks had been carefully rehearsed, and he was now ready for his work. A number of electric batteries had been purchased in

London, and when attached to the arm under the coat, communicated with a band of ribbon which passed over the palm of the white brother's hand, and when he gave the black brother a cordial grasp of the hand the black brother was greatly surprised to find his white brother so strong, that he nearly knocked him off his feet in giving him the hand of fellowship. When the native inquired about the disparity of strength between himself and his white brother, he was told that the white man could pull up trees and perform the most prodigious feats of strength. Next came the lens act. The white brother took from his pocket a cigar, carelessly bit off the end, held up his glass to the sun and complaisantly smoked his cigar to the great amazement and terror of his black brother. The white man explained his intimate relation to the sun, and declared that if he were to request him to burn up his black brother's village it would be done. The third act was the gun trick. The white man took a percussion cap gun, tore the end of the paper which held the powder to the bullet, and poured the powder and paper into the gun, at the same time slipping the bullet into the sleeve of the left arm. A cap was placed upon the nipple of the gun, and the black brother was implored to step off ten yards and shoot at his white brother to demonstrate his statement that he was a spirit, and, therefore, could not be killed. After much begging the black brother aims the gun at his white brother, pulls the trigger, the gun is discharged, the white man stoops . . . and takes the bullet from his shoe! By such means as these, too silly and disgusting to mention, and a few boxes of gin, whole villages have been signed away to your Majesty.

When I arrived in the Congo, I naturally sought for the results of the brilliant program: "fostering care", "benevolent enterprise", an "honest and practical effort" to increase the knowledge of the natives "and secure their welfare". 1 had never been able to conceive of Europeans, establishing a government in a tropical country, without building a hospital; and yet from the mouth of the Congo River to its head-waters, here at the seventh cataract, a distance of 1,448 miles, there is not a solitary hospital for Europeans, and only three sheds for sick Africans in the service of the State, not fit to be occupied by a horse. Sick sailors frequently die on board their vessels at Banana Point; and if it were not for the humanity of the Dutch Trading Company at that place —who have often opened their private hospital to the sick of other countries—many more might die. There is not a single chaplain in the employ of your Majesty's Government to console the sick or bury the dead. Your white men sicken and die in their quarters or on the caravan road, and seldom have Christian burial. With few exceptions, the surgeons of your Majesty's Government have been gentlemen of professional ability, devoted to duty, but usually left with few medical stores and no quarters in which to treat their patients. The African soldiers and laborers of your Majesty's Government fare worse than the whites, because they have poorer quarters, quite as bad as those of the natives; and in the sheds, called hospitals, they languish upon a bed of bamboo poles without blankets, pillows or any food different from that served to them when well, rice and fish.

I was anxious to see to what extent the natives had "adopted the fostering care" of your Majesty's "benevolent enterprise" (?), and I was doomed to bitter disappointment. Instead of the natives of the Congo "adopting the fostering care" of your Majesty's Government, they everywhere complain that their land has been taken from them by force; that the Government is cruel and arbitrary, and declare that they neither love nor respect the Government and its flag. Your Majesty's Government has sequestered their land, burned their towns, stolen their property, enslaved their women and children, and committed other crimes too numerous to mention in detail. It is natural that they everywhere shrink from "the fostering care" your Majesty's Government so eagerly proffers them.

There has been, to my absolute knowledge, no "honest and practical effort made to increase their knowledge and secure their welfare." Your Majesty's Government has never spent one franc for educational purposes, nor instituted any practical system of industrialism. Indeed the most unpractical measures have been adopted against the natives in nearly every respect; and in the capital of your Majesty's Government at Boma there is not a native employed. The labor system is radically unpractical; the soldiers and laborers of your Majesty's

Government are very largely imported from Zanzibar at a cost of £10 per capita, and from Sierra Leone, Liberia, Accra and Lagos at from £1 to £1/10 per capita. These recruits are transported under circumstances more cruel than cattle in European countries. They eat their rice twice a day by the use of their fingers; they often thirst for water when the season is dry; they are exposed to the heat and rain, and sleep upon the damp and filthy decks of the vessels often so closely crowded as to lie in human ordure. And, of course, many die.

Upon the arrival of the survivors in the Congo they are set to work as laborers at one shilling a day; as soldiers they are promised sixteen shillings per month, in English money, but are usually paid off in cheap handkerchiefs and poisonous gin. The cruel and unjust treatment to which these people are subjected breaks the spirits of many of them, makes them distrust and despise your Majesty's Government. They are enemies, not patriots.

There are from sixty to seventy officers of the Belgian army in the service of your Majesty's Government in the Congo of whom only about thirty are at their post; the other half are in Belgium on furlough. These officers draw double pay—as soldiers and as civilians. It is not my duty to criticize the unlawful and unconstitutional use of these officers coming into the service of this African State. Such criticism will come with more grace from some Belgian statesman, who may remember that there is no constitutional or organic relation subsisting between his Government and the purely personal and absolute monarchy your Majesty has established in Africa. But I take the liberty to say that many of these officers are too young and inexperienced to be entrusted with the difficult work of dealing with native races. They are ignorant of native character, lack wisdom, justice, fortitude and patience. They have estranged the natives from your Majesty's Government, have sown the seed of discord between tribes and villages, and some of them have stained the uniform of the Belgian officer with murder, arson and robbery. Other officers have served the State faithfully, and deserve well of their Royal Master.

From these general observations I wish now to pass to specific charges against your Majesty's Government.

FIRST.—Your Majesty's Government is deficient in the moral military and financial strength, necessary to govern a territory o 1,508,000 square miles, 7,251 miles of navigation, and 31,694 square miles of lake surface. In the Lower Congo River there is but One post, in the cataract

region one. From Leopoldville to N'Gombe, a distance of more than 300 miles, there is not a single soldier or civilian. Not one out of every twenty State-officials know the language of the natives, although they are constantly issuing laws, difficult even for Europeans, and expect the natives to comprehend and obey them. Cruelties of the most astounding character are practiced by the natives, such as burying slaves alive in the grave of a dead chief, cutting off the heads of captured warriors in native combats, and no effort is put forth by your Majesty's Government to prevent them. Between 800 and 1,000 slaves are sold to be eaten by the natives of the Congo State annually; and slave raids, accomplished by the most cruel and murderous agencies, are carried on within the territorial limits of your Majesty's Government which is impotent. There are only 2,300 soldiers in the Congo.

SECOND.—Your Majesty's Government has established nearly fifty posts, consisting of from two to eight mercenary slave-soldiers from the East Coast. There is no white commissioned officer at these posts; they are in charge of the black Zanzibar soldiers, and the State expects them not only to sustain themselves, but to raid enough to feed the garrisons where the white men are stationed. These piratical, buccaneering posts compel the natives to furnish them with fish, goats, fowls, and vegetables at the mouths of their muskets; and whenever the natives refuse to feed these vampires, they report to the main station and white officers come with an expeditionary force and burn away the homes of the natives. These black soldiers, many of whom are slaves, exercise the power of life and death. They are ignorant and cruel, because they do not comprehend the natives; they are imposed upon them by the State. They make no report as to the number of robberies they commit, or the number of lives they take; they are only required to subsist upon the natives and thus relieve your Majesty's Government of the cost of feeding them. They are the greatest curse the country suffers now.

THIRD.—Your Majesty's Government is guilty of violating its contracts made with its soldiers, mechanics and workmen, many of whom are subjects of other Governments. Their letters never reach home.

FOURTH.—The Courts of your Majesty's Government are abortive, unjust, partial and delinquent. I have personally witnessed and examined their clumsy operations. The laws printed and circulated in Europe "for the Protection of the blacks" in the Congo, are a dead letter and a fraud. T have heard an officer of the Belgian Army pleading the cause of a white man of low degree who had been guilty of beating and stabbing a black man, and urging race distinctions and prejudices as good and sufficient reasons why his client should be adjudged innocent. I know of prisoners remaining in custody for six and ten months because they were not judged. T saw the white servant of the Governor-General, CAMILLE JANSSEN, detected in stealing a bottle of wine from a hotel table. A few hours later the Procurer-General searched his room and found many more stolen bottles of wine and other things, not the property of servants. No one can be prosecuted in the State of Congo without an order of the Governor-

General, and as he refused to allow his servant to be arrested, nothing could be done. The black servants in the hotel, where the wine had been stolen, had been often accused and beaten for these thefts, and now they were glad to be vindicated. But to the surprise of every honest man, the thief was sheltered by the Governor General of your Majesty's Government.

FIFTH—Your Majesty's Government is excessively cruel to its prisoners, condemning them, for the slightest offenses, to the chain gang, the like of which can not be seen in any other Government in the civilized or uncivilized world. Often these ox-chains eat into the necks of the prisoners and produce sores about which the flies circle, aggravating the running wound; so the prisoner is constantly worried. These poor creatures are frequently beaten with a dried piece of hippopotamus skin, called a "chicote", and usually the blood flows at every stroke when well laid on. But the cruelties visited upon soldiers and workmen are not to be compared with the sufferings of the poor natives who, upon the slightest pretext, are thrust into the wretched prisons here in the Upper River. I cannot deal with the dimensions of these prisons in this letter, but will do so in my report to my Government.

SIXTH.—Women are imported into your Majesty's Government for immoral purposes. They are introduced by two methods, viz., black men are dispatched to the Portuguese coast where they engage these women as mistresses of white men, who pay to the procurer a monthly sum. The other method is by capturing native women and condemning them to seven years' servitude for some imaginary crime against the State with which the villages of these women are charged. The State then hires these woman out to the highest bidder, the officers having the first choice and then the men. Whenever children are born of such relations, the State maintains that the women being its property the child belongs to it also. Not long ago a Belgian trader had a child by a slave-woman of the State, and he tried to secure possession of it that he might educate it, but the Chief of the Station where he resided, refused to be moved by his entreaties. At length he appealed to the Governor-General, and he gave him the woman and thus the trader obtained the child also. This was, however, an unusual case of generosity and clemency; and there is only one post that I know of where there is not to be found children of the civil and military officers of your Majesty's Government abandoned to degradation; white men bringing their own flesh and blood under the lash of a most cruel master, the State of Congo.

SEVENTH.—Your Majesty's Government is engaged in trade and commerce, competing with the organized trade companies of Belgium, England, France, Portugal and Holland. It taxes all trading companies and exempts its own goods from export-duty, and makes many of its officers ivory-traders, with the promise of a liberal commission upon all they can buy or get for the State. State soldiers patrol many villages forbidding the natives to trade with any person but a State official, and when the natives refuse to accept the price of the State, their goods are seized by the Government that promised them "protection". When natives have persisted in trading with the trade-companies the State has punished their independence by burning the villages in the vicinity of the trading houses and driving the natives away.

EIGHTH.—Your Majesty's Government has violated the General Act of the Conference of Berlin by firing upon native canoes; by confiscating the property of natives; by intimidating native traders, and preventing them from trading with white trading companies; by quartering troops in native villages when there is no war; by causing vessels bound from "Stanley-Pool" to "Stanley-Falls", to break their journey and leave the Congo, ascend the Aruhwimi river to Basoko, to be visited and show their papers; by forbidding a mission steamer to fly its national flag without permission from a local Government; by permitting the natives to carry on the slave- trade, and by engaging in the wholesale and retail slave-trade itself.

NINTH.—-Your Majesty's Government has been, and is now, guilty of waging unjust and cruel wars against natives, with the hope of securing slaves and women, to minister to the behests of the officers of your Government. In such slave-hunting raids one village is armed by the State against the other, and the force thus secured is incorporated with the regular troops. I have no adequate terms with which to depict

to your Majesty the brutal acts of your soldiers upon
such raids as these. The soldiers who open the combat
are usually the bloodthirsty cannibalistic Bangalas,
who give no quarter to the aged grandmother or
nursing child at the breast of its mother. There are
instances in which they have brought the heads of
their victims to their white officers on the
expeditionary steamers, and afterwards eaten the
bodies of slain children. In one war two Belgian
Army officers saw, from the deck of their steamer, a
native in a canoe some distance away. He was not a
combatant and was ignorant of the conflict in
progress upon the shore, some distance away. The
officers made a wager of £5 that they could hit the
native with their rifles. Three shots were fired and the
native fell dead, pierced through the head, and the
trade canoe was transformed into a funeral barge and
floated silently down the river.

TENTH.—Your Majesty's Government is engaged in
the slave-trade, wholesale and retail. It buys and sells
and steals slaves. Your Majesty's Government gives
£3 per head for able bodied slaves for military
service. Officers at the chief stations get the men and
receive the money when they are transferred to the
State; but there are some middle-men who only get
from twenty to twenty-five francs per head. Three
hundred and sixteen slaves were sent down the river
recently, and others are to follow. These poor natives
are sent hundreds of miles away from their villages,
to serve among other natives whose language they do
not know. When these men run away a reward of

1,000 N'taka is offered. Not long ago such a recaptured slave was given one hundred "chikote" each day until he died. Three hundred N'taka—brassrod—is the price the State pays for a slave, when bought from a native. The labor force at the stations of your Majesty's Government in the Upper River is composed of slaves of all ages and both sexes.

ELEVENTH.—Your Majesty's Government has concluded a contract with the Arab Governor at this place for the establishment of a line of military posts from the Seventh Cataract to Lake Tanganyika territory to which your Majesty has no more legal claim, than I have to be Commander-in-Chief of the Belgian army. For this work the Arab Governor is to receive five hundred stands of arms, five thousand kegs of powder, and £20,000 sterling, to he paid in several installments. As I write, the news reaches me that these much- treasured and long-looked for materials of war are to be discharged at Basoko, and the Resident here is to be given the discretion as to the distribution of them. There is a feeling of deep discontent among the Arabs here, and they seem to feel that they are being trifled with. As to the significance of this move Europe and America can judge without any comment from me, especially England.

TWELFTH—The agents of your Majesty's Government have misrepresented the Congo country and the Congo railway. Mr. H. M. STANLEY, the man who was your chief agent in setting up your authority in this country, has grossly misrepresented the character of the country. Instead of it being fertile and productive it is sterile and unproductive. The natives can scarcely subsist upon the vegetable life produced in some parts of the country. Nor will this condition of affairs change until the native shall have been taught by the European the dignity, utility and blessing of labor. There is no improvement among the natives, because there is an impassable gulf between them and your Majesty's Government, a gulf which can never be bridged. HENRY M. STANLEY'S name produces a shudder among this simple folk when mentioned; they remember his broken promises, his copious profanity, his hot temper, his heavy blows, his severe and rigorous measures, by which they were mulcted of their lands. His last appearance in the Congo produced a profound sensation among them, when he led 500 Zanzibar soldiers with 300 camp followers on his way to relieve EMIN PASHA. They thought it meant complete subjugation, and they fled in confusion. But the only thing they found in the wake of his march was misery. No white man commanded his rear column, and his troops were allowed to straggle, sicken and die; and their bones were scattered over more than two hundred miles of territory.

CONCLUSIONS Against the deceit, fraud, robberies, arson, murder, slave-raiding, and general policy of cruelty of your Majesty's Government to the natives, stands their record of unexampled patience, long-suffering and forgiving spirit, which put the boasted civilization and professed religion of your Majesty's Government to the blush. During thirteen years only one white man has lost his life by the hands of the natives, and only two white men have been killed in the Congo. Major Barttelot was shot by a Zanzibar soldier, and the captain of a Belgian trading-boat was the victim of his own rash and unjust treatment of a native chief. All the crimes perpetrated in the Congo have been done in your name, and you must answer at the bar of Public Sentiment for the misgovernment of a people, whose lives and fortunes were entrusted to you by the august Conference of Berlin, 1884—1 885. I now appeal to the Powers which committed this infant State to your Majesty's charge, and to the great States which gave it international being; and whose majestic law you have scorned and trampled upon, to call and create an International Commission to investigate the charges herein preferred in the name of Humanity, Commerce, Constitutional Government and Christian Civilization. I base this appeal upon the terms of Article 36 of Chapter VII of the General Act of the Conference of Berlin, in which that august assembly of Sovereign States reserved to themselves the right "to introduce into it later and by common accord the modifications or ameliorations, the utility of which may be demonstrated experience". I appeal to the Belgian people and to their Constitutional Government, so proud of its traditions, replete with the song and story of its champions of human liberty, and so jealous of its present position in the sisterhood of European States

—to cleanse itself from the imputation of the crimes with which your Majesty's personal State of Congo is polluted. I appeal to Anti-Slavery Societies in all parts of Christendom, to Philanthropists, Christians, Statesmen, and to the great mass of people everywhere, to call upon the Governments of Europe, to hasten the close of the tragedy your Majesty's unlimited Monarchy is enacting in the Congo. I appeal to our Heavenly Father, whose service is perfect love, in witness of the purity of my motives and the integrity of my aims; and to history and mankind I appeal for the demonstration and vindication of the truthfulness of the charge I have herein briefly outlined. And all this upon the word of honor of a gentleman, I subscribe myself your Majesty's humble and obedient servant, GEO. W. WILLIAMS Stanley Falls, Central Africa, July 18th, 1890."

Source: Hill, A. C. & Kilson, M. (2014).

That is some of what was revealed about the brutal rule of Leopold II in Congo. People were forced to produce what did not benefit to them; they were lied to up to the extent of thinking that the While Colonialists were extraordinary human being; they were totally controlled and abused; they learned to lead using lies, deceptions, discriminations, plunder, robbery, murder, etc. and all that with permanent use of fire guns to achieve their purposes.

Edmund Dene Morel noticed that during Leopold II's reign what was shipped to Congo was mainly composed by guns as if that was exchanged with the raw materials. Grove (2010, p.2) writes,

> "Edmund Dene Morel was a clerk for the British firm Elder Dempster that shipped goods for King Leopold II from Antwerp to the Congo. An intelligent and bilingual man, Morel realized that there was a massive trade deficiency. The vast amount of expensive raw goods that were coming from the Congo did not even closely equal the amount of goods being sent back to Belgium. The only items that were shipped back to the Congo were tools of war: guns, ammunition and knives. In Morel's mind, this meant only one thing: slavery."

This colonial mentality that was making the life of millions of Congolese difficult more than hundred years ago seems to have persisted in the DRC and in the whole AGLR. The 'mineral conflict' of the DRC as labeled by many has many similarity with Leopold II's outrageous enterprise in Congo.

Moreover, millions of innocent people died during Leopold's era of 'ownership of Congo' as mention in the section above and millions other fled into deep forests for fear of losing their lives. It can be assumed that no one could rescue those who flee and took refuge into the deep forests in regard to the cruelty used by Leopold's agents and the flow of European shipped fire gun in the Congo.

As a matter of fact, an outstanding documentary entitled 'Congo: White King, Red Rubber, Black Death' directed by Peter Bate gives some eloquent facts and testimonies of some of the survivors of the barberries committed by the agents of Leopold II in the Congo Free State. With clear narrative explanation given by the Elikia M'Bokolo, historian and professor at 'Ecole des Hautes Etudes en Sciences Sociales' in Paris, the documentary shows how Leopold II extended his power and glory at all cost.

With the creation of the pneumatic tire by John Dunlop, the rubber was in high demand and Leopold II used guns cruelly to get it. Hands were chopped for late delivery of rubber, heads were cut, psychological and physical tortures were done on daily basis, villages were burnt, black peoples of Congo were shot to death. Missionaries were the first to notice the atrocities committed by the King Leopold II in Congo, a man who was showing the world that he wanted to bring civilization and Christianity in Congo had transformed it into a large camp of forced-labor with 'human butcheries' in every village!

In the documentary, the diary of a Belgian officer – Louis Leclerq – during the year1895, the following information is given,

> "10 April 1895: Six natives killed. Village set on fire. Diner then return. 17 April 1895: Left with 80 men for Baurou. Around 15 people killed. 25 April 1895: Arrived at Iteke. Burned the village. And the same at Yambi. Ilongo. Burned the village and killed a native. Arrived at Bokolo at 6 p.m. Burned. Arrived at Yambumba at 11:40 a.m. I burned the village. Arrived at Likombe at 3 a.m. suddenly we were under attack. Two soldiers

were killed. After a substantial burst of rifle fire, the natives fled leaving 13 dead on the ground. I set fire to the houses. 8 June 1895 I headed towards Yamapete. I set fire to the village. After a good lunch, we returned to Basoko in triumph with our bloody trophies. 10 June. We reached Yambisi. We sent some groups of soldiers ahead. They returned some hours later with 11 heads and 9 prisoners. 22 June. They brought us 3 prisoners in the morning and 3 more towards the evening, along with 3 heads. A man running through the forest screaming for his wife and child was shot by one of our sentries. They brought us his head. Never have I seen such an expression of despair and fear. We set fire on Yambisi."

Source: Documentary on 'Congo: White King, Red Rubber, Black Death' directed by Peter Bate. New York: New York Daily News.

This is just one of true testimonies of people who worked to fulfill the desire of the King Leopold II. It is really alarming for that was the beginning of the problems that the DR Congo has been suffering from generation to generation. If people really want to solve the multiple problems that the country is suffering now, they must consider the atrocities committed by Leopold II in DR Congo; for it can be assumed that after Leopold II, the next generation of leaders took him as their role model even if their behavior was a little bit influenced by the international pressure and the human rights organizations.

- **Belgian Congo**

Due to the international pressure and the human right organizations, Leopold II was obliged to give the control of the Congo Free State to the Belgian government. Morel's initiative of denouncing the atrocities committed by Leopold's agents resulted in an important turning point for Congo. November 15, 1908, the country was renamed and put on direct control of Belgian authorities. So, Leopold's personal - rule ended and the Belgian administration took over (Dembour, 2008).

Their rule was based on what was called 'colonial trinity' that involved the Colonial Administration, the Missionaries, and Big Companies (Mpuila, 2012). These three institutions worked hand in hand to make sure their personal interests are protected in detriment of the general population of Congo.

For example, when there is a strike organized by the indigenous population against a private company, the state (Belgian political authorities) in Congo helped to break it and remove other barriers imposed by the workforce. The missionaries were also in harmony with the State. To make sure they continue to have the state's protection and help, they continued to use the policies given to them by Leopold II on how to behave during their missionary services to indigenous peoples. The content of the policy is found in the letter of Leopold II to the missionaries in 1883.

The full content of this letter that aimed to fake the teachings of missionaries is reproduced in chapter twelve of this book on section "Teachings of Christian religions during the colonial period". Asking missionaries to fake the message of the Bible shows unity between the State and the Christian religious leaders. They shared the same purposes: to work for the interest of Belgium and the missionaries, to teach indigenous people a 'blind obedience', to make sure they remain ignorant, and to fake the true teachings of the Bible to maintain the colonized eternally in ignorance and poverty.

In addition to that, the Belgian rule was very harsh and very direct in terms of authority and administration. Indigenous peoples were not given a chance to take part in positions of authority; in contrast to the other colonial powers in Africa like British and French who were training traditional leaders and other indigenous people in order to assume some posts of authority under the supervision of the colonialists. They offered an improved way of ruling their colonies called 'indirect rule' that the Belgian colonialists did not use, instead they used a discriminatory 'direct rule'.

So, indigenous people in Congo did not learn to rule with justice but were observing how their masters were ruling unjustly and cruelly; that was a very bad 'role model' for the colonized. In the 1940s and 1950s, the country experienced an important level of urbanization and various programs were implemented by the colonial administration to develop the colony. During that period a new middle class of Europeanized African called "*les évolués*" (developed or civilized) was formed in the cities. This was another serious problem created in the Congolese society by Colonialists. People who were trained to wear, to eat, to speak, etc. to live like colonialists could think of themselves to have been equipped and developed to cope effectively with the challenges of modernization or/and globalization.

Conversely, the formal education of colonial era was inadequate, as we are going to discuss about it in chapter twelve of this book, although the educated of that period seemed to behave as if they have become like their colonial masters and so different or separated from the general population of the country! That was an ugly lie, and still, it is today. Some Congolese who have undergone a certain level of formal education and become able to communicate with one or more of the languages of western countries (languages of former colonialists or official languages) think they are smarter than the average population. Thus, they end up by not being helpful in their communities because of thinking very higher of themselves. That is a form of barrier to the durable peace and prosperity in the DRC today with roots originating from colonial period; a change of mentality is really needed as it is suggested in chapter seven of this book.

Nzongola-Ntalanja (2002) writes, in his book 'The Congo from Leopold to Kabila', that the history of democracy movement in Congo consists of four major periods which are the independence struggle from 1959 to 10=960, the second independence movement from 1963 to 1968, the fight against Mobutu's dictatorship and reign of terror from 1969 to 1997, and the current struggle against new forms of dictatorship and external aggression.

In 1925, the Belgium annexed the mandated territory to the Congo to Create a single administrative entity known as Congo Belge et Ruanda-Urundi. In 1931, pende

345

uprising, one of the major rural revolts in the Belgian Congo, takes place in the Kwilu region against the economic hardships imposed by the colonial state and the concerning companies. On December, 4 – 9, 1941, UMHK mine-workers' general strike begins in Likasi and ends with the massacre of over one hundred strikers in Lubumbashi. From February to May 1944, there was insurrection by soldiers, workers, peasants and white-collar employees along the line of rail from Kananga to Lubumbashi. In 1945, dockworkers' strike and demonstration at Matadi. During this same year, Ruanda-Urundi becomes a UN trust territory under Belgian supervision.

In 1946 Joseph Kasavubu, a Kongo intellectual and middle-level civil servant, gives a lecture in Kinshasa on 'the right of the first occupant'. In 1948, the process of assimilating educated African elites or 'évolués' begins in the Belgian Congo with the introduction of the 'social merit card'. In 1950, Abako is established as an association for the promotion of Kongo language and culture. In 1951, Simon Kimbangu dies in jail at Lubumbashi after 30 years of detention. In 1952, another step in the assimilation process is taken with the introduction of the status of 'matriculation' or the designation of a certain categories of évolués as honorary Europeans.

In 1954, The controversy over the establishment of public schools in the Congo plays a major role in politicizing the évolués, who are now beneficiaries of the importation of Belgian political organizations in the colony. Kasavubu takes over the presidency of Abako with a determination to go beyond its original cultural agenda to deal with more general issues of social and political emancipation in the Congo.

In 1955, King Baudouin's visit to the Congo and his willingness to listen to the voices of the évolués helped to strengthen those advocating political liberalization and power sharing with the African elites. February, 1956, professor A. A. J. Van Bilsen's pamphlet with a 'thirty-year plan for the political emancipation of Belgian Africa' is published in French translation. 2 July, A group of Catholic intellectuals known as 'Conscience Africaine' responds favorably to the Van Bilsen plan, with a manifesto published in 'Courrier d'Afrique', a Kinshasa newspaper. 23 August, a counter-manifesto by Abako rejects the plan and in presenting the group's position, Kasavubu calls for 'immediate independence'.

In 1957, Abako wins an impressive victory in the municipal elections in Kinshasa. On April 20, 1958, at his inauguration as the mayor of the Dendale commune or municipality in Kinshasa, Kasavubu called for the recognition of the Congo as a nation. In October, Patrice Lumumba, Joseph Ileo, Cyrille Adoula, and Joseph Ngalula found the Mouvement National Congolais (MNC), a nation-wide political party. In December, Lumumba, Ngalula, and Gaston Diomi attend the 'All African People's Conference' in Accra, Ghana. On December 28, Lumumba held a mass rally in Kinshasa, to report to the nation on the Accra conference and to agitate for independence. On January 4, 1959, popular uprising for independence in Kinshasa. And on January 13, the Belgian King and government announced their willingness to consider independence for the Congo.

● **Post-colonial period (post-independence)**

The Belgian colonialists granted independence to Congolese in June 1960. Patrice Emery Lumumba became the government's prime minister while Joseph Kasavubu was president of the country. The Belgium did not prepare the Congolese elites for independence; they plundered the national treasury and handed the State to the newly independent government with debts. With the aim of having a hand on the rich copper belt of Katanga, the Belgian Colonialists supported Moise Tsombe to declare Katanga province independent. That happened just a few days after the independence of Congo.

The following chronology of events puts clear that the early period of post-independence of Congo had nothing peaceful and prosperous that could lead to a better future of self-governance. Nzongola-Ntalanja (2002) writes,

"11 July 1960: With Belgian support, Moise Tshombe, president of the Katanga provincial government, declares the secession of the province from the Congo. 12 July: President Kasa-Vubu and Prime Minister Lumumba appeal to the United Nations for UN troops to protect the country against external aggression and to restore its territorial integrity, an appeal to which the Un would later respond favorably. 8 August: Albert Kalonji proclaims the secession of South Kasai. 18 August: US President Dwight D. Eisenhower authorizes the assassination of Prime Minister Lumumba. August-September: ANC troops on their way to Katanga are given orders to end the secession of South Kasai, and their actions result in large-scale massacres at Mbuji-Mayi and Kasengulu. 5 September: Using the Mbuji-Mayi massacre and its characterization as 'genocide' by UN Secretary-General Dag

Hammarskjoold, President Kasa-Vubu dismisses Lumumba as primer minister, illegally. 14 September: With parliament having refused to endorse Kasa-Vubu's decision and renewed its confidence in Lumumba, ANC Chief of Staff Joseph-Desire Mobutu stages his first military coup and replaces the legitimate government with a college of commissioners composed of university graduates and students. 24 November: In a credentials vote, the UN General Assembly favors Kasa-Vubu's delegation over the one representing the democratically elected government, thus endorsing Lumumba's dismissal. 27 November: A virtual prisoner in his own official residence in Kinshasa, Lumbumba tries to break out of his isolation by fleeing to his political stronghold of Kisangani, where Deputy Prime Minister Antoine Gizenga had already established the legitimate government. (Nzongola-Ntalanja, 2002).

All that has been done not for the interest of the people of Congo because when 20,000 peacekeepers were sent to Congo after the request for assistance made by the newly formed independent government to the United Nations in July 1960, serious destructive conflicts had already made alive. The UN peacekeeping mission was called ONUC

(Opération des Nations Unies au Congo/United Nations Operations in Congo).

However, the ONUC mission was not successful and behaved as working on account of some western capitalist countries that feared the hegemony of communist countries in the rich independent Congo. That was the importation of the Cold War in Africa – in the Congo. And in September 1960, Lumumba was removed from power due to a coup d'état led by Col. Joseph-Désiré who was supported by Belgium and the United Nations. That paralyzed the government by arresting Lumumba. This nationalist man was handed over to his enemy Moise Tshombe in Katanga and there he was tortured and murdered on 17 January 1961.

To make sure the killers cover-up their crime, they unburied his body and cut it into pieces and after dissolved it in acid. That was the historical time when the country wanted to lead its own fate and destiny but failed. The seriousness of the situation resulted in the death of the UN Secretary-General Dag Hammarskjöld who was traveling to Zambia for peace talks in September 1961.

The colonialists who had been tormenting the people of Congo were not tired and wanted to maintain the position-power at all cost. That was the beginning of a new era of killing, stilling, and illegal exploitation of the country's riches. The activities that began with Leopold II did not end but took a different form making impossible durable peace and prosperity of the general population of the country.

In 1964, the Katanga province was again controlled by the central government, and the peacekeeping mission of UN was withdrawn. And then came the Mobutu era which was dictatorial and very murderous; Mobutu seized power in 1965 after his second coup d'état. This man was very dangerous for the peace of many in the country especially the intellectual elites who seemed to oppose his dictatorial regime and for the durable prosperity of the population of Congo. With the Belgian and American support with CIA, Mobutu established himself as a king. He made the country a nation of 'singers and dancers', and even some governors of the provinces could dance for him!

355

In 1966, the mining of the country was nationalized by Mobutu; he used nepotism too much that he put his family members and friend in charge of some important managerial positions of the organizations of the State. During the same year, he made much money – billions of dollars – through trade in copper, cobalt, diamonds, and coffee. On 4th June 1969, the students of the University of Kinshasa were massacred after demonstrating peacefully against the growing dictatorial regime of Mobutu. Some of the human rights violating decisions that were taken during the regime of Mobutu mentioned here.

> "1971 June: Kinshasa and Lubumbashi university students are forcibly enrolled in the army, for daring to commemorate the 1969 massacre. July: The Catholic University of Lovanium and the Protestant Congo Free University are nationalized to create a single state university with campuses at Kinshasa, Lubumbashi and Kisangani. 27 October: Mobutu

unilaterally changes the country's name from 'Congo' to 'Zaire'" (Nzongola-Ntalanja, 2002).

His power grew year after year; he had much support from the US government because of his willingness to serve as a springboard in the Cold War in Africa. For example, he facilitated the US operations against Soviet-backed Angola in 1971. He changed his name to Mobutu Sese Seko Nkuku Ngbendu wa Za Banga which can be translated into the following words: The powerful warrior who goes from conquest to conquest, leaving fire in his wake because of his endurance and inflexible will to win! In 1991, a national initiative for multiparty democracy started in the country. The National Sovereign Conference is open to discuss the transitional situation. That was possible due to the 'so-called end' of the famous Cold War in the world; the support of western countries to Mobutu became insignificant. So, internal and external pressure were put on him in order to democratize the country. Social, political, and economic situations of the country were discussed during the Conference. Its end resulted in the formation of a transitional government and Mobutu remained president with considerable power.

Practically, in the day to day activities of the State, no improvement was seen in the country. In fact, in April 1994, during the genocide in the neighboring country Rwanda, some 800,000 people were killed – mostly of the Tutsi ethnic group and the moderate Hutu – and about a million Hutu took refuge in DRC (Zaire by that time). We have witnessed some of the horrible events that occurred in DRC (and in the whole AGLR) from the time

Rwandan refugees entered in the country up to the failed regime of Joseph Kabila. Refugees from Rwanda were put in concentration camps where the conditions of living were worse; and in July 1994, it was reported that an estimated 50,000 people died out of cholera.

November 1994, due to the inability of the government of Zaire (DRC) to care for the refugees in the camps, there was a birth of a certain disorder that resulted in insecurity enabling the humanitarian organizations to stop working there. It was reported that former Rwandan Hutu soldiers controlled access to the camps and food distribution! In November 1996 to May 1997, the Alliance of Force for Democratic Liberation (AFDL) supported by Rwanda, Uganda, and Burundi invaded Zaire and took power. Millions of Rwandan refugees and other Congolese people were killed during the first and the second wars of DRC. Mubutu who was already weak physically because of sickness fled to Morocco when Laurent Desire Kabila, the leader of AFDL, seized the capital of the country Kinshasa in May 1997. Mobutu died of prostate cancer in September 1997.

The soldiers of the AFDL, most of them of Tutsi ethnic group, have killed many Rwandese Hutu refugees in DRC; and their massive killing was qualified as 'new genocide in RDC' in June 1998 by the UN investigation team. Some Hutu, ancient soldiers of Rwanda who escaped the killing run into deep Congo forest where they formed the Army for the Liberation of Rwanda (ALIR). This rebel movement has also made durable peace and prosperity of people impossible; its power was in the fact that they had members inside the country and outside. Many people have lost their lives due to the sporadic attacks of these ALIR in the DRC.

However, the President Laurent Kabila decided to expel his allies, the Rwandan Army, back to their country. The Tutsi working for his government lost their positions. The president's attempt to be independent from Rwanda and Uganda (the countries that supported him to take power in DRC) resulted in the formation of a new rebel movement composed by the Rwandan and Uganda armies. They invaded DRC in August 1998. The pretext behind that was that President Laurent Kabila had violated their agreement. Many Congolese civilians were victims of torture and murder because of their physical likeness with Hutu of Rwanda.

Terence Co gives a brief account of how it started by putting,

> "The Second Congo War began with the defection of Sylvain Mbuki, commander of the FAC (Force Armees Congolaises or Armed Forces of the Congo) 10th Brigade, on 2 August 1998. Mbuki went on the radio to announce: 'The army of the DRC has taken the decision to remove President Laurent Desire Kabila from power.' In the next few days FAC brigades in the eastern Congo joined the uprising. Supported by Rwandan troops, the rebels quickly took over Goma, Bukavu (capital of South Kivu province) and Uvira (second-largest city in that same province) without much fighting. At that moment, UPDF (Ugandan People's Defense Force) troops crossed the border into the DRC on the grounds they were going after some local guerrillas. Then, on 5 August, the conflict escalated when the RPA (Rwandan Patriotic Army), the UPDF, and the rebels in the eastern Congo coordinated an operation that involved some 25,000 troops in an airlift to Bas-Congo province just to the west of Kinshasa." Terence Co (2013, p. 31).

To stop the progress of this rebel movement (the second war of DRC of 1998), Laurent Desire Kabila sought support from Zimbabwe, Namibia, and Angola to avoid seizure of Kinshasa the capital of the country by the rebels. But with the presence of soldiers from Rwanda and Uganda, the RDC government remained unable to control a large part of the east of the country.

The fighting did not stop; the Hutu rebel movement ALIR joined the president Kabila in the fight against the RDC primarily led by Tutsi politicians and officials. In August 1998, a peace-talk was held in Lusaka the capital of Zambia. A ceasefire agreement is signed, but the parties involved failed to stop fighting. Many people in the eastern part of DRC lost their properties, their family members, their lives, etc. because nothing changed in the country after the peace-talk that was boycotted by the rebel leaders.

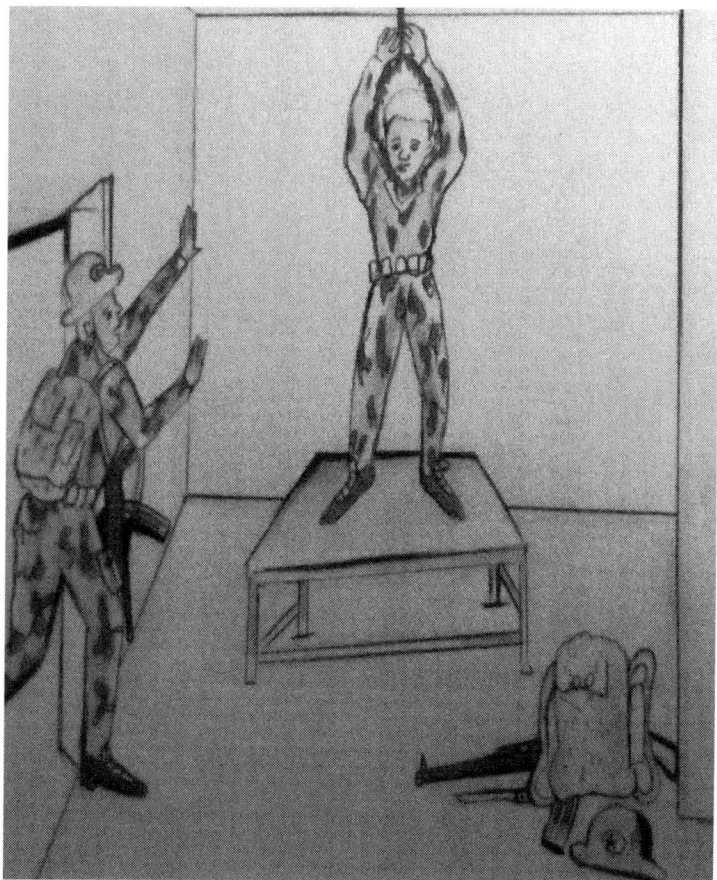

And even the establishment of a peacekeeping mission called MONUC in November 1999 with 500 military observers; this mission failed to put an end to the misery of the general population caused by wars and insecurity in the regions where the rebels were doing their dirty business that cost the lives of millions.

In February 2000, the UN Security Council added more 5,537 peacekeeping troops to strengthen their peace operations in DRC; but MONUC remained unable to eradicate the activities of the rebels. People were still raped, tortured, killed, etc. by the belligerents. The fighting between Laurent Desire Kabila regime and the Rwanda-Uganda aggressors was very bloody. Many innocent civilians lost their lives. Some were even buried alive in some village of DRC.

And the natural riches of the country continued to be stolen and illegally exported to foreign countries. Efforts were made to stop that, but nothing changed. For example, in May 2000 the diamond industry launched with campaign groups in Kimberley in South Africa to discuss the possibility of stopping the trade in conflict diamonds. And during the same year in June, the United Nations appointed a panel of experts to investigate on the illegal exploitation of country's mineral wealth and how it relates to the state of the conflict between the belligerents.

In May 2000, the ALIR re-named their rebel movement to the Democratic Forces for the Liberation of Rwanda (FDLR). The next month, in June, the Rwanda and Uganda troops fight for six days with the aim to take control of Kisangani province. About 150 civilians were killed, and 700 others were injured (The Associated Press – June 11, 2000). The battle was qualified war crimes by the UN – Uganda and Rwanda were asked pay the consequences – but astonishingly nothing was done neither by the Congolese government nor by the accused countries. A Rwandan officer known by the name of Karenzi Karake who was involved in that battle was later appointed to serve as deputy commander of the UN peacekeeping mission in Darfur. "The decision was taken despite General Kamanzi having served as one of the most senior military figures in Rwanda when the country supplied troops and weapons to a brutal militia in eastern Congo." (Rever, 2015).

Was he rewarded for what they have done in the DRC? The people who should pay penalties are being promoted to new post of responsibly! The death toll was high because during the month of June 2000, the International Rescue Committee reported that more than 1.7 million people had died since the year 1998 as a result of the war in RDC; the same report was updated in June 2001 showing that 2.5 millions have lost their lives with an important loss of children in the country (Coghlan, B. at al., 2006, p.1)..

It is not only the millions of people who had been killed many trees and wild animals have also lost their lives. And more other people continue to die to this date as a result of what has been happening in DRC. On 16 January 2001, one of the bodyguards of the president

Laurent D. Kabila shot him to death. His sun Joseph Kabila took power at a very young age of 29.

In April 2001, the first detailed report of UN panel of experts on illegal exploitation of the riches of the country was published; it denounced the military officials and companies implicated in the illegal trade and suggested sanctions to them. But, as the accused have been enjoying the state of impunity for no action was taken; could we assume that the riches that were stolen belonged to nobody or the owners were at the same time involved in other kinds of robbery or guilty of another type of crime that they feared to follow up? A country cannot expect durable peace and prosperity of its population if no one is responsible enough to punish the guild or to take serious care of its national riches.

DRC which had been plundered by the colonialists in the past has been object of new strategies of robbery; and sadly, some of its so-called political leaders cooperating with some people of foreign countries to get by force its minerals with the blood of their brothers and sisters as the national price to pay... If the DRC and its neighboring countries do not have companies that need the natural minerals to function? Can we presume that the AGLR countries are put into conflict by the buyers of minerals?

In February 2002, a second peace talk was held in Sun City in South Africa. It was called the Inter-Congolese dialogue and lasted for 52 days. Among the main groups, two signed an agreement but the rebels with support from Rwanda were excluded. In April 2002, DRC became a member of the International Criminal Court (ICC) by ratifying the Rome Statute. And in June 2002, the Human Rights Watch published a report entitled 'The War Within the War' showing that rape was used as a weapon of war in the eastern part of the country. Millions of women were raped and some suffered atrocious consequences and some even died after that act.

Day after day, people were killed and nothing was done; no intervention at all. Life of a human being in the RDC has become useless for the government. In September 2002, it was reported that an estimated number of 3,000 civilians were brutally killed in the town of Nyankunde in Ituri district in the Kisangani province. Astonishingly, some bodies of human beings were eaten by some militias as goat-meat.

That loss of human lives in DRC was said to be the largest massacre of the second Congo war. The international community made pressure on Rwanda; the result of that was the withdrawal of 20,000 Rwandan troops out of DRC and the peacekeeping troops were increased to 8,600 (Human Rights Watch, 2009). Although those troops left RDC in October 2002, they have already trained some networks of armed militias that continued to do business on their behalf. And during the same month, the UN panel of experts listed 85 international companies that were not respecting the international business norms in the country.

The DRC has been looking its resources for the profit of international companies and foreign individuals. People who could be used to protect the country have been used for a long time to serve for the interest of foreigners. Even the peace deals are faked for the interest of the people in business but not for the general population.

In December 2002, the rebels supported by Rwanda and Uganda agreed to sign a peace agreement with the government that resulted in the formation of a government of transition in which the power was shared. The DRC had then one president who was Joseph Kabila and four vice-presidents among them two were former leaders of rebel groups. The presence of these people in the political management of the country did not change the situation of the general populations. It was like all of them were working for their own interest and the sake of their former parties or rebel groups.

The victims of insecurity, civil war, and military barbarism continued to increase. The reports of the International Rescue Committee gave a death toll of 3.3 million of victims since 1998 up to April 2003. What was astonishing was that by the moment the government of transition was working to manage the politics of the country other armed foreign group was also doing its business on the territory of the country.

Due to the power of the international diplomatic pressure, the foreign armed group from Uganda was obliged to withdraw. They departure gave birth to an inter-ethnic unrest in Ituri. There occurred a fighting in which thousands of civilians lost their lives; that happened in May 2003 and in June 2003 European troops were deployed to Ituri to help the UN peacekeepers protect civilians who were targeted by ethnic groups in rebellion.

In a report entitled 'Ituri: covered in Blood', the Human Rights Watch organization showed how the human rights of people were severely violated by the ethnic groups in rebellion. During the same period in July 2003, the UN Security Council gave the authorization to add more soldiers to the peacekeeping troops to reach 10,800 and gave them mandate to use force for the sake of protecting civilians.

Although the work of the government of transition, the effort of NGOs to denounce the atrocities committed by rebel groups, and the mandate of UN peacekeepers to use force to protect civilians, etc. the country did not recover by following the paths of durable peace and prosperity of the general population. People were still suffering from poverty and insecurity as it is up to date. In July 2003, while it was already announced that the government of transition will work for two years before the democratic elections, the fighting continued in the eastern parts of DRC. The pillage of the natural resources continued and was facilitated by the citizens, national or international organizations as it is always the case.

To make it clear on the eyes of the general public, in October 2003 the UN panel on illegal exploitation puts, in its final report, that the robbery of the minerals of DRC continued and was one of the major causes of conflict. The panel made recommendations to scrutinize some 33 companies that were already denounced in their previous report. So, the transitional government made a request to the International Criminal Court (ICC) to investigate the crimes committed in the DRC since July 2002; the request was made in March 2004. Some Congolese found that request interesting with the hope that it will reduce the violation of human rights. But surprisingly, in May 2004 some media in the country reported a number of cases of sexual abuses made by MONUC (United Nations Organization Mission in the Democratic Republic of the Congo) peacekeepers!

The people who came to protect civilians started to abuse them. Rwanda still hungry for what they had already been doing in the DRC supported a certain Tutsi general Laurent Nkunda who took control of the town of Bukavu in the South Kivu province saying he was protecting

Tutsi civilians under attack. This happened during the period of May – June 2004; many people lost their properties and others lost their lives including a classmate who died in our hands at school by a stray bullet.

But Laurent Nkunda was forced to leave the town after four days due to considerable diplomatic pressure. The general population gathered themselves in crowds to protest against the MONUC staff who appeared unwilling to use its peacekeeping soldiers to stop the progress of Nkunda and his soldiers. In the middle of all those rebel businesses, in June 2004 the ICC announces to open its first investigation on crimes committed in DRC with focus on Ituri.

In August 2004, one of the four Vice-Presidents Azarias Ruberwa of Tutsi ethnic group and leader of a former rebel movement RCD stopped his participation in the transitional government because of the 160 Congolese Tutsi who were massacred by Burundian Hutu in a refugee camp in Gatumba – Burundi. But Azarias did not delay to reintegrate the government of transition due to diplomatic pressure. UN peacekeeping troops kept on increasing in number; in October 2004, the UN Security Council decided to add more 5,900 troops for the peace operation in DRC (UN Security Council, 2005 – Press Release).

So, MONUC had a total number of 16,431 troops in the country for its mission of protecting civilians. The contrast was that while the UN troops are increasing the death toll was also mounting and it reached 3.9 million dead according to the International Rescue Committee fourth mortality survey of December 2004 (Coghlan, B. at al., 2006).

Some of those deaths were due to the impossibility to access medicine and nutrition as the consequence of insecurity, rebellious atrocities, and wars. It was very sad that the leaders who were at the center of the problems that the populations were facing could sometimes be promoted to new posts of responsibility. For example, in January 2005 the human rights organizations in DRC denounced the appointment of five former Ituri rebel military leaders with cruel records of abusing the rights of civilians as generals in the army of the country. Was that a recompense for the blood they have shed in Ituri?

Was the government happy what they had done to civilians in Ituri?

The country had been since long ago in the hands of blood-shaders. It is still like that up to this very day; some people on power think human blood make safe leadership. Even the UN peacekeepers were sometimes killed. In February 2005, nine peacekeepers were trapped in an ambush and lost their lives; that was done by militias in Ituri.

The people who were sent in the DRC to protect civilians seemed to be in need of protection too! The country appeared to be like an unprotected and open field where everybody is free to do any business! The government trying to show its responsibility to protect civilians had arrested Thomas Lubanga and Floriber Njabu in March 2005 (UN Security Council, 2015 – Press Release). These two guys accused of war crimes in Ituri were arrested by Congolese authorities and transferred to Kinshasa the capital of DRC and to the ICC.

June 2005, a report by the Human Rights Watch entitled 'The Curse of Gold' informed that armed groups and multinational companies were illegally taking profit of the gold mining areas of the country, especially the eastern parts of DRC, and were the cause of the widespread human rights abuses. Another denouncement of plunder was made by a Congolese parliamentarian commission that many mining contracts were either illegal or gave no benefit to the State. Surprisingly, in June 2005, the report of that parliamentarian commission was seen missing some copies during its distribution to parliament. Did some copies of the report go missing because of stressing on judicial actions against senior political and corporate actors?

Some citizens especially the political leaders in the DRC can be held the first responsible for the situation of the country. The outrageous hunger for power and money had been destroying the country since long ago. Was it not the same egoistic hunger for power and money that led the politicians in the transitional government to delay the elections that were supposed to be held in 2005? In July 2005, in the capital of DRC Kinshasa, thousands of civilians demonstrated to protest against that delay. The police dispersed them with tear gas.

However, the borders of the DRC were very fragile because unprotected by the government. In September 2005 while the general populations were complaining about the delay of the elections, the Lord's Resistance Army (LRA) penetrated in the country installing themselves in Garamba National Park. The Uganda government threatened to enter DRC to pursue the LRA that was a long-lasting and powerful rebel movement in Uganda at that time. The United Nations did not stay silent about that.

In October 2005, the ICC made public the first arrest warrants for five senior leaders of the LRA, and in the same month, MONUC was supplied with more peacekeepers making their total number to over 17,000 (Human Rights Watch, 2009). That made the UN peacekeeping mission in the DRC the largest in the world at that time. In November 2005, a rebel movement Mai Mai that was doing its operations in Katanga province and led by a former ally of Kabila, Gedeon Kyungu Mutanda, was attacked by the Congolese army; it was reported that there were atrocities on both sides and the civilians were victims of that.

Regardless the sufferings resulting from rebel movements in the country, people were to adopt the project of the law that was to become the new constitution in a referendum in December 2005. While that was being done, the International Court of Justice said Uganda had committed human rights violations and illegal pillage of the resources of DRC during the period of 1998 and 2003 when its military troops occupied some parts of the country. The Court stressed that Uganda should pay the compensation, but they did not. The armed rebel group from Uganda, LRA, was attacked by the UN peacekeepers in Garamba National Park in January 2006. The peacekeepers failed to arrest the LRA leaders and some eight Guatemalan peacekeepers were killed.

But in March 2006, one of the most dangerous rebel leaders, Thomas Lubanga was transferred to the ICC after an arrest warrant that accused him of war crime and recruitment of children to make them soldiers. He was kept in jail or custody by the ICC. The next month, in April 2006 another killing of a Nepalese peacekeeper was signaled in Ituri and seven others were taken in hostage, but they were released a month later after negotiations. Were the militias in Ituri telling the peacekeepers that they were not able to provide security to civilians while they also needed to be secured? Or that was part of their games? DRC started to register the candidates for elections in April 2006, but that registration was made slow by the fighting in the east of the country.

That delayed the elections that were boycotted by an opposition political party 'Union for Democracy and Social Progress (UDPS). They said elections cannot be free and fair in the middle of terrible violations of human rights and the bloody activities of rebel groups in the east of the country. To help in the election process, the UN Security Council agreed on the deployment 2,000 soldiers from the European Union to support the UN peacekeepers during the elections. They entered the DRC in April 2006 and remained there until the end of November 2006.

The campaign for elections started in June 2006. There were 33 presidential candidates but the winner was Joseph Kabila. While it was being reported that Kyungu Mutanga is handed over to the Government of Kinshasa, other rebel movements were still operating in the country and other prepared to start!

> "On 16 May 2006, MONUC handed Kyungu Mutanga over to the Armed Forces of the Democratic Republic of Congo. The Superior Military Auditor Lubumbashi then became seized

of the matter. Kyungu Mutanga was detained under the authority of the military court but was not immediately charged." (Trial International, 2016).

Mr. President,

Don't worry. I am in charge of all the dioceses of the country. I will make sure all my Christians vote for you again... the second mandate is yours! Give the money.

... Thank you so much for securing our partnership. I am sure the Church and my government will cooperate to continue our win-win situation for the next 5 years that I am going to rule the country.

Corrupt leaders will never help build durable peace and prosperity.

One month later in July 2006, Laurent Nkunda started a new rebel movement in North Kivu province of DRC. They called their movement 'the National Congress for the Defense of the People (CNDP). Whom were they defending? The general population or their egoistic interests? While the country had been transformed into an 'unprotected field' where people harvested by force what did not belong to them, the transitional government managed to make 70 percent of voters to vote in August 2006.

The results showed that the president Joseph Kabila had 45 percent, his main challenger who was one of the vice-presidents of the country, Jean-Pierre Bemba, had 20 percent, and the other vice-president Azarias Ruberwa won less than 10 percent of the vote. Following the announcement of that result, more than 15 people have been killed in the capital of DRC, Kinshasa (Gettleman, & Sundaramaug, 2006). The Independent Electoral Commission (CEI) organized the second round of the vote because none of the candidates won 50 percent of the vote as required by the Constitution of the country at that time.

The supporters of Kabila being unhappy with that, they ordered soldiers to spread out in Kinshasa. Frightened by that situation, the soldiers of the security guards of the vice-president Bemba exchanged fire, and some people were killed. The gun-bullets exchange between the two rival groups was so dangerous that it took the intervention of the UN peacekeepers to save some ambassadors from Bemba's dwelling place where they were trapped by soldiers' firing.

After a cease-fire, it was reported by the media that there were 23 deaths. Watch Human Rights Watch (November 25, 2008) reported about that by putting,

> "The government of President Joseph Kabila has used violence and intimidation to eliminate its political opponents beginning in the immediate aftermath of the election's inconclusive July-August 2006 first round. In his first interview after his victory in the October runoff against former vice-president Jean-Pierre Bemba, Kabila said that he would be "severe" in governing Congo. He has matched his actions to those words. (…)
>
> "The worst of the repression took place in the capital, Kinshasa, and in the province of Bas Congo, areas where Kabila failed to win an electoral majority. In Kinshasa, Kabila launched what were in effect military operations (qualifying as internal armed conflict under international law) against his electoral rival Bemba in August 2006 and again in March 2007. Soldiers and Republican Guards interviewed by Human Rights Watch who participated in the

military operations said that they had received and interpreted their orders in March 2007 as needing to "eliminate Bemba." The military operations against Bemba and his often ill-disciplined guards were brutal and sudden. The use of heavy weapons during the busy work day in central Kinshasa left hundreds of civilians dead through the indiscriminate use of force by both sides, and left many others injured."

So many people were victims of what happened in the country during that period if not all the majority of the population of the country because the use of fraud and violence benefit none, although some may not agree with that reality. The tension remained so high between the rivals and Laurent Nkunda took advantage of the revelries between Joseph Kabila and Jean Pierre Bemba to expend his area of control in the east of the country.

In November 2006, the CEI announced the victory of Kabila with 58 percent of the vote and 42 percent for Bemba (BBC News, 2006). The results were not accepted by Bemba who accused Kabila of having smuggled the vote, but he was later obliged to accept the decision of the Supreme Court that granted his rival the first position as it was already published by the media. This man who had already led the country as the president of the transitional government did not succeed to bring the country to durable peace and prosperity of the general population regardless the huge and very rich natural resources of DRC. Insecurity and conflict continued regardless the democratic elections.

From December 2006 to January 2007, the president Kabila tried to negotiate in secret a peace deal with

Nkunda, but that was done in vain. Nkunda's rebel movement that was asked to mix with the national Congolese army by a message given the DRC head of the air force at the time, General John Numbi, to Nkunda in a meeting in Rwanda failed to produce a good result. Bemba, the big political rival of Kabila, became the leader of a democratic opposition to Kabila after his election as senator. At the same time, a political and religious movement that was allied with Bemba, Bundu Dia Kongo (BDK) in Bas Congo province was dispersed in February 2007 by the police force when protesting against the provincial elections judged to be faked by fraud (Human Rights Watch, 2008).

Strategically, the president Kabila nominated the old and elderly Congolese politician Antoine Gizenga as Prime

Minister of the government. But the Congolese population of the west of the country who supported Bemba was not appeased by that, although Gizenga was also a man of the western part of DRC. In February 2007, a commission of inquiry to make investigation about what happened in Bas Congo was set by the National Assembly of the county, but its work was hindered by some political leaders. And in the east of the country, the cease-fire process that was initiated to mobilize CNDP to integrate with the Congolese army met with some problems that made it ineffective.

The press interview of Bemba made his relationship with Kabila more and more critical in March 2007. Bemba accused Kabila of corruption and attempted to kill him. In Kinshasa, his security guards of some 400 soldiers refused to join the Congolese army; that refusal resulted in a fighting between the Congolese army with Bemba's soldiers. The fighting killed hundreds of civilians; 150 security guards of Bemba were instantly killed; and many of people who were supporting him were arrested and tortured and his headquarters was destroyed. He took refuge in the South African embassy. Was it a government in another government? What is sad and troubling is that it is the innocent or ignorant civilians who are often victims of all those kinds of barbarism. The innocent people always die during the fighting; and the ignorant are manipulated by the politicians to serve their egoistic interests.

In April 2007, Bemba was able to leave the country a certain night escorted by the UN peacekeepers to the airport going to Portugal to seek medical treatment. That was made possible by the diplomatic intervention. After the events of the west of the country that made an end to Bemba's activities in Kinshasa. In May 2007 Nkunda took the turn by interrupting the integration of his rebel troops into the Congolese national army. By the way, he continued recruitment in Rwanda and in the areas that were in his control in DRC.

The government seemed not to keep silent on that; in August – September 2007, the Congolese army fought the CNDP of Nkunda. The result of that made 200,000 people to flee their homes. The main donor countries of DRC met in New York to discuss the deteriorating situation in the country – but Rwanda refused that they were helping CNDP to make war in DRC.

While the Congolese president had agreed to start military operations against the LRA in Garamba in agreement with Uganda in Tanzania in September 2007, the UN human rights experts reported that Kabila's guards had committed serious human rights violations during the fight of March in Kinshasa against the security guards of Bemba. But that report was not published according to the decision of the top UN officials.

The same president whose bodyguards violated the human rights tried to seek a ceasefire agreement between Laurant Nkunda rebel movement in North Kivu, but they refused and told him to stop supporting the Rwandan Hutu rebels, the FDLR, before any peace-negotiation with them. That happened in October 2007. And the next month, November 2007, the Congolese government signed an agreement in Nairobi the capital city of Kenya with the Rwandan government. DRC agreed to stop all form of support to the FDLR and to begin asking them to return to their country voluntarily; the use of military force was the last agreed solution in case of refusal of voluntary repatriation.

Although that agreement between Rwanda and DRC, Laurent Nkunda rebel movement did not stop their activities in the country. Civilians continued to die day after day. The soldiers of Nkunda's rebel movement who were defeated in an offensive Congolese army attack in December 2007 with support from UN peacekeepers. They asked for a peace-talk with the government. But did they cease to exist on the territory of DRC as rebels?

It sounds important to remind that in January 2008 when the peace conference was organized in Goma, the death toll was said to be of 3.4 million since 1998 according to the report of the International Rescue Committee. During that peace conference, the government signed a peace-agreement with Laurent Nkunda rebel group and with some 22 other armed groups. That was a time when some inhabitants of the eastern provinces of the country hoped durable peace and prosperity with the mobilization of almost the most destructive armed groups to the peace conference.

The event was followed by the arrest of the Ituri warlord Mathieu Ngudjolo Chui by the government and handed him over to the ICC in February 2008. It also gave more hope for peace to people as it was an act of non-impunity.

But the hope people had for peace was suddenly turned into desolation in March 2008 when more than 200 people were killed in a second attack made by the government against the Bundu Dia Kongo (BDK), a political and religious movement in the Bas Congo province. The corpses of the victims were thrown in the river and they were accused of being armed but there was no evidence.

What kind of government was that claiming to sign a peace deal to protect civilians and that used fire-guns to kill other innocent people at the same time? The time for irresponsible government is over. The time to kill because of fire is over. People have right to live the lives that their Creator wants them to live. DRC should cease to be a human butchery. Its soil is now full of the blood of its own children. Enough is enough! The UN Human Rights Council, instead of denouncing the crimes committed by the government, terminated the mandate of the independent expert on human rights for DRC, they said that the country had made a political progress and stabilization.

More other people who had committed war crimes was arrested by the ICC during 2008 such as Bosco Ntaganda (April 2008 unsealed arrest warrant), Jean-Pierre Bemba arrested in May 2008 in Belgium but his supporters said that was political and not war-crime. In September 2008, the president Kabila restarted the strike against the LRA rebels in the North of DRC. The military operations began the LRA responded. The result was very disastrous; 160 people were killed and more than 300 children were kidnapped in the villages near the LRA headquarters in Garamba National Park in the country. And the Human Rights Watch (2009) reported that "in late December 2008 and into January 2009, the Lord's Resistance Army (LRA) brutally killed more than 865 civilians and abducted at least 160 children in northern DRC".

Laurent Nkunda rebels continued to progress militarily. They took possession of an important military base in the North Kivu province in October 2008; the UN peacekeepers were criticized by the government for not doing much to stop the progress of Nkunda rebels. In contrast, the report of the UN group of experts of the October 2008 gave evidence that the FDLR was receiving support from the Congolese government and the CNDP (M23) was being supported by the government of Rwanda. In November 2008, a massacre of 150 people was perpetrated by a troop of CNDP commanded by Bosco Ntaganda in the town of Kiwanja in the North Kivu province. Thousands of other civilians fled the region making the North Kivu province in need of more humanitarian aid.

In November 2008, the UN peacekeepers were added. There were 3,000 additional troops for MONUC, and reached 20,000 soldiers (Global Research, 2008). No other country in the world had ever requested for such number for peace operations; that made it the largest UN peacekeeping mission in the world! And the United Nations appointed the former president of Nigeria Olusegun Obasanjo as its special envoy to help put an end to the Congolese crisis. During the same period of history, the report by Human Rights Watch entitled *'We Will Crush You'* denounced the anti-democratic management of the president Kabila and his government including the executions, tortures, and arbitrary arrests.

In reaction to that report, the government held a press conference saying that what was reported was not true. And the parliament stressed on full inquiry about that. But the killing of civilians continued, when the LRA rebels were attacked by a joint Ugandan, Southern Sudanese, and Congolese troop in December 2008 with support from the US, the country lost 800 people and tens of thousands of civilians were displaced. In January 2009, the CNDP military leader Bosco Ntaganda (chief of staff – but on warrant arrest of ICC) declared that his rebel movement was to integrate the Congolese national army to help fight the FDLR. The Congolese government welcomed that and made Ntaganda a general in the Congolese army although he was wanted to be arrested by the ICC. The Congolese parliamentarians were not pleased by the decision of the government. The same month, the Rwandan troops crossed the border to enter the DRC.

In February 2009, they jointly attacked the FDLR with the Congolese troops. The FDLR were pushed far from their regular bases. After that event, Rwandan troops withdrew from DRC. But some weeks later, the FDLR retaliated against civilians in the DRC killing hundreds of them and tens of thousands were displaced. At the time, the LRA continued their attacks in northern parts of the country. Civilians had always been the victims of all kind of military or rebels business in the DRC. The country has been suffering a serious loss in all areas of its economy – the loss of human capital is the most serious.

Do most of civilians in the DRC think there can be hope for durable peace and prosperity without strong connections to a powerful source of power that will stop the people who were supposed to bring security and stability but are corrupted, and have been working for their own egoistic interests? While the Congolese government was signing a peace deal with CNDP to transform it into a political party in March 2009, the FDLR and the LRA continued to exist as rebel armed groups.

But the UN eager to continue their operations in the country was ready to support the Congolese army to pursue their attacks against the FDLR and the LRA. And Rwanda refused to send Laurent Nkunda to the trial in DRC as demanded by the government. The atrocious acts continued as daily barbarism in the DRC including sexual violence; during that historical period of the country, MONUC adopted a strategy to fight against sexual violence. Was that effective and efficient?

However, the economic situation of the country was becoming more and more worse. The general population was not able to manage their daily businesses well especially in the eastern part of the country because of insecurity and wars. A rural exodus was observed; people living in villages and forests were forced to flee towards towns and townships fearing the sporadic attacks of armed militia. That made the towns and townships very crowded and with insignificant supply in food and other needed basic items. The people of the villages who were producing crops to sell them to towns decreased and so the crop supply from villages.

The price of renting houses increased in towns and the even the price of buying a plot of land to build a house galloped very high. A new dangerous and non-negligible plot-conflict occurred especially in the eastern parts of DRC. The people who worked for the State especially the civil servants, teachers, police, and soldiers were complaining about not being paid their salaries. In the middle of that economic crisis, the International Monetary Fund (IMF) approved for the DRC, as reported by Reuters, a loan of USD 550 million which made the country eligible for IMF debt relief program. "The debt relief, which will cut the DRC's overall stock of public and publicly-guaranteed debt, will be reduced to about $4 billion from $13 billion, a senior IMF official said." (Reuters Africa, 2009).

That seems to be what Congolese political leadership is all about. Winning money even if they are losing people it's alright! That being putting money first and not caring about the durable peace and prosperity for all in a country that makes sure the people and their goods are safe. While the money-winners are busy counting the money in their offices, in April – May 2009, a report of the UN agencies mentioned that 800,000 people were forced to flee their homes during the operations of armed rebel groups and the Congolese army in eastern Congo. The soldiers who were not paid by the government continued to loot and to rape (Human Rights Watch, 2009).

While the attacks of FDLR and LRA continued in May 2009, the Congolese parliament was trying to pass an amnesty law rebel groups in the South-Kivu and Nork-Kivu provinces of DRC. But the war crimes or crimes against humanity was not concerned by the amnesty. Amazingly, without shame the president Kabila celebrated in June 2009 the Independence Day in the capital city of North-Kivu, Goma, saying that peace has finally come home! During the same month, a report by the Human Rights Watch put that there was increasing human rights abuse since the beginning of military attacks against the rebels of FDLR and LRA.

The report showed that both government soldiers and rebels were committing war crimes, but the government denied it. The government was unable to adequately control even the administrative areas where there were no militias. There was unacceptable disorder for a country; for example, some military leaders played the role of administrative officers in charge of collective taxes from the population.

A country in which soldiers are doing business asking people to pay taxes to them cannot achieve durable peace and prosperity of its general population. That is to build a military government in a so-called democratic government – an autonomous government in another autonomous government – of irresponsible leaders!

The DRC had registered several cases of insecurity and human rights violation during the year 2010 as in the previous years. We may cite the death of the human rights advocate Floriert Chebeya, the reported mass rapes in North Kivu province for which the both the rebels and the army were blamed by the Un envoy Margot Wallstorm (BBC News, 2016), fight against ADF-NALU (Allied Democratic Forces-National Army for the Liberation of Uganda), accusation of the networks within the Congolese army of promoting violence in East of the country to profit from mining, smuggling, and poaching (BBC News, 2016).

It was during the year 2010 in November that the greatest political challenger of Kabila, Jean-Pierre Bemba was set to the International Criminal Court for accused of allowing his troops to rape and kill in Central African Republic for the period of 2002 – 2003. That happened while the country is getting prepared for the 2011 elections. Was something done by the ruling party to make sure he could not appear in the political scene in the DRC for the next elections?

Many commentators considered that as one of the several events that made increased Joseph Kabila's chance to win the 2011 elections. Other favorable events prior to the 2011 elections are but not limited to the changes in the Constitutions of January 2011, the Court ruling against Lt-Col Kibibi Mutware for 20 years in jail for mass rape in Eastern Congo in February 2011, the trial of Ignace Murwanashyaka (Rwandan Hutu Rebel) in Germany for crimes against humanity in DRC in May 2011 (BBC News, 2016).

Unfortunately, almost all that happened by government's efforts or NGOs' interventions in the DRC prior to the November 2011 elections did not lead to durable peace and prosperity for all. Many people commented that the government of DRC has been doing all its best to make sure its members remain in power to serve their own interests. And that is very dangerous for the future of the country and the AGLR.

> "The 2011 elections should have consolidated a fragile democratic process, but they were organized by a regime which primarily wanted to consolidate its own power. It did that by making use of its complete control over the security forces and the electoral machinery (including the commission, led by Kabila's counsellor pastor Mulunda Ngoy) against an opposition which was institutionally and strategically fragile and very

divided. The review of the Constitution in January 2011 decreased the opposition's chances even further. The 2011 elections had no added value in stimulating the emergence of democracy nor the return of political stability." (Riche & Berwouts, 2014).

The presidential election was won by Joseph Kabila who started another term in the office. The country did not have a chance of experiencing a different type of political leadership on the presidency. Just one year later in November 2012, the troops of M23 enter the town of Goma but they withdraw when they are promised that some of their supporters will be released (BBC News, 2016). Does it not sound like a game?

Promising rebels a favor so that they may withdraw from a city of a province but not withdrawing from the territory of the country seems like paying a game! There had been so many atrocious acts committed by numerous rebel movements and Mai Mai groups in the East of the DRC; many remained unpunished and unnoticed. It appeared like having so many small governments in a country controlled by a 'failed bid government'. It is like spending much of their time thinking about how to stay in power has been their number one priority.

Some of the recent events in the DRC are eloquently speaking to any good hearer; the games of political leaders (both in leading and opposition parties) of the country have never been played to serve the interests of the people of the country. When learning that dozens of people were killed in protests against proposed electoral law changes in January 2015 (BBC New, 2016), we wonder whether the people who are trying to change the law and those who are inciting people to go and die in the reads and streets bear the true identity of political leaders who are supposed to lead the people of DRC.

Don't we really have many 'small Leopold IIs' covered with black skins in the DRC? If we look at what has been happening in the DRC on the political scene, can't we just conclude that most leaders doing business for personal egoistic gain? The people of DRC need to have clear and true knowledge of the aims of the political leaders of the country. Maybe it is not amazing to see an ex-faithful ally who strongly campaigned and maybe danced for a Chief appear to be among his number one opponents in less than five years!

Maybe it doesn't convey any amazing message to see a politician expresses his or her purpose of running for presidential election, and later he or she is put in jail or attacked, and forced to leave the country! And yet both parties (the attacked and the attacker) are saying to be willing to work for the interests of the people! Who can then lead the people of DRC to durable peace and prosperity if they don't turn to a different different source of power? We need the True Source of revolutionary power. What Source it that? Can every know have clear knowledge and understanding of the Source and use its power to archieve durable peace and prosperity for all in DRC, and in the whole AGLR?

Those are some of the questions that this book gives answers to from the sixth to the fifteenth chapters. We don't need to put our hope in a human beings who have been working for their own bellies for about more than four hundred years now (four centuries) in the DRC. When it seems like everything falls apart that the victims find new and excellent ways of leading to better situations if they are awakened for the November 2016 signed deal between President Kabila's ruling coalition and the opposition to delay the presidential election until 2018 as reported by media cannot be a good news for a population that has been experiencing political mis-leadership for many years.

Chapter Four
Overview of Republic of Burundi

4.1. Country Profile

● **Location and Population**

Burundi is also a small country in size like Rwanda. It is
27,834 sq km (10,747 sq miles). A latest UN estimation
of 2015 mentions that the population of Burundi is
11,726,719 (Worldometter, 2016). This makes Burundi a
high population density country of 450 per Km2 (1,165
people per mi2).

- ✓ The capital: Bujumbura
- ✓ National language: Kirundi
- ✓ Official language: French

Neighboring countries: Rwanda to the north, Democratic
Republic of Congo (DRC) to the west, and Tanzania to
the south and east.

Map of the Republic of Burundi

Source: United Nations – Department of Field Support - Cartography
Section, November 2011.

4.2. Natural Resources

● **Land and agriculture**

The arable land in Burundi is estimated at 1,351,000 hectares; that represents about 52.6 percent of the total land area of the country (Virtual Knowledge Africa, 2016). Mostly, the agriculture practiced in the country is of subsistence farming. About 90 percent of the populations of Burundi earn their living by practicing agriculture.

The part of the total production of agriculture which is marketed represents about 15 percent. It earns a non-negligible foreign exchange for the country; for example, the agricultural sector represented 48 percent of the total exports of the country and contributed up to 51 percent of the GDP in 2004. Coffee, cotton, and tea are the main crops that produce the majority of foreign earnings for the country. Other crops cultivated in Burundi include manioc, bananas, sorghum, beans, sweet potatoes, and corn.

The agricultural Production in 2004(14) was as follows (Abbuco Gabson LLC., ND).

- ✓ Bananas 1,600,000 tons;
- ✓ manioc, 710,000 tons;
- ✓ sweet potatoes, 834,000 tons;
- ✓ beans, 220,000 tons;
- ✓ sorghum, 74,000 tons;
- ✓ corn, 123,000 tons;
- ✓ peanuts, 8,800 tons;
- ✓ and yams, 9,900 tons.

- ✓ The main crops for export that were produced in 2004 Burundi are

- ✓ coffee 20,100 tons;

- ✓ Seed cotton 3,000 tons;

- ✓ cotton fiber was about 1,300 tons;

- ✓ and tea 6,600 tons.

The arable land in Burundi generally suffers from soil erosion, irregularity of rainfall, and lack of fertilizer that impact negatively the agricultural production.

● **Forests**

According to official statistics in Burundi, forests occupy a surface area of 152 000 ha. That is about 6 percent of the country's total land on which the natural forest covers about 14 percent, and the 86 percent are the plantation forest as reported by USAID (Nduwamungu, 2011). The expansion of agricultural lands and the high demand for wood products (mainly firewood) have led Burundi to considerable lost of much of Burundi's forest land. Mostly, the natural forests of the country have been replaced by plantations; it has been reported that during the period between 1990 and 2010, there was a lost of an average of 5, 850 ha or 2.02 percent of the Burundi forest per year. Making the country to lose 40.5 percent of its forest during a period of 10 years (Nduwamungu, 2011).

● **Fisheries**

In Burundi, the fishing is practiced on the Lake Tanganyika. The Lake Tanganyika has about 32,900 km^2 of the Western branch of the East African Rift Valley. Its deepness is 1470 and makes Lake Tanganyika the second deepest lake in the world. Its length is of 673 km and the width is of 48 km. This lake is shared by four countries which are countries Burundi (8%), D.R. Congo (45%), Tanzania (41%) and Zambia (6%). All of these four countries practice fishing on Lake Tanganyika. The fishing sector in Burundi is artisan. And the total lake-wide catches during the year 2013 was estimated to be of the order of 200,000 tons annually, of which about 10% is caught in Burundi (Roest, nd). Thus, the fishing constitutes an important source of income generation for many Burundians.

One of the great innovations in the fishing sector is the 'rack dry system' that was initiated by the non-government organization FAO. The rack system of drying fishes has helped the fishers to reduce or eliminate the post-harvest losses. It was introduced in 2004 by an 18-moths FAO project in Burundi; a center was constructed near Mvugo fishing village to train people of the fishery sector the rack-drying techniques (FAO, 2004). "From an average of 500 women who dried fish on the sand in 2004, today there are some 2 000 people directly involved in the improved drying operations in Burundi, an increase of 300 percent. It is estimated that over 12 000 family members are fed from this income generation. Improved production has also increased opportunities for dealers who buy the dried fish (*ndagala*) and re-sell it in other locations around the country. Additionally, small-scale industries have sprung up to provide materials and build racks. The small premises built by the project now serves as a pilot center for training and advisory services managed by a local fisher-based organization (FAO, 2004).

- **Livestock**

The majority of the human population of Burundi depends on agriculture and livestock to earn a living. The animal statistics of 2012 inform that there are 1,200,000 farmers among them 700,000 are livestock farms. The livestock sector contributes up to 14 percent to the national GDP. The country raises different kinds of animal which are 20 percent cattle, 45 percent small ruminants, 5 percent pigs (Mutunungu, 2013). So, the Burundi livestock population in 2012 were numbered as follows:

- ✓ Cattle: 695724
- ✓ Goats: 3214581
- ✓ Sheep: 329813

✓ Pigs: 363244

✓ Chickens: 1 0833676

✓ Rabits: 342294

✓ Bees: 389838

(Source: Butunungu, 2013)

However, the sociopolitical crisis in Burundi had a negative impact on poultry activities in the county (Sebushahu, 2008). Civil wars do not care about the kind of activity or sector to let it safe; they are always destructive and do touch almost all the economic sectors of a country. For example, Sebushahu (2008) shows the negative impact of wars in Burundi on animal rearing by putting that the numbers of chicken were estimated at 2 200 000 in 1992, but in 2000 they were only about 698 589. He mentions that during the same year it was shown that there was a loss of 32 percent of cattle, 40 percent of goats, 51 percent of sheep, 1 percent of pigs, and 80 percent of chickens. The conflicts that lead to civil wars can never allow the prosperity of the nation. They cost not only the lives of human population but also those of animals!

Burundi is naturally blessed with three agricultural seasons per year. The season A that runs from September to January; mostly, it produces about 35 percent of the total annual production of the country. The season B that start in February and finish in May; it gives about 50 percent of the national agricultural production. The season C that begins in June and ends in September; it provides the country with 15 percent of the total production (Ministere de l'Agriculture et de l'Elevage, 2005).

- **Minerals**

Burundi is not naturally blessed with abundant minerals. But there can be found some minerals such as Nickel, Gold, Iron-Titanium-Vanadium, Tin-Tantalum-Tungsten, Rare Earths, Phosphates, Kaolin, Limestones, Marble, Dolomites, Peat, Platinum group metals, and Hydrocarbons. Despite the list of minerals, they only contributed to the GDP of the country at 0.90 in 2013, according to the World Bank (Trading Economics, 2016). The mining sector of Burundi was estimated to be providing jobs to about 10,000 workers in 2009; gold mining about 4,000 workers; niobium, tantalum, and tin about 2,000 workers; and tungsten 1,600 workers (Yager, May 2013). Burundi also produces cement. The Burundi Cement Company (BUCECO) is operational in the country. It opened its new cement plant in Cibitoke Province in February 2011 with a capacity of producing 100,000 tons per year (Yager, 2013).

● **Tourism**

Burundi tourism is still in the infancy phase, but it can be highly developed to generate important funds for the country when there are a permanent peace and a good organization of the sector. The country has several nice places to visit such as capital city Bujumbura, Lake Tanganyika, Gitega, the former capital, with its museum and traditional handicraft center; and the Mosso area in the southeast, with its fairly abundant wildlife (RROfIT, 2007).

There is also a great variety of tropical birds, a rich folk art, and some dancers and drummers of the Tutsi ethnic group that can attract the attention of the visitors. Tourism sector is under the responsibility of the Burundi National Tourism Office (Office National du Tourisme) which is under the Ministry of Amenagement du Territoire, du Tourisme et de l'Environnement. In Burundi, the contribution of travel and tourism to the GDP in 2013 was 2.1 percent. It contributed directly to the employment of the country by giving 33,000 jobs to the population; that was about 1.8 percent of the total employment of the country. (WTTC, 2014).

● **Energy**

The energy used in Burundi is about 86 percent biomass. Wood, charcoal, and peat are mainly used to produce the domestic energy needed by the general population to survive. The country import only about 11 percent of petrol products; the electricity consumption reaches only 2 percent. The sector of energy in Burundi is progressively deteriorating the environment as it mostly depends on cutting trees. Only 0.1 percent of the population had access to electricity in 1999, and in 2016 the percentage was of 6.5 (World Bank, 2016).

The energy sector in the Burundi is under the management of the Directorate General of Energy (DGE) of Ministry of Energy and Mines. Most of the country's power-plants are owned by REGIDESO (Regi des Distribution d'Eau et d'Electricite), a company which works under the supervision of the Ministry of Energy and Mines, and assures the distribution of the plants' electrical production in urban areas. But the Direction General de l'Hydraulique et des Energies Rurales (DHER) is in charge of developing electrification projects in rural areas of Burundi.

So, there is still too much to do in the hydro-electrical domain taking into consideration the needs of the population. But in a report on 'African Economic Outlook 2012', we can read "In the energy field, the government has begun work on a hydroelectric generating station of 10.4 megawatts so as to reduce its energy deficit, which depresses investment and growth. It

will propose other hydroelectric schemes to its partners."
(AfDB & OECD & UNDP & UNECA, 2012).

✓ **Water**

Like other countries of African Great Lakes Region, there is abundant water in Burundi. But despite that, the country is still facing high demand for potable water and sanitation services are very limited. So, the water supply and sanitation sector in Burundi has been destructed by civil wars for many years. For example, resulting from conflicts and civil wars several kilometers of water pipes, connections, and 80 percent of installed meters were destroyed (USAID, 2010). The Ministry of Water, Energy, and Mines (MWEM) is in charge of management the Water supply and sanitation (WSS) sector of the country through its Directorate General for Water and Energy (DGEE).

The Directorate of Water Resources (DRH) within DGEE works to develop strategies to sustain the water resources of the country. It is also responsible for working on the water tariff and of maintaining the Water Mater Plan of the country. And the REGIDESO working under the MWEM is in charge for the catchment, treatment, and distribution of water in the urban areas while the Communal Water Authority (RCEs) is responsible of doing the same work in the rural areas. The RCEs are numbered 34 (USAID, 2010).

● **Transport in Burundi**

Burundi as other countries of AGLR does not have adequate systems of transport. That is one of the principal hindrances to the prosperity of the general population of the country. Transportation is done on roads, airports, and waterways. The total of the roads makes 12,322 kilometers in 2004 and only 7 percent of them are open – the rest are considered to be local roads or tracks (International Business Publications, 2011). The paved roads represent 1,286 km and the unpaved ones 11,036 in 2004 (Revolvy LLC., 2016). With the main port in the Capital Bujumbura, the Lake Tanganyika is used for the water transportation. Burundi has eight airports. The principal airport is Bujumbura International Airport. The runways of those airports are not all paved; only

Bujumbura International Airport is paved and its length exceeds 3,047m (International Business Publications, 2011).

Air Burundi is the national airline of Burundi possed by the State, but it has stopped working since 2007. This airline began its activities in 1975 after being established in April 1971 and was called 'Transports Aériens du Burundi'. It reopened its daily fights in 2008, but in September 2009 it stopped again due to inability to secure adequate funding to overhaul its aircraft led to the airline's suspension of operations. So, the different airlines such as Kenya Airways, South African Airways, Brussels Airlines, and Ethiopian Airlines connect the country to other international airports. There are no railways in the country.

4.3. Education (Schooling)

The education system of Burundi has four levels that are considered to be formal. The four educational levels are the following: pre-primary or kindergarten, primary level, secondary educational level (lower secondary, upper secondary, and technical secondary), and higher education (Hare, 2007).

✓ Pre-primary education

Most of the schools that organize pre-primary education in Burundi are private owned. This level of education enrolls children aged from three to six years.

✓ Primary education

The primary education in Burundi enrolls children aged six years. It lasts for six years, and at the end of the education program, pupils are granted a 'Certificate of Elementary Education' (Certificat d'Etudes Primaires).

✓ Secondary education

The secondary education in Burundi is organized into two levels. The lower secondary education that lasts for four years and the upper secondary education that takes three years to complete. The lower secondary education enrolls students who pass the National Entrance Examination. A certificate called 'Diplôme d'Etat' is allocated to students who finish the upper secondary level; it gives them the possibility of joining higher education settings.

✓ Technical secondary education

It lasts seven years in Burundi.

✓ Higher education

It is principally provided by the University of Burundi. This university has an autonomous management although it is largely financed by the government of Burundi. The president of the Republic appoints the Rector of the University of Burundi to lead it for a period of four years (Hare, 2007). There are also private universities in the country that provide higher education to the people.

4.4. Religions

Christianity is the dominant religion with about 67 percent (with a population estimated at 8,508,000, in Burundi). Among the many subdivisions of Christianity, the Roman Catholics only represent the largest majority of the Christians of the country with about 62 percent. 5 percent represent the Protestants. Muslim are estimated to represent 10 percent and 23 percent are members of traditional indigenous religions. (Africa.com, 2016).

In Burundi, there is an apparent freedom of religion because it is guaranteed by the Constitution of the country promulgated in March 2005. There was no societal abuse or discrimination based on religious belief or practice in Burundi according to the US Government study of 2007 (Revolvy LLC., 2016). There is no religion that belongs to the state, and none of them is particularly favored by the government in detriment of others. So, discrimination based on religious belonging is prohibited. In Burundi, there is a requirement that all the religions should register to the Ministry of the Interior and maintain a headquarters in the country (US Department of State, 2008).

Regardless its denomination, each religious group has to be registered by giving the following information:

- ✓ the denomination or affiliation of the religious institution,

- ✓ a copy of its statutes,

- ✓ the address of its headquarters in the country,

- ✓ an address abroad if the local religious institution is a subsidiary,

- ✓ and information about the association's governing body and legal representative.

Failing to do that the preventive of the religious institution will run the risk of being penalized for about 6 to 5 years of imprisonment. Religious institutions are so valued in the country that the main leaders of religions are granted diplomatic status by the Government.

Another important religious impact in the country is the fact that the Government recognizes the holy days of the Catholic Church such as Assumption, Ascension, All Saints' Day, and Christmas; it has also made official the Islamic holy days such as Eid al-Fitr and Eid al-Adha (US Department of State, 2005). This really shows how valuable are religious congregations in Burundi and how they have been impacting the country.

4.5. Brief political history and conflict analysis

- **Historical settlement**

Historically, Burundi has a similar historical reality like Rwanda where people settled there at different times of history. As shown in the history of Rwanda, the Hutu migrated to Burundi and met the Batwa in the Region; and the Tutsi came after the Hutu. Concerning the

Kingdom, Burundi was unified and independent kingdom. The king was neither a Hutu nor a Tutsi. He belonged to Baganwa considered as a mixed ancestry (USIP, nd) writes about that by putting "Burundi was a unified, independent kingdom, occupying the central highlands, at the time of the German conquest in 1893. The royal caste, the Baganwa, was placed above both the Hutu and Tutsi and claimed to have a mixed ancestry. Under the King and other Baganwa, both Hutu and Tutsi exercised positions of power and prestige. There is no record of ethnic massacres from the pre-colonial period. Judicial authority was exercised by the King himself, by the local chiefs appointed by him, and by wise men designated by consensus on each hill, the Bashinganhaye." (USIP, nd). It is good to note that Burundi was first visited by the European explorers and missionaries in 1856, and in 1899 Burundi became the colony of the German with its East African Administration.

- **Colonial Period of Burundi**

As it is also the case of Rwanda, it was during the colonial period of Burundi that the seeds of damaging ethnic conflict were planted in people's mind. The two country were colonized with one colonial administration and known as Ruanda-Urundi. We learn, from the history of Africa, that the two countries (Ruanda-Urundi) together with Tanganyika (called today Tanzania) were under the German colonial administration before the World War I. The League of Nations (United Nations today) decided to involve the Belgian colonial administration in the management of Burundi and

Rwanda (BBC, 2016; History World, 2016; World Atlas, 2016).

From 1945 to 1962, the Belgian Colonialists had the monopoly of colonization over the whole region. Both German and Belgian colonialism in Burundi had created nonconstructive systems that progressively deteriorated the traditional strong social ties and the harmonious cohabitation that existed between the Hutu majority (85% of the population) and Tutsi minority (15 per cent of the population).

Nonetheless, the Belgian colonialists allowed two rival political parties to officially function in Burundi: the multi-ethnic party UPRONA (Union pour le Progrès National/ Union for National Progress) that was created during the 1950s and led by the Tutsi Prince Louis Rwagasore (Maula, 2012), and the PDC (Parti Démocrate Chrétien/Christian Democratic Party) that was supported by the Belgium. To prepare the Burundians for self-government, Belgian colonialists created a local government.

The Belgian colonial administration, with its political philosophy of dividing peoples, had made Tutsi feel more important than Hutu all over Rwanda-Urundi that was administratively considered as one country until January 20, 1959 when Mwami Mwambutsa IV Bangiriceng demanded their separation to create what is known today as Burundi and Rwanda (Fortune of Africa, 2014). By the fact that the colonialists needed to remain the 'rulers' over the colonized people and were against the decolonization movements that were becoming more and more powerful during the 50s in Africa, the PDC in Burundi could not be supported by Belgium anymore because led by a Tutsi Prince with all the power to demand immediate independence.

So, the Belgians who had already given more power to the Tutsi became opposed to them and turned their support to Hutu people who were considered inferior to Tutsi by the same colonialists! Thus, the victory of the UPRONA in legislative elections resulted by the assassination of the Prince Louis Rwagasore in 1961

(BBC, 2016 & History World, 2016). However, on July 1, 1962, when Burundi claimed independence, the parliament had both Hutu and Tutsi as members. During that time, the power was held by Mwami Mwambutsa IV with his regime that was a constitutional monarchy with a Hutu prime minister, Pierre Ngendandumwe, who was assassinated on January 15, 1965 (Lemarchand & Martin, nd). His death resulted in a number of destabilizing Hutu revolts and government suppression.

The sad reality was that Mwambutsa IV regime was dissolved by Prince Ntare V in 1966 and after the Captain Michel Micombero who was Prime Minister made a coup. This Tutsi leader took the power and established a military dictatorial regime by abolishing the monarchy in

Burundi. The country became a republic. That was just a succession of coups in which Tutsi leader was replacing another Tutsi leader. Were they in conflict among themselves? The Tutsi of Burundi in that time might had had a certain fear of losing power by giving a Hutu leader the opportunity of ruling the country and then retaliate to kill or discriminate people of Tutsi ethnic group as that was the case of the neighboring country Rwanda where the 'Social Revolution' of 1959-1961' made the Rwandan Tutsi exposed to murder by the new government of Gregoire Kayibanda who was a Hutu.

The political situation in Burundi was very tricky at the time when Michel Micombero led the coup against the King Mwambutsa. During that time, there was a multi-ethnic government in Burundi that was the result of first elections after which the Hutu politicians dominated the two houses of the parliament. Unhappy with that, the Tutsi King Mwambutsa abolished the legislature for fear of the Hutu hegemony; the consequence of the King's act gave way to the revolt of the army that was dominated by Hutu. Amazingly, the King was deposed by the coup of the Tutsi offers led by Michel Micombero and replaced by his son Ntare V. The prince Ntare V did not assume the power for a long period; he was dismissed by Micombero and about 5,000 Hutu were killed during the riot.

Micombero built a centralized government. And Ntare V fled the country. The new regime led by military officers of Tutsi ethnic group develop a policy that discriminated against the Hutu. Many Hutu elites lost their lives; especially during the year 1969. It has been reported that during September 1969, there was another attempt of a coup that failed and the Tutsi regime's response to that situation made 50,000 Hutu lose their lives and the entire Hutu political leadership was executed (The Combat Genocide Association, nd).

During the year 1972, Ntare V was arrested by Micombero with the help of the President of Uganda Idi Amin; he was put in custody where he silently died. Again Burundi entered a new phase of killings; during an unrest that killed 2,000 top Tutsi officials, the President Micombero instructed the military to murder Hutu. It was reported that 100,000 Hutu died; the educated ones were the most targeted (World Atlas, 2016 & History World, 2016). About 100,000 Hutu fled to neighboring countries. Other sources like the Commission on Human Rights of the United Nations Economic and Social Council puts that an estimated 100,000 to 200,000 Hutu were killed and 300,000 went into refuge in Rwanda, Tanzania, and Zaire – the actual DRC (UNESC Commission on Human Rights, 1995).

The president Micombero's power was gradually increasing; and in 1974, he revised the constitution of the country to make UPRONA the only officially accepted political party in Burundi – the one-party state. In 1975, the prosecution that was opened by the UN Commission on Human Rights against the officials of the government of Burundi because of their human rights violations against Hutu had no punitive action. The case was later forgotten and dropped as if no human rights were violated. A year later in 1976, the president Micombero was toppled by a military coup led by Colonel Jean-Baptiste Bagaza (BBC, 2016 & History World, 2016).

But the power remained in the hands of a Tutsi elite supported by the army, civil servants, and UPRONA. After deposing Michombero, Jean-Baptiste Bagaza became president but with less power because of many powerful opponents. So, in 1985 Bagaza organized repression against all the oppositions to this political hegemony including the Roman Catholic Church. Just after a year in 1988, another military coup happened in Burundi; Pierre Buyoya overthrew Jean-Baptiste Bagaza. The country was characterized by many and sporadic ethnic atrocities.

As mentioned in the previous paragraphs, the 1960s was characterized by civil unrests, and so was in the following decades of Burundi. The outrageous seeds of conflicts that were buried in the minds and hearts of some Hutu did not spoil to death, but they found a favorable soil that allowed them to spoil and die for rebirth and growth! In 1988, in the north of Burundi, other attacks against the Tutsi were registered. It seemed that some Hutu groups unsatisfied because their plan failed in 1972 wanted to restart killings. Were Burundian parents teaching conflicts to their kids to make sure killings continue? Does the following drawing convey a meaningful message to us?

More other people lost their lives in Burundi during the period from 1987 to 1988. In fact, that happened after Major Pierre Buyoya had overthrown Colonel Bagaza and decided to dissolve opposition parties by suspending the 1981 constitution. His ruling CSMN (Comité gouvernant Militaire du Sauvetage National/Military Committee for National Rescue) was instituted and the tensions among the populations increased. About 150,000 people were reported killed and tens of thousands of went into refuge in the neighboring countries (US Department of State, 2005).

The killings continued to be reported across the years. For example, in 1988 the army killed about 525,000 Hutu in retaliation for the Hutu killings of many Tutsi in the north of the country. It reported that an estimation of 60,000 Hutu fled to the neighboring country Rwanda and another 100,000 became homeless in Burundi (Gale, 2007). In 1991 there was again violence in Burundi when the PALIPEHUTU (Parti pour la Libération du Peuple Hutu/Revolutionary Party for the Liberation of Hutu) instigated new attacks.

However, one of the more remarkable characteristics of the president Buyoyo was the increase of the participation of Hutu in the government. Many governmental posts especially the ministries became dominated by Hutu. But although their massive presence in politics of the country the power was still rested in the hands of the all-Tutsi with the CSMN (Military Committee of National Salvation). While a step to positive change tried to take place in the country with a new constitution that opened the way for multi-party elections in 1992, the next year in 1993 gave birth to new violence that made the scheduled elections impossible. Once more, many people lost their lives, and about 175,000 refugees took refuge to Rwanda (Stedman & Tanner, 2003).

From 1993 up to 2005 there were many ethnic unrests and killings in Burundi. There were massacres that were called genocide followed by civil wars that brought the country to serious ruin. In fact, the assassination of President Ndadaye by some Tutsi military extremists in October 1993 made a rapid negative change in the country's security. Some people of the Hutu ethnic group retaliated by killing Tutsi. The Tutsi army did not stay inactive in the matter; they organized the killing of thousands of Hutu. That was very sad that the ethnic killings are being organized and supported by leaders. The people who are supposed to understand the importance of ethnic diversity have been since long ago the authors of ethnic discrimination and slaughter. What kind of leadership is that?

The story of the killings continued by the murder of the president Cyprien Ntaryamira who succeeded Ndadaye. That happened in Rwanda when a plane bombarded in which both presidents of Burundi and Rwanda died. That incident made the conflict in Burundi more destructive; and more Tutsi were killed by Hutu. After the assassination of the president Ntaryamira, it was announced by the media that there was a newly formed Hutu army 'Armee Populaire' (People's Army) that was operating in the region of Kamenge north of the capital of the country. In May 1, 1994, about 10,000 persons were arrested in an operation launched by the government with the aim of checking and confiscating illegal arms in the Kamenge region.

However, the Hutu who constituted the majority of the population in Burundi were able to win the first seemed democratic elections in the country in 1993 in which Melchior Ndadaye was elected President of the country.

The elections that were supposed to bring peace back home in the country became a turning point that allowed new ethnic violence to take place. In October 1993, the Hutu elected president Ndadaye was assassinated by some members of the Tutsi dominated army (Global Security, 2016). As a result, new ethnic-based killings occurred in Burundi between the Hutu and the Tutsi. Most victims were Tutsi during the killings.

Does it not seem like the human creatures are the most losers of lives than any other creatures in Burundi? It is sad that the more intelligent creatures seem to be the more violent ones. Was that country created to be an endless 'human butchery' in which one ethnic group is firmly determined to finish another? Can that be possible? The history of Burundi had registered another very depressing event in 1994 when another elected Burundian Hutu President Cyprien Ntaryamira was killed with the Rwandan Hutu President Juvenal Habyarimana in a plane.

The airplane was shot, and that was the beginning of new ethnic massive killings in Burundi and Rwanda. So, for more than 40 years Burundi has been losing its children; not by foreign aggressors, but civil wars based on ethnic divisions and discrimination. Many peace talks happened trying to end the civil wars in Burundi but were never successful to bring durable peace in the country. Like today, there had been times for cease-fire but that has never set the country on the path of durable peace and prosperity.

After the death of the president Ntaryamira, there was a certain power-sharing in Burundi between the Tutsi who dominated the army and the Hutu leading the presidency of the country. But in July 1996 Pierre Buyoya of Tutsi ethnic group took power in a military coup (BBC, 2016). With some Hutu militias fighting against a Tutsi regime in a civil war, the peace of the nation was buried once again. So, in 2000, there was a peace negotiation in Arusha between the government of Burundi and the militias; that was made possible by the international diplomatic pressure.

The peace agreement that was to be signed stressed on having an army that was ethnically balanced (with a fair mixture of Hutu and Tutsi), a government that fairly involved both Hutu and Tutus, and democratic elections. But the CNDD-FDD (Conseil National pour la Défense de la Démocratie-Forces de Défense de la Démocratie/National Council for the Defense of Democracy–Forces for the Defense of Democracy) and the FNL (Forces Nationales de Libération/National Forces of Liberation) refused to sign the peace agreement (BBC News, 2001).

FNL and CNDD-FDD continued to fight. The CNDD-FDD accepted to sign a peace agreement in November 2003. They become part of the government of transition.

And the FNL accepted to stop fighting in 2006 by signing a cease-fire deal (IRIN, 2016); but they continued to hold guns and some civilians continued to be victims. The civil war seemed to tend towards an end in Burundi but the country did not recover in terms of peace and economy due to the significance of the negative impact of civil wars and ethnic conflicts on people, and the mindsets of many Burundians especially the leaders.

Although the signature of the peace and reconciliation agreement there continued to happen several cases of massacres in Burundi; they were mostly perpetrated by armed groups that did not attend the peace talks. For example, the Agence France Presse announced on January 1, 2004, the death two soldiers and six civilians during a clash between the government soldiers in West Burundi (Preventing Genocide, 2004). On April 10, 2004, Xinhua News Agency also reported the death of 21 people among them 6 soldiers during clashes between the FNL militias and the government soldiers.

Many other people were killed by different rebel groups even the government soldiers in the country. For example, Violette Nzitonda who was reported murdered by Palipehutu-FNL members because her husband was a member of CNDD-FNL; two civilians who were killed and three other persons wounded by the FAB (Forces armées de Burundi) after being suspected to have contacts with the Palipehutu-FNL in June 8, 2004; on July 26, 2004, the Palipehutu-FNL killed Paul Ndabanukiey for giving information to security forces; in

August 13, 2004, the CNDD-FDD (a former Hutu militia that joined the government) beat to death Albert Ntahomyukire and beat surely his sun because they were only suspected to be members of the Palipehutu-FNL; on October 2004, Palipehutu-FNL was said to have killed a Catholic priest in Burundi; etc. (US Department of State, 2004).

Those are just a few of the massacres and atrocities that took place in Burundi while some international and regional peace actors were trying to seek a total cease-fire to cover all the armed groups in the country. The Agence France Press announced in February 1, 2005 that the Palipehut-FNL was ready to negotiate peace with the Burundian Government without more conditions while on February 18 of the same year the US Department of

State's reported that Palipehutu-FNL cut off arms, legs, and head of a farmer they accused of passing information to the FDN (government troops). The report mentioned several other inhuman acts such as threat, beating, kidnapping, raping the civilians (US Department of State, 2005). That sounds to be a stranger and contrast reality; leaders who announced to seek peace of civilians and who continue to torture and kill them cannot be trusted!

✓ **Peace Negotiation in Burundi**

In Burundi, during the years 1993 and 1994 to negotiate peace was not an easy task. The propaganda of genocide was increasing its ampler on daily basis. But the involvement of the UN in the situation through the appointed Special Representative of UN Secretary-General, Ahmedou Oudl-Abdallah, stepped the country towards the process of peace talks. Ahmedou who represented Boutros Boursos-Ghali expressed the UN viewpoint publicly by saying that the propaganda of genocide or the incitement of people to mass atrocities was intolerable and unacceptable. So, the first phase of peace talk started with the facilitation of Julius Nyerere in November 1995 (Centre for Humanitarian Dialogue, 2011).

Nyenyere was appointed by the heads of states of the region. The UN and the OUA (Organisation de l'Unité africaine/Organization of African Unity *today* AU: African Union) were to help as important actors to support the peace process. The peace actors perceived the Burundian conflict as being political with ethnic background. So, the peace talks were managed taking into consideration two important dimensions which were political and military.

> "The two-track conflict management efforts had both political and military elements. The political track aimed at bringing together all political players to hammer out a political compromise, and the military track involved protection of key political players and demobilization sites." (Ayebare, nd).

The report of the Security Council of 1996, after investigation conducted by the UN Department of Political Affairs, confirmed that there were acts of genocide in Burundi committed by certain Burundian parties. So, the Security Council report made it clear that Burundian conflict had ethnic roots that led some people to perpetrate genocidal acts in the country. Should one ethnic group be eradicated by the other so that the country may set its foundations on the path of durable peace? Or the country was to be divided into two parts: one for the Tutsi and another one for the Hutu?

The task of the peace actors and facilitators cannot be easy in a conflict motivated by racial or ethnic discrimination or hate. The peace talks facilitated by Nyerere in Arusha-Tanzania had the following 19 Burundian delegates who represented different political parties (All Africa, nd).

- ✓ The Government of the Republic of Burundi,
- ✓ The National Assembly,
- ✓ The Alliance Burundo-Africaine pour le Salut (ABASA),
- ✓ The Alliance Nationale pour le Droit et le Développement (ANADDE),
- ✓ The Alliance des Vaillants (AV-INTWARI),
- ✓ The Conseil National pour la Défense de la Démocratie (CNDD),

- ✓ The Front pour la Démocratie au Burundi (FRODEBU),
- ✓ The Front pour la Libération Nationale (FROLINA),
- ✓ The Parti Socialiste et Panafricaniste (INKINZO),
- ✓ The Parti pour la Libération du Peuple Hutu (PALIPEHUTU),
- ✓ The Parti pour le Redressement National (PARENA),
- ✓ The Parti Indépendant des Travailleurs (PIT),
- ✓ The Parti Libéral (PL),
- ✓ The Parti du Peuple (PP),
- ✓ The Parti pour la Réconciliation du Peuple (PRP),
- ✓ The Parti Social-Démocrate (PSD),
- ✓ The Ralliement pour la Démocratie et le Développement Economique et Social (RADDES),
- ✓ The Rassemblement du Peuple Burundais (RPB),
- ✓ The Union pour le Progrès National (UPRONA).

These representatives of parties have signed a peace and reconciliation agreement in Arusha on the 28th of August 2000 under Nelson Mandela facilitation effort. That agreement has five main protocols that all the 19 parties signed for and that constitute the integral part of the peace accord. The protocols include the nature of the conflict, problems of genocide, and exclusion and their solutions; the democracy and good governance; peace and security for all; reconstruction and development; and guarantees on the implementation of the agreement (Hatungimana & Theron & Popic, 2014).

Generally, in the AGLR, people who sign peace agreements always seem to accept the content of the nice articles of the agreement, but when it comes to their personal and egoistic interests their memories about peace of the community seemed to fed away, and they seemed to signore their signatures. As it is the case of other countries of AGLR, Burundi has also excellent articles in its peace agreements. If they were deeply inscribed in the minds and hearts of the signatory parties, the country could, without doubt, be a place where peace and prosperity will find a nice home. But because the words of the articles of the agreements do not have life and healing power in them, they fell to heal the parties that signed them.

It seems like the wounds created by the colonialists in the hearts of ancestors of Burundians have been inherited by their children up to present generations. It can be wondered why some of the country's leaders claim to know where their problems come from, but are not seriously committed to put a final end to them. Those leaders claim to know the truth, but are not willing to communicate it correctly to their followers. But do they really know the truth? Are they really free because of the truth they know?

For example, the article 2 of the first protocol of the 2000 Arusha peace and reconciliation agreement reads,

"Article 2 Colonial period,

- ✓ The colonial administration, first German and then Belgian under a League of Nations mandate and United Nations trusteeship, played a decisive role in the heightening of frustrations among the Bahutu, the Batutsi and the Batwa, and in the divisions which led to ethnic tensions.
- ✓ In the context of a strategy of "divide and rule", the colonial administration injected and imposed a caricatured, racist vision of Burundian society, accompanied by prejudices and clichés relating to

morphological considerations designed to set the different components of Burundi's population against one another on the basis of physical characteristics and character traits.

✓ It also introduced an identity card which indicated ethnic origin, thus reinforcing ethnic awareness to the detriment of national awareness. This also enabled the colonizer to accord specific treatment to each ethnic group in accordance with its theories.

✓ It manipulated the existing system to its advantage by resorting to discriminatory practices.

✓ Moreover, it undertook to destroy certain cultural values that until then had constituted a factor for national unity and cohesion.

✓ On the eve of independence the colonizer, sensing that its power was threatened, intensified divisionist tactics and orchestrated socio-political struggles. However, the charismatic leadership of Prince Louis Rwagasore and his colleagues made it possible for Burundi to avoid political confrontation based on ethnic considerations and enabled it to attain independence in peace and national harmony." (Peace Maker, 2000).

This is one of the interesting articles that was signed by leaders delegated to the peace and reconciliation agreement of Arusha on 28 August 2000 in the presence of several political and influential regional actors and some high profile with the facilitation of Nelson Mandela, the former president of South Africa, who replaced Nyerere in December 1999. It puts it clear that everyone who signed that agreement agreed on behalf of their parties that non-ethnic group created the ethnic conflict in the country. It was created by colonialists who are not colonizing the country anymore today!

Should Africans keep everything that the colonialists created? Are they forced by the westerners to do that today? Do all Burundians know the content of the peace agreement that the leaders of the political parties they support signed? There is an article in the peace agreement that states that it should also be written in Kirundi. Every citizen, especially the youth, is encouraged to be reading the laws and agreements of the country to avoid being deceived and/or manipulated by egoistic leaders. The agreement was thus used as the basis for power-sharing between the armed groups. But is it always in the interest of the general population of the country or for the leaders of armed groups?

Likewise, in early 2002, Jacob Zuma who was the Deputy President of South Africa replaced President

Mandela as facilitator of the long-lasting peace process of Burundi. He continued the work of his predecessors and was given additional mandate to achieve a cease-fire agreement between the government of transition with the armed grouped that were still in civil wars. We read some of what he observed in his mediation leadership and what he observed behind the Burundi civil wars in the following quote.

> "Zuma's approach to mediation was different from the strategy pursued by both presidents Nyerere and Mandela in the sense that he was more discrete in his mediation efforts, and he also directly involved the African Union and the United Nation envoys to Burundi into the talks. He realized that the armed groups in Burundi were part of the web of armed groups spanning the entire Great Lakes region. Many violent actors in the region were being supported by some regional governments. For this reason he concluded that he needed support from the entire international community to achieve a sustainable solution to the armed conflict in Burundi." (Ayebare, nd).

After a summit of the regional heads of states on December 4, 2008, chaired by the president of Uganda Yoweri Museveni, the result of Zuma's facilitation effort recorded some positive facts summarized in the established Burumjura Declaration. The Declaration included the obligation for the Burundians to release all the political prisoners, the decision to make 33 posts available in the government for the Palipehutu-FNL so that they may stop their rebellion and join the government institutions.

The militias of Palipehutu-FNL were asked to leave the civil war and join the demobilization process; also, they were asked to change their name that was calling for ethnic division or discrimination. The process of establishing peace and reconciliation agreements continued until the year 2006 that marked the end of civil wars when the last armed group accepted to sign the cease-fire agreement with the government. Signed on 17 January 2009, the Bujumbura Declaration have the following decision of the Palipehutu-FNL rebel group.

> "The PALIPEHUTU-FNL responded positively to the call of Burundians, the Region and the International Community, to sit for negotiations that led to Agreements signed in Dar-Es-Salaam on 18 June and 7 September 2006, respectively, between the Government of Burundi and the PALIPEHUTU-FNL. According to these Agreements, the PALIPEHUTU-FNL would be transformed into a political party. The PALIPEHUTU-FNL also signed the Magaliesberg Declaration of 10 June 2008, whose spirit and words enjoined both parties to be more flexible in dealing concurrently with both military and political issues. This spirit was supplemented by the Ngozi Declaration of 29 August 2008, which recommended the Political Directorate to assist parties in reaching a common ground as far as the registration of the PALIPEHUTU-FNL and its integration into national life are concerned. In conformity with the Declaration of 4 December 2008, the PALIPEHUTU-FNL undertook on Sunday 4 January 2009 a campaign to explain to

its members the obligations related to the accreditation of the political party and to hold consultations so that a new name could be found for its registration as a political party. After consultations with our militants and exchange of various views and considerations: Considering the pressing time factor; Considering also the high interest for durable peace all Burundians aspire to; We agree to sacrifice ourselves and cut our identity up by changing the name of our party. From now on, the PALIPEHUTU-FNL becomes "FNL": Forces Nationales de Libération (in English National Forces for the liberation). We would like to request the Government to be also flexible and register this new party with no conditionality, whatsoever. It is for this reason, in this very decisive moment of the history of Burundians, we would like to hold as witnesses, Burundians, the Political Directorate, Member countries of the Regional Initiative, as well as the International Community involved in the Burundi Peace Process, who were looking forward to this big event. As for any new organizations, we hereby would like also to request the support of the International Community in different areas. Done in Bujumbura, this 9 January 2009 Agathon Rwasa, Chairman." (African Security Analysis Program ISS, 2009).

The history of Burundi informs that during the month of

February 2007 the UN closed its peacekeeping mission

and became interested in helping the country to economically recover. It donated USD 35 million to Burundi; that money was to be used on infrastructure, on rebuilding the army, on promoting democratic practices, and on human rights (Icirore C'amahoro, nd).

The genocides and civil wars left serious consequences on the population of Burundi. Those who could not be killed by genocide and civil wars, hunger and disease like HIV killed them! A sample post-civil war tasting of HIV showed that HIV positive represented 20 percent of the urban population and 6 percent of the rural people (Barry, 1998). The UN made an estimation that 25,000 deaths in 2001 were due to HIV. And there were about 45,000 deaths due to HIV in 2003 according to Oxfam. (Triposo, nd).

Likewise, Burundi has been experiencing a cease-fire but its foundations are not yet set on the path of durable peace and prosperity. Its history records some political progresses like the adoption of the post-transition constitution on the referendum of 28 February 2005 and the elections of June, July, and August 2005 that led Pierre Nkurunziza on the presidency of the country. During the Nkurunziza reign in April 2009, the Forces for National Liberation (FNL) accepted to be transformed into a political party after laying down their guns. A new sign of hope towards peace was felt by the population.

Another good sign was the presence of both main ethnic groups (60 percent of Hutu and 40 percent of Tutsi) in the government as stipulated in the constitution of the country. But the situation of the country remained fragile. In 2010, Pierre Nkurunziza was re-elected as president of the country. But the opposition parties claimed that the election was fraudulent; they boycotted the polls (New York Times - Kron, 2010).

The 'UN Integrated Office in Burundi' was started as a new UN mission in Burundi in January 2011. The aftermath of the elections made people fearful of news killings. Agathon Rwasa, the leader of the FNL, entered the hiding; some people thought he wanted to start a new rebellion. From that time there had been a number of brutal and sporadic killings in which some civilians were victims, the murders of politicians, the attack at Gatumba with 39 deaths in September 2011 (HRW, 2013), etc.

Apart from FNL, the members of the political party *imbonerakure* – the youth league of the ruling national council for the Defense of Democracy – Forces for the Defense of Democracy (CNDD-FDD) – appeared to be violent in the country by committing killings, beatings, threats, and rape. The government said they would punish the perpetrators of such acts but they did not. In 2012, some human rights organization reported a serious state of impunity in Burundi. That is how it seems to be there as in all the other countries of the AGLR.

However, the year 2014 in Burundi has registered many violations of human rights and threats to oppositions. The country is not on its way to durable peace and prosperity yet although the end of civil wars. The mentality that created civil war is still seen in the behavior of many peoples in Burundi especially some political leaders. Some acts of restriction of people's freedom of assembly, harassment, murder, and intimidation tend to impede the build-up to the 2015 elections in the country. Amnesty International report of 2014 deplores it by writing

"Political space in Burundi is shrinking. In the build-up to the 2015 presidential, legislative and communal elections, Amnesty International has documented an increase in violations of individuals' rights to freedom of association and peaceful assembly, including the harassment and intimidation of critical voices by the Government of Burundi. The authorities routinely and arbitrarily deny groups authorization to hold meetings and demonstrations, whose purpose is often to discuss or raise concerns in relation to political developments or state accountability for human rights. The Government of Burundi has denied political opposition groups, the press, the Burundian Bar Association and civil society organizations their rights to association and peaceful assembly."

This situation suggests that what is happening in the minds of some leaders in Burundi will never allow durable peace and prosperity to set its roots in the country unless there is a positive change of mentality. The mind that created genocides and civil wars that cost millions of Burundians' lives is still alive in the country. How can a country dream to build durable peace and prosperity if its ruling party is encouraging acts that are likely to push opposition parties to create new civil wars?

In fact, during the year 2014, as reported by Amnesty International, the youth wing of the ruling party CNDD-FDD called the *Imbonerakure* had intimidated members of political opposition parties, prevented political meeting and attacked some members of political opposition parties. And that happened without any punishment at all; the government did nothing about that (Amnesty International, 2014). Another peace frustrating issue was the proposed amendments to the Constitution of the country by the Government with the aim of allowing the president of the country to be legally allowed to go for the third term instead of two terms as stated by the actual law. That is one of the two main causes of the nature of the conflict in Burundi as stated in the 2000 Arusha Peace and Reconciliation Agreement for Burundi on its fourth article. It reads,

> "Article 4 Nature of the Burundi conflict
> With regard to the nature of the Burundi conflict, the Parties recognize that:
>> (a) The conflict is fundamentally political, with extremely important ethnic dimensions;
>> (b) It stems from a struggle by the political class to accede to and/or remain in power.
> In the light of the foregoing, the Parties undertake to abide by the principles and implement the measures set forth in Chapter II of the present Protocol."

People who are aware of what they have agreed to respect and do not abide by it will always be dangerous for the future of their nations because a 'hidden threat' does not mean 'no threat' at all. Should the Burundians always be expecting the leaders who know the laws and agreements of the country but once on power forget about them and start leading with their desires and feelings?

It is time to see the unseen. It is time to wake up for durable peace and prosperity. It is time to divorce with all the fake leaders who teach people ethnic conflict so that they may become rich for themselves. It is time to build a nation where everybody will fill okay to live. It time to crucify the old egoistic 'self', and make it resurrect into a 'self' that takes care of the need of the whole community

for a better future for all.

It was reported that when president Nkurunziza was told that the law does not allow him to run for the third presidential term, he argued that had not been elected the first time saying that being elected by the parliament did not count (Telegraph Media Group Limited, 2015). On July 21, 2015, there was an election which was boycotted by the opposition in Burundi. And international observers also said it was neither fair nor free. That happened after a failed coup and generalized public unrest that led to violence making about 300,000 people to flee to neighboring countries such as Tanzania and Rwanda (Telegraph Media Group Limited, 2015).

Moreover, it is time for all Burundians together with other populations of the whole AGLR who were ignorant of the danger in the 'faked political leadership' in the region to learn about it. The corrupt leaders of the region always sustain their dirty ideology and hunger for riches and power by creating ethnic or regional divisions among the citizens. That unchanging behavior has become for some an incurable disease that is why conflict and hate do not leave their minds; that is why even during the time of cease-fire or absence of civil wars or genocide millions of people in the foreign countries are reluctant to go back to their home countries of the AGLR.

Can it be suggested that most the people on power in the AGLR should be consulting the laws and agreements they signed to respect before going to the office? Does the office work steal from their memories laws and agreements? It seems like once on power, they tend to consider their positions as 'traditional kingdom' where the power is their private possession and may hand it to their children at their death! That very ugly attitude is poison to durable peace and prosperity in our developing and global world today.

Chapter Five
Overview of Republic of Uganda

5.1. Country Profile

● **Location and Population**

Uganda is located in the eastern African plateau; its total area is 241,551 sq km (93,263 sq miles). The population of Uganda, according to a census of November 2014, is of 34.6 million which had increased of 10.4 million within 12 years period with reference to the population senses of 2002. The density is 174 inhabitants per sq km (Uganda Bureau of Statistics, 2016).

✓ The capital: Kampala

✓ National languages:

About 40 languages are spoken on regular basis in Uganda (Kaji, 2013). They may be classified into three main categories: Bantu languages, Nilotic languages, and

Central Soudanic. Luganda is the most spoken local language in Uganda; it is mostly used in the urban areas of Kampala the capital city and in town and localities in the region of Buganda. The Runyankore-Rukiga and Lusoga languages are spoken predominantly in the southeast and southwest of Uganda constitute the second variety of languages that are widely used by Ugandan peoples. Other local languages are used but not very widely.

✓ Official languages: English as the first official language since independence, and Swahili as the second since 2005.

Neighboring countries: Sudan to the north, Democratic Republic of Congo (DRC) to the west, Tanzania and Rwanda to the south, Kenya to the east.

The post-colonial period of Uganda has seen a considerable increase in population; in 1969, there were about 9.5 million of people. So, the population of Uganda has increased of about 25.3 million since the independence of the country. It has increased of 10.6 million persons over a period of about 12 years.

According to Ugandan Bureau of Statistics (2016), the population of Uganda increased from 9.5 million in 1969 to 34.6 million in 2014. And between 2002 and 2014, the population increased from 24 million to about 35 million representing an average annual growth rate of 3.0 percent. Also, by mid-year 2016, the population was projected to be 36.6 million. The population density, which is measured with consideration to the degree of crowding of an area in terms of persons per square kilometer, has also increased at a high rate. The Ugandan population density given in the census of 2014 is 174 persons per square kilometer while in 1969 it was of 48 persons per square kilometer.

Population Density of Uganda, 1969 – 2014

Index	1969	1980	1991	2002	2014
Population (Millions)	9.5	12.6	16.7	24.2	34.8
Population density (Persons per sq km)	48	64	85	123	174

Source: Uganda Bureau of Statistics, 2016.

Uganda is a country of many ethnic groups that are sometimes manipulated by some political leaders to create conflicts between peoples to serve their egoistic purpose. The principal ethnic groups in Uganda, according to the Uganda Bureau of Statistics, are as follows.

- ✓ Acholi: 4.7% (of the total population of Uganda),
- ✓ Baganda: 16.9%
- ✓ Bagisu: 4.6%
- ✓ Bakiga: 6.9%
- ✓ Banyakole: 9.5%
- ✓ Basoga: 8.4%
- ✓ Iteso: 6.4%
- ✓ Langi: 6.1%
- ✓ Lugbara: 4.2%
- ✓ Banyoro: 2.7%
- ✓ Other 29.6%.

Since the independence of Uganda, there had been a number of interpersonal communications resulting into conflicts among the Ugandans due to their ethnic diversity. Although some conflicts have inter-ethnic aspect that they often hide, most of the conflicts that murder peace there is mainly hiding it enter-ethnic aspect. And it can be argued that there are only two big ethnic groups in latent conflict in Uganda as in other countries of AGLR: The Nilotic peoples and the Bantu peoples. People judge others by the shape of the noise or by the size (height) of their bodies, etc.

That kind of behavior is very antiquated and will never help any leader to establish durable peace and national prosperity. Unfortunately, it has always been the case of all the other countries of the African Great Lakes; things that could enrich them are the things that are used to divide them. A deep observation on what is happening in the African Great Lakes Region may push me to argue that national peace and prosperity in the region depend primordially on the following three spheres that any country of the region, like Uganda, should not neglect: natural resources, education, and religions. These are the main sectors containing riches, knowledge, skills, teachings, practices, and beliefs that can unite people and divide them. They can make people love each other; they can also make them hate each other up to the extent of killing each other. They are often productive of atrocious acts, and they can also make people productive or lazy.

Let's have a look at those sectors in Uganda by trying to look at the following questions. What kind of Natural resources are there in Uganda? How huge are they and how are they managed? How is education in Uganda? And what kinds of religions are there, and how many adepts each has with reference to recent statistics in percentage?

5.2. Natural Resources

✓ **Land and Agriculture**

In Uganda, the land occupies a space of 200,523.2 sq km while the total area of the country is of 241,550.7 square kilometers. The altitude above sea level ranges from 620 meters (Albert Nile) to 5,111 meters (Mt. Rwenzori peak). The country shares Lake Victoria with Kenya and Tanzania and Lakes Albert and Edward with the Democratic Republic of Congo (DRC). Uganda has other lakes such as lakes Wamala, Bunyonyi, Katwe, Nakivale, Mburo, Kyoga, George and Bisina. Both the Eastern and Western borders are marked by the mountains; the Rwenzori mountains, often called the Mountains of the

Moon), form about eighty kilometers of the border between Uganda and Congo.

Further south, the northernmost of the Mufumbiro volcanoes reach 4,132 meters and mark the border with Rwanda and Congo. In Eastern Uganda, the border with Kenya is also marked by volcanic hills including Mount Elgon which rises to reach a height of 4,324 3,085 meters (Uganda People, 2012). The Imatong Mountains with 3,029 meters with South Sudan. Land area estimates by type of cover as updated from the Remote Sensing Survey carried out in 2010 indicated that agricultural land occupies 38%, the water 15%, the glass land 22%.

The most important economic factor that supports the lives of most Ugandans is agriculture practiced on land.

The supreme law of the Uganda defines four systems of land possession for the country which are freehold, leasehold, mailo, and customary (State House, Constitution of the Republic of Uganda, 1995). The land in Uganda is progressively suffering from degradation such as soil nutrient loss and soil erosion that pose socioeconomic and environmental threats, it constitutes one of the most crucial natural resources on which people practice agriculture.

The agricultural sector of Uganda provides the country with 30.3 percent of GDP (situation of 2006), and in 2015 it was 25.3 percent (CIA, 2016), and constitutes a profession for more than three-quarters of the people of Uganda. It also constitutes 50% of the total exports. The economy of the country depends more on agriculture than any other exploited sector in Uganda (Uganda Bureau of Statistics, 2012).

That is why the land on which agriculture constitute the main socioeconomic activity is done should attract the attention of people that would like to see Ugandan people live in durable peace and prosperity for all. And Ugandan land is not without considerable risk because scientific studies indicate that Uganda loses about 11 percent of its Gross National Income per annum as a result of excessive soil erosion alone. And although, poverty levels in Uganda decreased significantly between 2002 and 2005, the African Development Bank still estimates that 51 percent of Ugandans live in extreme poverty (Failler & Karani & Seide, 2016). Because of the considerable growing number the population that is putting pressure on agricultural natural resource with its traditional farming methods, the agricultural productivity is running the risk declining due to the effects of deforestation, wetland degradation, soil erosion, and water and land pollution.

Although, almost 70 percent of agricultural production is used for subsistence purposes in Uganda, the loss of soil productivity results in USD 39 to 56 per hectare per year. (UWS, 2010). So, the threat is serious, but it can be managed well to avoid disaster in the future; this is happening in Uganda but the whole African Great Lakes Region because that had always been one of the main cause of migrations in Africa. And it most of the time causes destructive conflicts. Also, the whole region is to be concerned about that environmental menace in

Uganda because the population is day to day increasing there and the land is also progressively deteriorating as if there were a curse on it! And deforesting one country of AGLR will always have a negative impact on its neighbors, even on the whole Africa, on the whole world. However, the main grown crops that provide revenue to the country include

- Coffee
- Cotton
- Horticulture
- Tobacco
- Raw sugar
- Cocoa

✓ **Forests**

Forests in Uganda are non-negligible contributors to the ecology of the country and its needs of energy. Ugandan forest resources contribute 6 percent of the GDP of the country. The forestry gives jobs to many people in Uganda. About 100,000 persons are directly employed by the sector, and approximately other 750,000 are indirectly given employment by the same economic sector (NEMA, 2014).

Another important fact about forests is that they supply the household of Uganda with the majority of the energy their need in their daily activities. They also support the lives of animals and other sorts of biodiversity and guarantee a considerable amount of foreign exchange (FOREX) is earned by Uganda through tourism. The

National Forest Authority (NFA) is responsible for the management of the central forest reserves of the country; and the Uganda Wildlife Authority (UWA) is in charge of national parks and wildlife reserves. There are 698 gazetted forest reserves in Uganda; they are a total of national and local forest reserves of the country. The local forest reserves are under control of local governments. As it was mentioned concerning the land, forest reserves are also under significant danger of deterioration and disappearing.

According to the District Forest Services, Uganda lost 27% of its original forest reserves during a period between 1990 and 2005 (Kiying, 2010). That means that the country had lost 1,329,570 hectares which made a loss of 88,638 hectares each year. If this situation of yearly deterioration of forest continues with the same rate and nothing special or extraordinary is done to stop it or to alleviate it, in 2050 all the forestry of the country will probably be null; for all the forest reserve will be exhausted. And how will be the economy of the country in 2050 if the State together with their partners don't work hard for the improvement of that sector?

Is the future of the country prosperous and peaceful with such situations? Are all leaders of the country aware and serious about this vital issue? Are they awakening people about that on a daily basis for a change of mind and a general initiation of joint preventive action? Are all the spiritual and religious leaders talking to their adept about that in their daily meetings? Are they praying to God to make new trees and wild plants to grow fast, to always stop earthquakes and soil erosion, and other natural calamities to make sure the environment remains supportive of life? Be aware of this issue all the people of AGLR; the problem or disaster of your neighbors are also yours in a way or another. Durable peace and prosperity in the AGLR are strongly linked to God-given natural resource, to God's frequently intervention in the nature and the countries, and to human adequate care of the God-given natural resource of the region.

✓ **Fisheries**

The fisheries in Uganda are significant employment-giver sector that occupies the second position in terms of earning foreign exchange for the country. The fisheries sector employs about 700,000 people (Atukunda & Ahmed, 2012); and it exports a considerable quantity of fish. For example, in 2008 the sector exported 24,965 tons of fish with a consequence of earning about UDS 124 million in export revenues (Bagumire, 2009). There is an estimation of UDS 200 million of investment in the fisheries sector in Uganda.

This sector is also being threatened by the decreasing of fish stocks and the value of fish in Uganda is falling. For example, the fisheries sector contributed over USD 117 million in export revenue in 2007, but in the previous year, the revenue was of USD 142.69 million (UWS, 2010). The principal lakes on which that activity is done are Lake Victoria, lake Kyoga, lake Albert, lake Edward, and lake George.

✓ Livestock

According to the Uganda national livestock census of 2008, the country has 4.5 million households that rear at least one kind of livestock or poultry. That figure represents 70.8 percent of households in Uganda (UBOS, 2008). But it was reported that 99.1 percent of the livestock-rearing households have family members as a primary source of labor; that may be considered as an indicative fact of the small herd size of livestock-rearing in Uganda and as being of subsistence. In Uganda, in 2008 the national cattle herd was estimated to be 11.4 million, the milked cows were estimated to be 1.52 million (UBOS, 2008).

✓ **Wildlife and Biodiversity**

Uganda has a rich biological diversity; it ranks within the top ten in the world. (Fauna & Flora International, nd). There are many animals of different sorts in Uganda; there are also a rich and wide variety of aquatic and terrestrial ecosystems. They make the sector of tourism very productive for the country. It earned in 2008 about USD 560 million of foreign exchange from wildlife tourism. (UWS, 2010).

✓ **Minerals**

Uganda is among the African countries that have several types of minerals. It is blessed with over 50 different types of minerals although most of them have never been exploited up to their viability level (Fortune of Africa, 2013). To the 'question what minerals exist in Uganda?', the chamber of mine and petroleum in Uganda give the following chart with details on where they are located and who is exploiting them.

Minerals	Location	Reserves/ Grade	Comment
Copper	Kilembe in Kasese District; Boboong in Kotido District, Kitaka in Bushenyi District and Kampono in Mbarara District	Reserve at closure was about 6 million tonne at 1.77% Cu	Government signed concession agreement with a Chinese company Tibet Hima to develop the copper resources at Kilembe mines
Cobalt	Kilembe in Kasese District	5.5 million tonnes with grade of 0.17% of cobalt	Kasese Cobalt Company Limited has been processing cobalt stockpile which is nearly exhausted.
Beryl	Kazumu in Ntungamo	Under evaluation	Under exploration

	District, Mutaka in Bushenyi, Bulema and Ishasha in Kanungu District and in Rukungiri District; Mbale Estate in Mubende & Lunya in Mukono District		
Chromite (associated with platinum precious metal)	Nakiloro in Moroto District.	Under evaluation	Under evaluation
Gold	Districts of: Bushenyi, Mbarara, Kabale Kisoro, Rukungiri Kanungu, Busia, Mubende, Moroto, Hoima, & many	Five (5) million ounces of gold in Mubende District by Anglo Uganda Corporation.	Mining Leases granted to 1. M/s Greenstone resources at (Tira, Busia District)

	streams of West Nile	One (1) million ounces of gold estimated at Mashonga	2. M/s Anglo Uganda Corporation (AUC Mining, Mubende District) 3. M/s Kisita Co. Mining (Mube nde District) and 4. M/sJan Mangal (U) Limited in Moroto District
Iron ore	Districts of: Muko, Kabale, Kisoro, Mbarara, & Hoima Tororo (Magnetite in Bukusu and;	50 Mt at Muko, Kabale 2 Mt in Mugabuzi, Mbarara 23 Mt at	4 Mining Leases, granted for development of iron ore resources 1. Great Lakes

	Sukulu), Moroto (Napak) & Kotido (Toror) Recent discoveries are in Bufumbira County, Kisoro, Nangara, Karukara, Buhara in Kabale District, Butologo in Kanungu District & Kateera in Mityana.	Bukusu and 45 Mt at Sukulu; Tororo District 50 Mt at Buhara in Kabale District (new dicovery) 55 Mt at Butologo in Kanungu District (new discovery) 8 million tonnes in Bufumbira, Kisoro (new discovery)	Iron & Steel Company Limited, 2. Kigezi Steel Company Limited, Uganda 3. Uganda International Mining Company Limited 4. Sino Minerals Investment Company Limited
Lead	Kamwenge District (Kampono, Kanyambogo and Kitaka in	Under evaluation	Under evaluation

	Kitomi Forest), Isingiro district (Kikagati)		
Lithium	Ruhuma in Kabale District; Mwerasandu, Rwamwire and Nyabushenyi in Ntungamo District; Lunya in Mukono District; Nampeyo and Mbale Estate in Mubende District.	Under evaluation	Pegmatite deposits suitable for small scale mining
Columbite Tantalite (Niobium-Tantalum)	Ntungamo District; Bushenyi District; Kanungu District; Kisoro district and Lunya in Mukono District. Sukulu in	130 million tons of Niobium at Sukulu	The Sukulu phospahate deposit is potentially the most important source of Niobium.

	Tororo District (230 million tons of which Bukusu Complex in Mbale District; Napak in Moroto District and Toror in Kotido District.		
Tin	Mwerasandu, Kaina, Nyinamaherere in Ntungamo District; Kikagati in Isingiro District, Ndaniyankoko, Kitezo in Mbarara District, Burama Ridge on the Kabale/ Ntungamo border, Rwaminyinya in Kisoro District.	1.0 million tons at 2.5% tin estimated in Ntungamo and 2.5 million in Isingiro by First Mining Company Limited	Under-developed. Two mining leases: Zarnack holdings and First Mining company Limited

Titanium	Bukusu Complex in manafwa District (22% TiO2) and Sukulu in Tororo District (13% TiO2).	Grade of titanium is 22% TiO2 and (13% TiO2 in Bukusu and Sukulu respectively.	Undeveloped
Tungsten	Nyamuliro (Bjordal Mine) and Ruhija in Kabale District; Kirwa, Mutolere, Rwamanyinya and Bahati in Kisoro district; Kyasampawo in Mubende District and Buyaga in Rakai District	Kirwa wolfram resources are at 801,300 metric tonnes with average grade of 68.67% WO3, One (1) million tones and possible reserves of 355 million tonnes at Nyamuliro with ore grade at 0.1%	(3)mining leases granted: 1.Krone Uganda Limited , 2.Berkeley Reef Limited 3.Sino Minerals investment

Silver	Silver occurs in association with galena at Kitaka in Kamwenge District and Mubende granite in Mubende District	Under evaluation	
Zinc	Zinc occurs with galena at Kitaka in Kamwenge District	Under evaluation	
Rare Earth Elements (REE)	Isolated pegmatites in SW Uganda, Carbonatite centres in Eastern Uganda (Sukulu, Butiriku, Bukusu, Napak)	REE grade at Sukulu is 0.32% La2O5	Unexplored, but Sukulu is now under exploration
Limestone/ Marble	Muhokya in Kasese District	14.5 million tonne	production on large scale in Kasese, Tororo

	and Dura in Kamwenge District, and Hima in Kasese District. Sukulu and Tororo in Tororo District; Napak and Katikekile in Moroto District and Toror in Kotido District; Moyo Districts.	s at Hima, Kasese and 11.6 million tonnes at Dura, Kamwenge Vast resources of marble in Karamoja region	and Moroto Districts
Phosphates	Sukulu in Tororo District and Bukusu in Mbale District, Lolekek in Napak	230 million tons at Sukulu with grade of 13.1% p2o5 ; 50 million tons at Bukusu with grade of 12.8% p2o5	Investment in fertilizer manufacturing plant viable Apatite with magnetite, vermiculite, pyrochlore, barite, zircon,

			uranium, titanium,Niobium and rare earth elements.
Vermiculite	Sukulu in Tororo District and Bukusu Carbonatite Complex (Namekhara, Nakhupa, Surumbusa, Kabatola and Sikusi) in Mbale District	54.9 million tonnes at Namekhara	Mine developed at Namekhara Investment in fertilizer manufacturing plant viable
Kaolin	Namasera, Migadde and Buwambo in Wakiso district; Mutaka in Bushenyi District, Kisai in Rakai District and Kilembe in Kasese District	2.8 million tonnes at Mutaka, Bushenyi. One (1) million tonnes at Kisai(Koki), rakai	On demand by local industrial sector

Gypsum	Kibuku in Ntoroko Distict, Lake Mburo in Kiruhura District and Kanyatete in Lake George basin Kasese District.	2 million tons in kibuku	Available market
Salt	Kibiro in Hoima District; Katwe and Kasenyi in Kasese District	22 Million tonnes of trona at Katwe and Kasenyi, Kasese District	Mined for animal and human consumption locally. Industrial production opportunities available
Feldspar	Bulema in Kanungu District; Bugangari in Rukungiri District; Mutaka in Bushenyi District; Nyabakweri in	Under evaluation	Development and investment in downstream industries viable

	Ntungamo District and Lunya in Mukono District.		
Glass sand	Diimu and Bukakata in Masaka District; Lwera in Masaka District, Nalumuli Bay, Nyimu Bay and Kome Island in Mukono District	The highest quality 99.95% SiO2 at Kome islands, 2 Mt at Dimu and Bukakata (99.93% SiO2)	Viable investment
Kyanite	Kyanite occurs at Ihunga and Kamirambuzi hills in Rukungiri district; new prospect around Murchison Falls	Under evaluation	Not explored
Diatomite	Panyango, Alui, Atar and Amboso River near Packwach in Nebbi District	Under evaluation	Un developed
Dimension	Marble occurs	Over 300	Tiles in

538

stones	in Karamoja Regio Granite in various colours and textures occur in various parts of the country.	million tonnes of marble in Karamoja (Rupa, Kosiroi, Tank Hill, Forest Reserve, Matheniko, Pule and Lolung)	Uganda are 100% imported. A Mining Lease granted to Building Majesties (u) Limited (BML) to process granites in Mubende into dimension stone
Clays, aggregates and hard cores	Various parts of the country		Stable demand, viable investment.
Others potential minerals	Nickel at Kafunzo in Ntungamo District; Rugaga in Isingiro	Unknown	Further exploration and development being

	District. Platinum Group of Metals at Nakiloro in Moroto District, Bweyale in Kiryandongo District Diamond potential in Kibaale, Butare in Buhweju District, areas around Lake Kyoga, indicator minerals occur in Katakwi and Karamoja		undertaken

Source: The Uganda Chamber of Mines and Petroleum, 2016

That is the list of minerals that are reported to exist in Uganda. It is good to see the whole list in the above chart and notice how some of the Ugandan minerals are under-evaluated, some under developed, and some unknown. And yet Uganda has been accused by many NGOs and observers to have been taking part in the conflict in the DRC; a conflict that was qualified 'mineral conflict'.

That sounds amazing. Does it seem reasonable to spend time, means, and efforts to take part in the plunder of one's neighbor's minerals because they are discovered and evaluated instead of investing more in working on one's own minerals to well evaluate, develop, and exploit them for the general interest of all the people of the country?

✓ **Tourism**

Uganda is a country that attracts tourists. As the country has been experiencing a certain absence of civil war, there has been an increase of visitors and investors. The tourism sector contributes about 9.0 percent to GDP. In 2010, the sector contributed US$ 773 million to generate foreign exchange in the country (MTWH & World Bank, 2012).

About 225,300 t0 522,000 people are employed by the tourism sector. And 1,151,00 visitors arrived in Uganda in the year 2011 (MTWH & World Bank, 2012). In 2013, the number of visitors to national parks of Uganda increased from 152,000 in 2012 to 214,000 in 2013 and a total of 1.6 million arrivals and 1.5 million departures was recorded during the year 2013 (Uganda Bureau of Statistics, 2014).

✓ **Energy**

The energy sector in Uganda plays a crucial role of revitalizing other productive socioeconomic sectors of the country. The main sources of energy, that constitute the engine for economic growth and development, are hydroelectricity, biomass, and petroleum. These sources provide respectively 2%, 96.5%, and 1.5% of the total energy consumed in the country (AWE Environmental Engineers, 2012). There are other sources of energy in the country but their contribution to the national energy balance is very low and insignificant.

The Ugandan population is almost unserved by the electricity supply available in the country. About 97 percent of Uganda's population does not have access to electricity and many towns, especially in the North of the country are without electrical power (HELIO International, 2009).

In the rural settings of the country, only about 1% of the households are connected to the national power network, and yet it is where 85% of the total population live (Muhoro, 2010). Generators, solar photovoltaic, and rechargeable batteries sometimes help other categories of people to satisfy their needs of power. The inability of the country to exploit its natural hydro-power potential seems to be the main cause of the national power shortage. Although the country possesses a huge hypo-power potential estimated at 3000 MW, only less than 10% is exploited. (Hivos, nd).

Baanabe (2012), commissioner at the ministry of energy and mineral development, presented the following information concerning the sources of energy in Uganda at a workshop on 'promoting sustainable transport solutions for East Africa' on 1 August, 2012.

Energy Sources in Uganda:

1. Biomass – Constitute 93% of energy consumption (mainly in traditional form).

2. Hydropower (1% of energy supply)

    – Installed capacity 683 MW (Bujagali 250MW,

       Nalubale 180MW, Kiira 200MW, and

       Mini hydros combined 53MW),

    – Current generation 400 - 450MW

    – Potential sites

       • Isimba 140MW

       • Kalagala 450MW

       • Karuma 600MW

       • Ayago 600MW

- Murchison Falls 600MW
- Orianga 450 MW

3. Fossil Fuels

– All fossil fuels currently used in Uganda are imported.

– Energy mix has 100 MW from thermal

– Exploration program in the Western Rift Valley area or the Albertine Graben has led to the discovery of commercial petroleum reserves.

4. Renewable/Alternative Sources of Energy

– Solar

- Uganda is blessed with constant sunshine throughout the year.
- A lot of potentials to generate electricity from solar.
- Over 30,000 solar PV system installed.

– Geothermal

- Estimated potential of 450MW concentrated in Western Uganda.
- There are 41 potential sites identified on small rivers in the country.
- These have potential of generating over 150MW of electricity

– Wind

- Wind speeds are high on mountains tops in places like Karamoja
- This can be used for water pumping and generation of electricity.

This is one of the countries that has been seriously and voluntarily involved in atrocious conflicts in the AGLR and yet cannot supply electrical power to its population. Maybe all is alright for a country making efforts invade the borders of its neighbors military but cannot make effort to serve electrical energy to the 99 percent of its people who live in rural areas and to the 95 percent of its total population who live without it at all!

How can leaders a country dare to think of achievement in terms of durable peace and prosperity for all in today's modern world while they are failing to exploit effectively and efficiently what they naturally have to produce enough energy for all? If the resources are not being managed well, can the Source of all be happy? It is known that Africans, in general, believe in the existence of the Source of all (God). But how do they express that belief into practice if the resources created by the Source for the good of all are mismanaged or are not managed at all?

✓ **Oil and gas**

There are five potential hydrocarbon exploration areas in Uganda:

- ✓ Kadam-Moroto Basin
- ✓ L. Kyoga Basin
- ✓ Hoima Basin
- ✓ The Albertine Graben
- ✓ L. Wamala Basin

These are the areas where important natural resource lie; if exploited adequately, they may bring a huge amount of money to the economy of the country. For example, the exploration done in the Albertine Graben has informed that there are large amounts of petroleum there. Among the 39 wells that are there, the exploration was done on 37 and has revealed commercial quantities of oil and gas rest there! There is an estimation of more than 2 billion barrels of petroleum reserves in Albertine Graben. With that, the area can produce 100,000 barrels of oil per day in Uganda and that can last 20 years (Kraemer-Mbula & Wamae, 2010).

In his article, Karugaba (2011) puts "Uganda's oil potential now stands at two billion barrels from just 45 percent of the potential area. If Cabinet adopts the feasibility report by the Ministry of Energy, which recommends the construction of a $2 billion worth oil refinery plant, Uganda will be producing 60,000 to 120,000 barrels per day. (…) If Uganda is to produce 120,000 barrels per day, and going by the current price per barrel (159 litters) of $90, (around Shs200,000) Uganda could get an annual $3b (over Shs6.8 trillion)."

5.3. Formal Education

Formal education is legally recognized in Uganda as a right for each citizen. The 1995 Constitution (amended) states that each child is entitled to a basic education which is the responsibility of both parents of the child and the State (Unicef & FIDA Uganda, nd). Apart from what the Constitution stipulates, there are some other legal documents that put emphasis on the right of

550

children to be educated. For example, the Children's Act highlights that all children must be educated by demanding the parents to make sure the children attend schools and the state to provide needed resources (Unicef & FIDA Uganda, nd).

Also, the National Development Plan (NDP) (2010/11 to 2014/15) considers education as one of fundamental social sectors that help the country to build its national social capital (Republic of Uganda, 2010). Thus, Uganda is a country that legally values education. But how are the schools in Uganda? Does the government support them adequately?

In Uganda, all schools were asking their students to pay fees until 1997 when the government introduced a program known as Universal Primary Education (UPE). With the UPE, the government could support the primary education freely up to four children per family. Most schools are managed by the Government and the education is not compulsory (UNESCO & IBE, 2010); the missionaries have also some schools that they manage. Primary education lasts for seven years and it begins at six years of age. And secondary education lasts for four years for the first cycle, and two years for the second, making a total of six years. The beginning age is 13 years.

The report of a survey conducted in 2010/2011 by the Uganda Bureau of Statistics (UBOS), on its section concerning primary education, shows that most of commonly used schools are managed by the government and their facilities overall are not of good qualities. The report puts,

> "The findings show that Government-owned schools remained the most commonly used schools compared to Other schools. Also, only two percent of the available teachers' houses and only 14 percent of the available toilet/latrine facilities were reported to be adequate. Spring/Rain water followed by the boreholes were the most commonly used sources of water at primary schools while close to three in every ten primary schools (28%) reported that they provided toilet facilities for physically impaired children during both survey periods (UBOS, 2013).

5.4. Religions

There many religions in Uganda and the dominant are Christianity and Islam. Other religions include traditional indigenous religions, different branches of Hinduism, Judaism, Baha'i Faith, etc. Among the Christian missionaries that are active in the country, we can cite the

Catholic church missionaries, the Pentecostal Church, the Baptist Church, the Church of Christ, the Mormons, and the Episcopal Church/Church of Uganda.

The statistics of CIA (2016) World Fact Book shows that the population of Uganda is divided among different religious groups as follows. The Christian Protestant represent 45.1% (Anglican 32.0%, Pentecostal/Born Again/Evangelical 11.1%, Seventh Day Adventist 1.7%, Baptist 3%), the Roman Catholic Christians 39.3%, the Muslim 13.7%, other 1.6%, none 0.2% (2014 est.). So, the Christianity has the largest number of adherents in Uganda with 84.4 percent of the population.

5.5. Brief Political History and Conflict Analysis

- **Pre-colonial Uganda**

The history enlightens that when Jesus Christ was born the Bantus people had already migrated in Uganda. Their migrations are very old because they are said to have started at around 500 B.C., they migrated in South West Uganda from the west. The earliest states in Uganda may have been organized between the 13th and 15the centuries by the Chwezi, a group of pastoral rulers whose legends consider to be supernatural beings.

But the study of their remains by archaeologists has shown that the Chwezi were human beings. And they are suspected to be the ancestors of the people known today as Hima or Tutsi of Rwanda and Burundi (Wikivisually, nd).

Around 1500, the Nilotic-speaking Luo people migrated in Buganda and formed Bito dynasties of Buganda, Bunyoro and Ankole (The Gale Group, 2010). They were from the present-day southeastern Sudan. The Luo-speaking peoples, ambitious and organized, later during the 16th century were able to conquer the North of Uganda and formed the Alur and Acholi ethnic groups. The Langi and Iteso migrated in Uganda during the 17th century.

During the historical period from the 16th to the 17th century, the dynasty of Bunyoro was the leading state in the South Uganda. It was controlling an area that extended into present-day Rwanda and Tanzania. But about 1700, the dynasty of Buganda started to enlarge gaining more control than the Bunyoro dynasty (The

Gale Group, 2010). The expansion of the state of Buganda made the Banganda able to control a large territory that bordered Lake Victoria from the Victoria Nile to the Kagera River. Their supreme chief was *Kabaka* (King) who had all the power to appoint regional administrators, to command a powerful army, and to be in charge of a large bureaucracy in his day to day administration of the state. Their economy rested mainly on cattle, ivory, and slaves.

As matter of fact, ivory and slaves were exchanged with firearms, cloth, and beads between the Buganda state with the Muslim traders who reached Buganda from the Indian Ocean coast in the 1840s (Ekitibwa kya Buganda, 2013; BBC News, 2016; The Ugandan Space Agency, nd). Those were the Kabaka of Buganda with other business men of the state exchanging their African brothers and sisters in order to get more power and riches (firearms)! Imagine the state of inner peace of the family members of the slaves who were sold for good. How did those family members felt about their own lives and the lives of people of their color and creed who were selling them? What kind of feeling had the victims about themselves?

The same way the African people in power were selling their own brothers and sisters to get power and goods, the same way some political, religious, and other leaders are ready to kill and destroy their communities in order to get riches and personal power. It's a pity because the African leadership has not changed although the times are changing across history. Change is needed; not only in

Uganda but in the whole African great lakes region. Because the situation of the countries of AGLR is the result of what was done in the past; and the future will only look like what people are doing now, at the present time of their lives. In other words, the national and community life in the countries of AGLR reflect exactly what the leaders believed, thought, communicated, and did for the region in the past; and the future depends on what they believe, think, communicate, and do today. A person cannot plant beans and expect to harvest sweet potatoes!

In the 1862, British explorer John Hanning Speke becomes the first European to visit Buganda. The earlier history of Uganda also reveals that the Buganda dominant state in Uganda was challenged by the state of Bunyoro at the beginning of 1869. The Bunyoro which was ruled by Kabarega was possession of firearms that they obtained in doing trade with the traders from Khartoum that they used to compete against the expansion of Buganda.

- **European exploration and Arrival of Religious Missions in Uganda**

John Hanning Speke, whose exploration aim was to establish the source of the Nile River, reached the Buganda state as the first European in the region in 1862 (BBC News, 2016). During his visit in Buganda, Speke was welcomed by the Kabaka Mutesa I who had inherited in 1856 the most powerful kingdom in Uganda. The inter-regional (or international) trade made his kingdom open to international influences. That is why, the Swahili and Arab traders were welcomed in Buganda to trade (to exchange) their cloths, guns, and other manufactured products for ivory and slaves. Some of these traders were from Zanzibar. From that inter-regional trade, Islam was imported to Buganda and made significant religious and cultural influences in that dynasty.

However, Christianity arrived in and by that time Islam had already made it impact in Buganda. That means that there were many converted Baganda Muslims in Buganda when Christianity arrived including the *Kabaka* (king) Mutesa. So, before the coming to Christianity in Buganda, the Baganda were already familiar with some concepts that are common in the imported religions in African (Islam and Christianity) such as a 'holy book', a 'Holy God', a 'holy day', a 'God above all gods', a 'new life after physical death', 'doomsday', 'paradise', 'hell', etc. Christian missionaries had good starting point to begin for even before the coming of Islam the Baganda had some belief similar to both Islam and Christianity.

For example, Kevin Ward (nd) writes that neither 'Islam nor Christianity needed to import a foreign name in order to proclaim their God. The Baganda already knew of Katonda, the Creator. But the status of this Katonda has been the subject of controversy within the religious historiography of Buganda. Was Katonda just one, very insignificant lubaale? Or had he always been regarded as superior to the balubaale (dome of the sky consisting of seventy gods), high above Mukasa, Kibuuka, and Muwanga, but remote from the life of the nation and of the individual, and therefore not the focus of a strong cult? Whatever the answer to these questions, it is certain that Islam gave a new prominence to Katonda, and that Christianity built on this growing significance.

King Muteesa made a rupture with Islam due to the fact that the force of Muslims from Egypt wanted to conquer all the regions surrounding the Nile (including Buganda) in the Egyptian Empire. When some Egyptians visited Buganda in 1876, there was a rupture of relationship between Islam and the king. Muteesa who has strongly supported Islam for ten years from 1867 to 1876, was obliged to stop being Muslim. Thus, there was a need of finding other external partners who could help him fight against the Egyptian attacks. Henry M. Stanly, who reached Buganda in 1875, made a proposal to the king to let the Christian missionaries enter his state (The Ugandan Space Agency, nd).

Fearful of the Egyptian Muslim attacks, the king Muteesa accepted the proposal and the members of the British Protestant Church Missionary Society were the first missionary to arrive in Buganda in 1877. In 1879, the representatives of the French Roman Catholic White Fathers entered Buganda (Lugira, 1999). The Christian missionaries worked hard to be able to gather some groups of new converts. Around the 1880s, there was a certain antagonism between the new Christian groups that belonged to different missions (Catholic and Protestant). And the third influential group was that of Muslims which was also growing day to day.

In 1884, Mwanga became the new *Kabaka* when Muteesa died. Buganda became so much influence by conflicting imported religions; and Mwanga fearing to lose his position began to persecute the Christians. Muslims and Christians deposed Mwanga in 1888 (The Editors of Encyclopedia Britannica, 2013). He lost his power and was replaced by his brothers. In 1889, he regained his power but lost it again to the Muslims in very few weeks. Because Buganda state was already full of chiefs who converted to Christianity, Mwanga who regain the full control of the state in early 1890 was weakened by the converted Christian chiefs.

- **Uganda Colonial Era**

The Great Britain is the country that colonized Uganda. The European activities in Uganda started after the year 1862 during which Henry visited that land as mentioned in one of the previous paragraphs. But it was in 1889 that a treaty of friendship was signed between Mwanga who was the *Kabaka* (king) of Buganda during that period with Carl Peters who was a German colonialist.

Fearing to lose or the risk of weakening its control on the Nile River, Great Britain signed a treaty with Germany in 1890; what was agreed upon in the treaty gave Great Britain the rights to control or to colonize a territory that is known today as Uganda. During the same year, some troops of British colonialists reached Buganda. And the authority of the Imperial British East Africa Company (IBEA) was established in the South of Uganda in 1892 by Frederick Lugard (Turner, 2014). This agent of IBEA helped the Protestant missionaries to the Roman Catholic in Buganda as they were in a serious competition.

The favored religious mission became the Protestant (Anglican Church) and the colonial administration in Buganda worked hand in hand with them. The British colonialist continued their conquest of controlling all the territory of Uganda by negotiating treaties with other kingdoms; that was done during the historical period from the 1890s to 1918. The kingdom of Buganda that was the most powerful in Uganda and the first colonized was declared officially by Great Britain a protectorate in 1894; and the same status was given to other small kingdoms like the Bugosa, Bunyoro, Toro, and Ankole.

The British colonialists gave more preference to the kingdom of Buganda than any other kingdom in Uganda; but Buganda it was also weakened by British when they deposed the king Mwanga who started to oppose to their hegemony. His son Daudi Chwa replaced him. In 1900, Buganda was made a constitutional monarchy controlled majoritarily by Protestant chiefs (Byrnes, 1990). From the time, several important colonial activities impacted Uganda. Among them we may cite,

- ✓ the transfer of the Eastern province of Uganda to British East Africa Protectorate (Kenya) in 1902 for administrative reasons;

- ✓ the beginning of cultivation of cotton in 1904 (it became the main export crop);
- ✓ the development or the growth of production of coffee and sugar in the 1920s;
- ✓ the settlement of many Asians who were mainly Indians, Pakistanis, and Goans (in the 1920s);
- ✓ the establishment of a legislative council for the protectorate in 1921, but accepted African members only in 1945 but in few number;
- ✓ the African members of the legislative council were given a considerable number of seats in the mid 1950s.

The British colonial administration was reducing gradually the sovereignty and self-government of Buganda. Mutesa II being unpleased with the decrease of his power and control on Buganda territory became reluctant to cooperate with the British. As a result, he was deposed in 1953 but regained his position in 1955; the relationship between Buganda and the rest of territory of Uganda was not healthy, there remained a rift between them.

In Uganda in 1954, there was a formation of a national movement, a Democratic Party (DP) that aimed a unitary independent state of Uganda and opposed the will of the Bagandas to continue having a dominant influence on the whole country even after independence. The Uganda National Congress (UNC), which was formed in 1952 by Ignatius Musazi and Abu Mayanja as its first Secretary General, pleaded for African control of the economy in the dependent state that they wished to be federal. In 1958, Uganda People's Congress (UPC) was formed by Dr. Milton Obote and some members of other political parties joined him (two members of UNC did it).

This political party was also opposed to the hegemony of the Southern Kingdom of Buganda even if it later signed a partnership with the Kingdom. In 1960, when many of the African countries had gained their independence, in Uganda there three main political forces that included DP led by Benedicto Kiwanuka, UPC led by Milton Obote, and the Lukiiko (legislature) of Uganda. In 1961, Uganda organized the first national election to the Legislative Council (Vision Group Uganda, 2015). Kiwanuka was appointed Chief Minister after his political party, the DP, won the majority of the seats. But the ruling elites of Buganda contested him.

As a result, a political party representing the interests of the Bugandan Lukuiko, called Kabaka Yekka, was formed. Kabaka Yekka (KY) means the King Alone. This political party allied with the UPC against the DP which was the winner of the election. When Uganda was granted self-government with Kiwanuka as Prime Minister, the collation UPC-KY worn the majority of seats in the pre-independence elections to a National Assembly in April. So, the UPC-KY formed a Government let by Obote.

In October 1962, Uganda gained independence from Britain and kept its membership to the Commonwealth (The Commonwealth, 2017). And on 9 October 1963, the country had the status of a Republic with the Kabaka of Buganda (Mutesa II) as President; but he was not fully in charge of the executive (non-executive).

- **Milton Obote Regime**

However, in 1964 the coalition UPC-KY was judged no more important by some members. UPC became weaker and was split between the conservative, the centrist, and the radical elements of the party. The rulership of the country changed dramatically in 1966, when Milton Obote, the Minister of Defense, and Colonel Idi Amin Dada, the second-in-command of the Army, were suspected to be involved in gold and ivory smuggling by the National Assembly. King Mutesa II (President of the country that time) of the Southern Kingdom of Buganda gave order to investigate about those allegations.

During the same month, the Obote made a coup against his accusers in the UPC (Lipschutz & Rasmussen, 1986). That situation resulted in

- ✓ arrest of five government ministers,

- ✓ suspension of the Constitution,

- ✓ deposit of the President,

- ✓ transfer of all executive powers to Obote.

In April 1966, Obote became head of state and an interim introduced Constitution gave him full executive power and it withdrew regional autonomy in the country. And in May, the Bugandan Lukiiko (the parliament of the Kingdom of Buganda) reclaim the restoration of the autonomy of Buganda Kingdom. But the government reacts oppositely on that and Amin commanded the government troops to attack the Kabaka who was able to escape the attack and fled abroad for asylum. A new Constitution that abolished the traditional rulers and legislatures was adopted in September 1967; it also established a unitary government.

The Obote regime was cruel and non-integrating; it was characterized by arbitrary detentions and military repressions. After the failed assassination attempt of Obote in December 1969 in which he was wounded, Amin Dada who was still commander of the Army took refuge to a military base in his homeland (village). That marked the rapture of good collaboration between Obote and Amin.

● **Idi Amin Dada Political Reign**

In January 1971, Obote traveled to attend a Commonwealth prime ministers' conference in Singapore. Idi Amin took that opportunity to take power (Lipschutz & Rasmussen, 1986). Obote took refuge in Tanzania with other 20,000 Ugandans. The following month, February, Amin proclaimed himself Head of state. To make sure his regime is strong and stable, Amin used massacres which was sometimes pointing some tribal groups. Jennings (2009, p. 1227) puts "Amin consolidated his military position by massacring troops and police (particularly those of the Langi and Acholi tribes) who had supported the Obote regime."

Amin regime appeared to be more barbarous, dangerous, and atrocious than Obote's. Among his many irrational decisions and atrocious act we can cite,

- ✓ murder of millions of civilians,
- ✓ suspension of any political activity in the country,
- ✓ suppression of most civil rights,
- ✓ dissolution of the National Assembly,
- ✓ rule by decree,

- ✓ extension of the military tribunal jurisdiction to cover the entire population,

- ✓ expulsion of all Asian people who were in Uganda (about 4,000),

- ✓ the nationalization of all British companies in Uganda without reimbursement in December 1972,

- ✓ Amin declares himself President for life (1976).

Yoweri Museveni, President of Uganda today, who was a senior officer in that time and David Oyite-Ojok, a former Chief of Staff, tried to fight against Amin's regime by invading in Tanzania in September 1972. In reaction to that, Amin retaliated by bombarding some towns in Tanzania. Amin regime was supported by Libya and URSS which was mainly militarily. The country's economy was dying and its infrastructures were decaying because the Western aids were completely stopped.

Idi Amin leadership was very absolute. He used violent act and oppressive control to establish his power permanently in the country. He persecuted anyone who was suspected to oppose him regardless their social status. Many people were killed; an estimated number of 300,000 to 500,000 people were murdered during his regime (Kalyegira, 2005).

In 1979, Amin attempted to invade Tanzania where some Ugandan opponents to his regime were in exile claiming the rightful possession of the Kagera salient. But Julius Nyerere, President of Tanzania, mobilized his army together with the exiled Ugandan on his territory to counterattack Amin regime and they succeeded to seize the power in Uganda. Amin fled to Libya and later to Saudi Arabia where he died in 2003. Thus, Amin was very despotic and so was Obote.

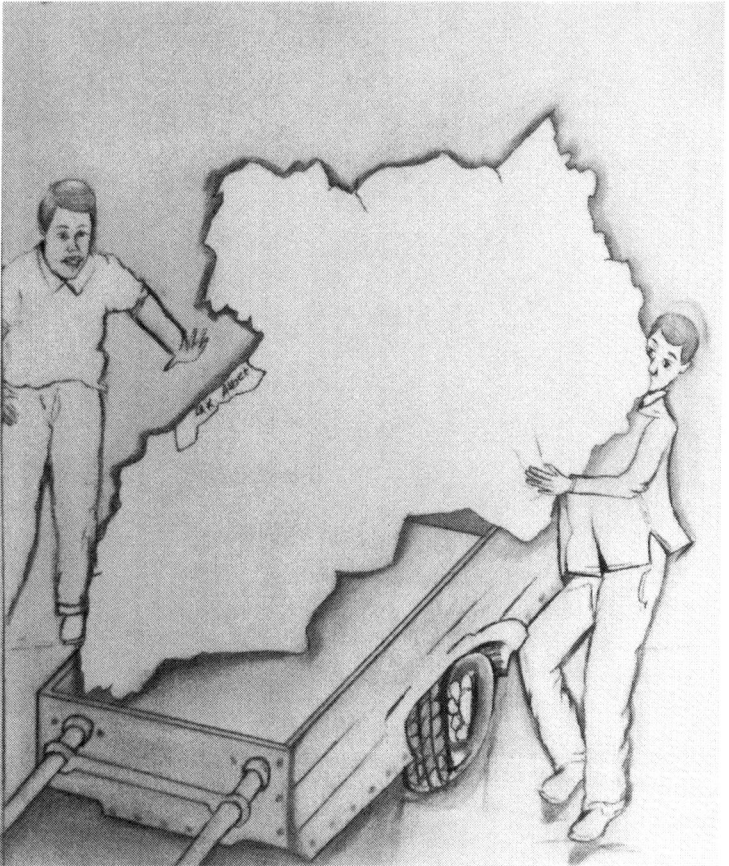

- **Period of the Government of Transition Followed by Obote and Okello Regimes**

After the Uganda National Liberation Army (UNLA) succeeded to boost out Idi Amin, there was an establishment of transitional government. A National Executive Council (NEC) was formed in April 1976; it was a coalition of 18 previously Ugandan exiled groups. Yusuf Lule was appointed as president of the NEC; he served also as president of Uganda for only 68 days. Lule, a former vice-chancellor of Makerere University, wanted to restructure the NEC in June 1979; but some members of the Uganda National Liberation Front (UNLF) did not agree with him.

So, Yusuf Lule decided to resign. He was succeeded by Godfrey Lukongwa Binaisa who was a former Attorney-

General. And in May 1980, Godfrey was overthrown by the Military Commission of the UNLF and the six-member military commission took control of the government on May 12, 1980 (UCA – Political Science, 2014). This commission was chaired by Paulo Muwanga and the vice-chairman was Yoweri Museveni. Paulo was an associate of Obote and he had the support of Oyite-Ojok.

The country had elections in December 1980 and the political party UPC gained the majority of seats and Obote became for the second time the President of Uganda. Other competing political parties who failed on the elections were Democratic Party (DP) under the leadership of Paul Ssemogerere, the Uganda Patriotic Movement (UPC) led by Yoweri Museveni, and the

Conservative Party (CP) that was the emanation of the Kabaka Yeka (KY) political party. Most of the contesters didn't accept the results of the elections. Their discontent pushed some to them to form 'armed groups' to fight against the new Obote regime. The three main groups were,

- ✓ Uganda National Rescue Front (UNRF): its members were the supporters of Amin,
- ✓ Uganda Freedom Movement (UFM): under the leadership of Balaki Kirya and Andrew Kayiira,
- ✓ National Resistance Army (NRA): under the leadership of Yoweri Museveni and Yusuf Lule. When Lule died in 1985, Museveni became the principal leader of the movement.

These liberation military movements didn't operate without important loss in the country. For example, when the Uganda National Liberation Army (UNLA) wanted to fight against the progress of the National Resistance Army (NRA) in March 1983, civilian refugees were victims of that. Attacks on a refugee camp made hundreds of people lose their lives and according to figure given by Michael Jennings' article 100,000 people were displaced (Jennings, 2009). In 1984, the UNLA repeated similar attacks fighting against the NRA; again many civilians suffered the consequences. It is estimated that during the second regime of Obote about 100,000 people were killed.

In July 1985, Milton Obote who belonged to the Langi tribe was deposed by a military coup led by Basilio Okello who belonged to the Acholi tribe. Obote sought asylum in Zambia where he was accepted to stay. Okello invited some members of the armed groups to join his national army, some accepted but one of the NRA/NRM joined. He also made an amnesty for people who supported Amin and who were still living in exile. But during the same year of the Coup (1985) in September, the NRA took control of a large part of the South of Uganda. The government in Kampala which lost control and the revenue from the cash crops of the South was obliged to sign a peace accord with the NRA in December 1985, but its violation pushed the NRA to continue their fight.

- **Yoweri Museveni Regime**

The NRA under the leadership of Museveni continued its conquest. In January 1986, they successfully took control of the capital city Kampala. That was the end of the

Basilio Okello regime. Museveni became the President of the country (Rule, 1986). And Samson Kisekka was appointed Prime Minister. There was a formation of a National Resistance Council (NRC) involving both the civilians and the members of armed groups.

The activities of political parties were suspended in March and the elections were postponed to three years. The victory of Museveni's NRA made some other changes that included,

- the announcement of the policy of national reconciliation,
- the mandate of a commission of investigation of the violations of human rights during the Amin regime, and the same was done for the regime of Obote and Okello,

- the reorganization of the police force after investigating their activities (more than 2,500 were fired in July 1986),
- the establishment of a system of resistance committees at local and district level with mandate: the maintenance of security and the elimination of corruption.

Nonetheless, the most significant resistance to Museveni rule after seizing power in Uganda was a religious one. In fact, a religious leader named Alice Lakwena, in her religious sect, was able to convince and attract many farmers from the tribe of Acholi and former soldiers of the Uganda National Liberation Army (UNLA). Alice, who proclaimed herself Prophetess, associated with the people who were attracted to her (Bridgland, 2007).

They formed a rebel movement known as the Holy Spirit Movement. Museveni regime fought back against it in the late 1987, and its leader Alice Lakwena fled to Kenya. But Joseph Kony, the nephew of Lakwena, who remained in the country with other members succeed to reorganize themselves and formed the Lord's Resistance Army (LRA). Kony took the leadership of the movement and made the north of Uganda 'a hell on earth' as some argue about their atrocious acts especially on children.

- **Museveni Regime, LRA and other armed rebel groups**

The armed movement in rivalry with Museveni regime which started as the Holy Spirit Movement and later became the Lord's Resistance Army (LRA) led by Joseph Kony was the only movement that engaged in a very long civil war in the north of Uganda causing an important loss to many civilians and the lives of many perished.

Kony and his followers wish to build a nation in Uganda that uses the Word of God as law – a nation in which the Ten Commandments given by God to Moses in the Bile are the cornerstone of any law that will be governing the country. This seems wonderful; but, it strongly contrasts with what the LRA did to the people they wanted to serve using the Word of God. Because since the 1990s, Joseph Kony had been accused of many atrocious acts and violation of human rights. Some of his acts include,

- recruiting children by force to serve as soldiers,
- taking children by force to work as sex slaves,
- (about 30,000 children were taken by force)
- murder of innocent civilians,
- mutilation, kidnapping, and death (estimation of more than 100,000 people),
- causing loss and displacement of civilians (estimation of about 1.6 million people from the Northern Uganda were displaced).

The Museveni regime has been ruling for a long period; it has been there for a longer period than any other previous regime in Uganda. It had many rivalries mostly composed of armed groups, but it survived. Since 1986 up to nowadays – that makes 31 years of reign –, Museveni has been playing on the political scene of Uganda as President of the country.

Many militant groups and armed groups have been operating against his power throughout the country, some disappeared with the course of time, others were terminated by Museveni regime, and some other exist today as political parties. Among his rival military groups, we may cite,

✓ The Allied Democratic Front (ADF): was doing its activities in the western parts of Uganda, in the districts of Bundibinyo and Kasese. This movement had bases in the border mountains of Rwenzori in DR Congo. Civilians in both Uganda and RD Congo were victims of the attacks of this rebel group. They sporadically attacked peoples in both countries causing important losses and deaths.

✓ The People's Redemption Army (PRA): this rebel group was also operating in the territory of DR Congo. They had strong partnership with some opposition political parties in Uganda

✓ West Nile Bank Front (WNBF): operated in the West Nile region.

✓ Uganda National Liberation Front (UNLF II): also operated in the West Nile region.

The both WNBF and UNLF II operated in and out of DRC and have ended when the government signed a peace agreement with them in 2001. Some other rebel groups in Uganda have also ended due to the amnesty (to members of Uganda Democratic Army – UDA) of the government, especially in eastern parts of Uganda and the Karamoja region. Moreover, apart from internal peace agreements, amnesties, and forceful disarmament, Uganda had also signed several peace agreements with its neighbors. The neighboring countries involving in diplomatic peace treaties are DR Congo, Sudan, Somalia, and Rwanda.

- **LRA and Museveni Regime Peace Talks**

There was a certain stability and cease of hostilities in the Northern region of Uganda in 2008 due to the peace talks initiated in Juba between the Ugandan government and the Lord's Resistance Army (LRA). The LRA seemed to agree with the government on different issues related to peace and development of the country and stopped a little bit their atrocities. Because the International Criminal Court (ICC) had accused Kony and other leaders of LRA for war crimes and crimes against humanity, they refused to sign the peace agreement and demanded the denial of the accusation made against them first.

And later on, they continued with their atrocious acts on civilians. Astonishingly, they become increasingly ambitious in their activities up to extending them over the borders of Uganda. They started operating in Eastern DRC, in some parts of Central African Republic, and in some region of Sudan. In December 2008, Uganda,

Sudan, and DRC made a joint military attack against the LRA (Enough, nd). The attack was very powerful that the LRA soldiers were scattered and made many civilians victims in their flight.

> "According to Human Rights Watch, in December 2008 and January 2009, the LRA brutally killed more than 865 civilians and abducted at least 160 children in northeastern Congo alone. From September 2008 to December 2010, reportedly more than 1,900 people were killed by the LRA in Congo, 2,615 were abducted (including 886 children), and 347,360 were internally displaced in Congo alone." (Enough, nd).

The LRA's record of atrocious acts is very critical. It is reported by The Resolve.org that the LRA has a serious key statistics record of human rights violation that includes,

✓ Deaths
- The LRA is responsible for more than 100,000 deaths over the course of the conflict.

Among the recent killings outside Uganda, the following facts were reported.

- More than 2,400 killed by the LRA in DRC, CAR, and South Sudan since 2008, as of December 2011;
- DRC: Over 1,900 killed between September 2008 and December 2010;
- South Sudan: 216 killed between December 2008 and November 2009;
- Central African Republic: 175 killed between February 2008 and November 2010.

✓ Abductions
- More than 3,400 abducted by the LRA in DRC, CAR, and South Sudan since 2008, including over 1,500 children as of March 2011.
- DR Congo: 2,615 people abducted, including 886 children, as of December 2010.
- South Sudan: 149 abducted between December 2008 and November 2009.
- Central African Republic: 352 abducted, including many children, as of November 2010.

- Uganda:
  - 66,00 people/youth between the ages of 14 and 30 from the mid-1990s to 2006

- and 30,000 children (under 18) abducted from 1988 to 2004.

✓ Displaced People

- 438,504 LRA-induced displacements in DRC, CAR, and South Sudan as of December 2011.
  - DR Congo: 347,360 IDPs in LRA-affected areas of DRC as of December 2011.
  - South Sudan: 70,000 estimated number of people displaced due to LRA violence as of December 2011.
  - Central African Republic: 21,144 displaced in Southeast Central African Republic as of December 2011.
- Uganda: approximately 1,700,000 internally displaced from 1986 to 2007.

Source: http://www.theresolve.org/the-lra-crisis/key-statistics/

And that is not all that the LRA can do to the people of central Africa because the movement is not yet totally eradicated in the region. Is that what their 'lord' has been telling them to do? Maybe the 'lord' is the lover of human blood and flesh, and he is always happy to see people suffering and dying!

- **The Period from 2009 to 2017 in Ugandan: Some of the Main Political Events**

The very recent history of Uganda suggests that there is an absence of civil wars, but that does not mean that the country has already set its feet on the path of durable peace and prosperity for all. Some of the reasons include but not limited to the Museveni regime has been reported to have implication in the conflicts in the AGLR that has cost the lives of millions of people, the instability of the neighboring countries, the political leaders' hunger for power.

The rebel movement members who seem to still have faith in themselves and their 'lord' to set 'Uganda free' are still a permanent threat to the security of people and their goods in the AGLR. UN Security Council President condemned their movement, the LRA, on January 16, 2009; and on March 18, 2009, they announced a cessation of military hostilities. The man who was appointed as UN Special Envoy for the LRA insurgency in Uganda, former President Joaquim Chissano of Mozambique, finished his work on June 30, 2009 (UCA – Political Science, 2014). That was the sign that the LRA was fragilized but not completely eradicated.

Likewise, while Uganda is preparing for the election of February 2011, the Government accused Kizza Besigye, the main opponent of Museveni, and ten co-defendants of treason. They were charged with plotting to forcefully overthrow the Ugandan government between 2001 and 2004; that was to happen for Besigye associated with the People's Redemption Army (PRA) that operates from the DRC as said by his accusers. But the Uganda Constitution Court dismissed the treason charges on October 12, 2010, and said that there was insufficient evidence and that the defendants' rights were violated by the state (Paulsworth, 2010).

So, Besigye continued his preparation for the presidential election to which he was a candidate. The results of the legislative elections of February 18, 2011, showed that the President Yoweri Museveni of the NRM (National Resistance Movement) was re-elected with 68 percent of the vote. The NRM won 263 out of 375 seats in the

National Assembly. Besigye's political party the FDC (Forum for Democratic Change) won 34 seats in the National Assembly (UCA – Political Science, 2014).

The election had many observers such as the Commonwealth that sent thirteen observers and five staff members who worked from February 10 to February 24, 2011; the EU (European Union) that sent seven election experts, 34 long-term observers, and 68 short-term observers who worked from January 15 to March 10, 2011 and were from 28 countries; the AU (African Union) sent 29 observers; a joint delegation of 70 observers from EAC (East African Community), COMESA (Common Market for Eastern and Southern Africa), and IGAD (Intergovernmental Authority on

Development) from 14 countries worked beginning on February 12, 2011 (UCA – Political Science, 2014).

It was reported by the Commonwealth that the 2011 elections were contested by more candidates compared to previous polls (Commonwealth, 2011). As it the custom of the AGLR countries, there are always victims of contested elections. The government police officers arrested the opposition leader Kizza Besigye on Aprile 28, 2011 and in Kampala at least two persons died in riots on April 28-29, 2011 (UCA – Political Science, 2014). However, in 2012 the military component of the RCI-LRA (Regional Cooperation Initiative for the Elimination of the Lord's Resistance Army) created by AU was launched together with the RTF (Regional Task Force) to combat the LRA. It had 5,000 troops from

Uganda, South Sudan, CAR, and DRC and was commanded by Colonel Dick Prit Olum of Uganda.

In an article on Uganda, the Political Science Department of the UCA (2014) shows some of the achievement of the RTF troops. They put,

> "AU RTF troops killed the chief bodyguard of Joseph Kony, a commander known as Binani, in the Central African Republic, on January 18, 2013. The president of the UN Security Council condemned the LRA and called for an immediate end to the violence in Uganda on May 29, 2013. US. Special Forces transported some 20 Ugandan government troops serving with the AU RTF into Central African Republic on November 22, 2013. Within one week, Ugandan government troops killed between five and ten LRA rebels, including senior LRA commander Colonel Samuel Kangul. The president of the UN Security Council condemned the LRA on November 25, 2013. Nineteen LRA rebels surrendered to AU RTF troops in the Central African Republic on December 6, 2013. On July 10, 2014, the African Union (AU) appointed Lt. General Kiprono Tuwei of Kenya as the AU Special Envoy for the LRA insurgency. Several thousand individuals,

including more than 2,500 civilians, have been killed during the government's conflict against the LRA. More than 400,000 individuals have been displaced during the conflict." (UCA – Political Science, 2014).

One of the members of the LRA, Dominic Ongwen, appeared before the International Criminal Court in January 2015. That was also one of the outcomes of the RTF. While the government of Uganda was making effort towards the eradication of LRA, the President Museveni appeared to be doing his best to have another term in the office for the February 2016 elections. Many people in Uganda seemed to be disappointed by Museveni's decision to run for another presidential mandate. President Yoweri Museveni who was already in office for 30 years was re-elected in February 2016 with 62 percent of votes. His main competitor, Kizza Besigye, had 34 percent. The FDC rejected the results and Besigye was arrested (Karimi & Ntale & Botelho, 2016). Sounds like a game; Besigye underwent the same situation during the elections of 2011.

Is there any hope for positive change in the future of Uganda? Can Ugandan people hope for true democracy that will to durable peace and prosperity for all? What can the people of Uganda do to have lasting peace and prosperity? Is that possible with reference to the bloody, atrocious, and troublesome history of Uganda? Can Uganda play its role well as a good neighbor for other countries of the AGLR? That is what this book will try to answer in the next chapters.

Chapter Six
Self-Awareness and True Knowledge of the Land and its People

"Colonialists stole not only the lands of African people and renamed them. They stole also their knowledge, so that they would know nothing about themselves."
(Motsoko Pheko)

6.1. Overview

The ignorance of 'self', others, and the land is one of the main causes of the challenging and atrocious situations that most people face in the African Great Lakes Region (AGLR). The accurate knowledge and use of one's real natural potentials, gifts, strengths, and identity in a well-known territory or land with well-known people as partners or neighbors make the core of the first fundamental principle that may reduce the difficulties that hinder people's capacity to live well when it is well applied in life. As known, since the exploration periods of Africa, the history is full of unfair and untrue facts about Africans that made some of them unable to discover and use their true abilities that may lead them to durable peace and prosperity.

The people of AGLR who appear to be the most disturbed by the lack of peace in Africa should rethink their future; they have to rediscover who they really are and think about what they have to do to change the situation for a better life for all. Thus, the people of the AGLR have to reasonably think about the following life fundamental questions to be ready to welcome other principles for durable peace and prosperity for all.

- As a human being, who am I? Why am I her on the planet earth? Why was I born in the AGLR?

- What are my thoughts and beliefs? What do I think about my tribe or ethnic group? What do I think about other ethnic groups or tribes of my country? Are my thoughts and beliefs based on truth or they are based on ignorance, lies, and stereotypes?

- Do I know the history of African migrations? Do I know the history of the people of AGLR? Do I know the impact of colonialism on Africa – on the AGLR?

- Do I know that the European Colonialists were overestimated by Colonized Africans who underestimated themselves and that hindered their fight for independence? Do I know the impact of cold war in Africa – in the AGLR?

- What gift(s) or talent(s) do I have?

- What goals do I have with reference to my gifts and beliefs? What do I like to do? Is what I like to do in accordance with what I was born to do?

- What about my values, attitudes, and virtues, and character? Are they helping me to live well?

- What is obedience to me? Up to what extent do I obey authorities or leaders?

- What do I know about racial discrimination during the colonial period of Africa? Is it still shaping the way I consider the other races up to nowadays? Are black peoples inferior to those of other races? Do I know the impact of African Stereotypes on Africans? Do I know what is believed by some non-Africans about Africa? What do I know about the land of Africa and its ethnic groups (especially those of the AGLR)?

- Do I recognize other people's potential? How much do I value them? At what extent do I neglect or despise others?

Reasonable answers to these questions may shed light on people's minds and help in the process of establishing durable peace and prosperity for all. What exactly these questions try to remind us?

6.2. Who am I? Why am I on the planet earth? Why was I born in the AGLR?

These questions that always seem difficult to have meaningful answers by many people in the world is to make the center of every single individual of the AGLR. The AGLR supports the lives of millions of people since long ago; most of them seem to have been living with much ignorant of 'who they are', 'why they were born there', and why 'they have been living there'. The most important discovery on planet earth is the genuine and straight answers to the question 'Who am I?' About that, there are some scientific explanations that have been given by some philosophers and thinkers, but their explanations show how much they are still very far from the unquestionable arguments because true answers defining human beings require God's inspiration and revelations rather than scientific or religious views.

In fact, there are many planets in the universe, but human beings found themselves living on the planet earth where their lives can be easily lived with the availability of the resources they need to live well. And the truth is that nobody chose to be living on earth – that exclude any possible idea of freedom to choose to exist – as a human being. Now the question is 'why should I kill, hate, or discriminate against a neighbor who didn't chose to be living near me? He or she did not choose to be on earth, and I did not choose that too! Why should I destroy him or her because of other people's opinions and stories? To avoid bad things to happen to us, we should seek to have ingenious ideas about 'who we are'. We have a Source and we are living on a planet that has a Source, a Creator, a Mighty God; that is one of the main reasons why we did not decide to be on earth.

Grudem (2000), in his book *'Systematic Theology: An Introduction to Bible Doctrine'*, summarizes the traditional proofs of the existence of a Supreme God who created everything that exists in the universe in four main types of arguments. He talks about,

- ✓ The cosmological argument: it takes into consideration the fact the everything that exists in the universe has a cause. And the universe itself must have a cause for its existence; thus, the cause of such a wonderful universe can only be God.

- ✓ The teleological argument: this argument stresses on the evidence of the existence of harmony, order, and design in the universe. It argues that the design and harmony in the universe produce confirmation that there is intelligence purpose. And as the universe is seen to be signed with purpose, there must be an intelligent God who created it to function with purpose.

- ✓ The ontological argument: this argument supposes that it is greater to exist than not to exist. The existence of creatures being people to have the ideas of a being who is "greater than which nothing can be imagined" and who exist also.

✓ The moral argument: it takes into consideration the man's inner sense of what is right and what is wrong. The human inner knowledge of what is right, wrong, and the need for justice to be done is a proof of the existence of a God who is the source of right and wrong and who will judge the human beings someday. By that, He requires that justice be done on earth.

It is good to mention that these arguments are not based on faith as it is the case of most religious arguments or statements; they based on the creatures – things and persons that are seen – that everyone can see or experiences with their natural human senses. These arguments show clearly that behind everything that exists there is a Master Creator. They show that there is a suppose for the existence of the universe; they also show that there is a noble purpose to the existence of human beings with justice being their day to day regulator of harmony in their social interactions or activities.

But what is the true purpose of the existence of human beings if the created things exist to make their lives possible on earth? What is the purpose of existence of humans who are allowed to kill millions of plants and other creators to live well? Were they exist to just consuming the oxygen and other earthly resources for nothing and then die? The humble and clear answer to this question is essential for any person who wants to live in durable peace with himself or herself and with other people in the society.

We are from the Creator and we exist on earth to manifest His glory by serving each other with love using the free gifts we got from Him without discrimination based on color, race, physical statures, opinions, religions, languages, creed, country, continent; and that should be done without expectation of being over-rewarded by the people we are serving (more explanation in chapter eight that deals with laws).

It seems to me that the purpose of human beings' existence on earth, which is inseparable with 'who they are', has been universally misunderstood or ignored by millions of human beings. And it is one of the main reasons why world peace is difficult to achieve. That is why millions of the people in the world are living under influences of liars, cheaters, robbers, egoistic leaders, killers, etc. and end up copying the behavior and attitude of their role models. That is why most people violate the basic principles of durable peace and prosperity.

Before looking at the possible answers that the dominant religions in the AGLR provide about these questions, it is important to recall here, as mentioned earlier, that we are noble creatures of God sent to the planet earth to fulfill his purpose of serving others in the community, using his love and justice in our daily living. Serving others honestly is the quintessence of man's existence on earth because of the power and joy which come from that; that is one of the main secrets that lies behind long-lasting personal inner peace.

When people have a deep understanding of this truth and apply it in their lives, they allow durable peace and prosperity to set its roots in the nation. Serving each other with integrity and honesty is supposed to be at the center of humanism for we don't need to be religious or to have religious beliefs to understand this reality. For example, it can be hard to believe that some Hutu people who had clearly understood that they exist to honestly serve all the Rwandans with discrimination, could involve themselves in the massive killing of people they are supposed to work for! That would clearly appear to them as killing themselves! But because of the ignorance of the 'self' people were making their existence useless. And the sad reality about civil wars and genocide in the AGAR is that even some religious leaders and many Christians are mostly involved in the planning and execution of violent acts.

Today, there are thousands of religions in the world; and all of them have some explanations that try to answer the questions "Who am I as a human being?" and "Why am I here on the planet earth?" The dominant religion in the AGAR is Christianity with about 90 percent of the population of the region. Their teaching about human beings' mission on the earth is constructive and powerful in terms of peace and prosperity archieving. I wander whether all the Christians in the AGAR are aware of the very power of the teaching of their religion on that issue. Let's have a look at some details of what Christianity teaches about human beings on earth.

About the existence of human beings on earth, the Catholic Church, the largest subdivision of Christianity in the AGAR, teaches that they were created by God by His free Will to share with them His blessed life. In the 'Catechism of the Catholic Church', we can read,

> "God, infinitely perfect and blessed in himself, in a plan of sheer goodness freely created man to make him share in his own blessed life. For this reason, at every time and in every place, God draws close to man. He calls man to seek him, to know him, to love him with all his strength. He calls together all men, scattered and divided by sin, into the unity of his family, the Church. To accomplish this, when the fullness of time had come, God sent his Son as Redeemer and Savior. In his Son and through him, he invites men to become, in the Holy Spirit, his adopted children and thus heirs of his blessed life.1" (Pope John Paul II, 1997).

So, God is a Creator who gives human being a blessed life and not a cursed one like that of many people of the African Great Lakes Region. Many people have been experiencing, since long ago, a life of curse although their membership in the Catholic Church. This religion explains that by the natural light of human reason God can be known because He created man in His image; and without that man cannot be able to welcome God. But the historical conditions of human beings had made it difficult for them to know God by the light of reason alone. The point 37 of the Catechism of the Catholic Church puts,

> "37 In the historical conditions in which he finds himself, however, man experiences many difficulties in coming to know God by the light of reason alone: Though human reason is, strictly speaking, truly capable by its own natural power and light of attaining to a true and certain knowledge of the one personal God, who watches over and controls the world by his providence, and of the natural law written in our hearts by the Creator; yet there are many obstacles which prevent reason from the effective and fruitful use of this inborn faculty. For the truths that concern the relations between God and man wholly transcend the visible order of things, and, if they

are translated into human action and influence it, they call for self-surrender and abnegation. The human mind, in its turn, is hampered in the attaining of such truths, not only by the impact of the senses and the imagination, but also by disordered appetites which are the consequences of original sin..." (Pope John Paul II, 1997).

This is some of the fundamentals the beliefs and teachings of the Catholic Church about human beings; a religion that has more members than any other religious group of the AGLR, and has been evangelizing for more than hundred years there. Created by God with natural reason and capacity to know Him, human beings throughout the history of their lives on earth have been unable by their inborn light of reason to fully recognize God's will. Although the printed law of God in their hearts, human beings are still stumbling to live according to the original purpose of God by their own inborn faculty.

That is why human beings need to be enlightened by God's revelation in order to access to the truth of God and to live according to His will. The following points may summarize what is supposed to be the teachings of Catholic Church about man (according to Catechism of the Catholic Church),

- ✓ "44 Man is by nature and vocation a religious being. Coming from God, going toward God, man lives a fully human life only if he freely lives by his bond with God.

- ✓ 45 Man is made to live in communion with God in whom he finds happiness: When I am completely united to you, there will be no more sorrow or trials; entirely full of you, my life will be complete (St. Augustine, Conf. 10, 28, 39: PL 32, 795}.

✓ 46 When he listens to the message of creation and to the voice of conscience, man can arrive at certainty about the existence of God, the cause and the end of everything.

✓ 47 The Church teaches that the one true God, our Creator and Lord, can be known with certainty from his works, by the natural light of human reason (cf. Vatican Council I, can. 2 § 1: DS 3026),

✓ 48 We really can name God, starting from the manifold perfections of his creatures, which are likenesses of the infinitely perfect God, even if our limited language cannot exhaust the mystery.

✓ 49 Without the Creator, the creature vanishes (GS 36). This is the reason why believers know that the love of Christ urges them to bring the light of the living God to those who do not know him or who reject him." (Pope John Paul II, 1997, Catechism of the Catholic Church. Second Edition. Vatican: Catholic Church).

Thus, we may say that the Catholic Christians of the AGLR believe that God is the cause and the end of everything. And without the Him, there cannot be life on earth. That is why, in light of his teachings, people are to live according to Him who is the cause and end of everything. Does he allow some Christians or Christians religious leaders in the AGLR to take part in the massive killing of innocents as it was the case during the genocides?

Does He allow some human being to put an end to the lives of others because of ethnic differences? Does He say that some Catholic Christians teach conflict and help rebel leaders to perform their acts in exchange for money or any other advantages? Do they know all who they are according to the teaching of their religions? The world needs to remember that Catholics are the majority of the populations of the AGLR. Their teachings and beliefs are supposed to be seen in their daily living and dominate the societies of the region.

6.3. What are my thoughts and beliefs? What do I think about my tribe, ethnic group? What do I think about other ethnic groups or tribes of my country? Are my thoughts and beliefs based on truth or they are founded on ignorance, lies, and stereotyped?

"Watch your thoughts, for they become words. Choose your words, for they become actions. Understand your actions, for they become habits. Study your habits, for they will become your character. Develop your character, for it becomes your destiny." - Anonymous

This is not the time for the people of the AGLR to think nor as during the colonial era neither as they have been thinking during the post-colonial era. There is a need of renewal of thoughts and beliefs in every single individual's mind. So, each person needs to ask herself or himself the following questions: What are my thoughts and beliefs? What do I think about my tribe or ethnic group? What do I think about other ethnic groups or tribes of my country? Are my thoughts and beliefs based on truth or they are founded on ignorance, lies, and stereotyped? These questions are to be addressed by every person in the AGLR who need to improve or correct his or her attitude towards the 'self' and others. What people believe of themselves direct their thoughts and guide their daily actions.

That is why revising one's beliefs may result in a positive inner state that can be healthier to durable peace and prosperity of the community. The state of people's beliefs can also determine their power to build or to destroy. They are the cornerstone of confidentiality and success. The type of success needed is the one that requires the use of the full natural potential of a person and full service to other people in the community. Individual success requires self-confidentiality and both allow personal peace and prosperity. So, people need to discover and to use their full self-confidence to serve themselves and their communities.

There are many theories that people can study about self-confidence and success. Books and articles have been written by experienced, gifted, and successful person in the world, sharing their thoughts and experiences about how to succeed and to secure successful achievements.

One of them is Steven Convey; in his book entitled 'Seven Habits of Highly Effective People', we find constructive principles that may help people lead their lives toward success if well applied. Stephen Covey produced Seven Habits of Highly Effective People in a book which was first published in 1989.

Daft (2015) explains them in his book, 'Leadership experience'. With reference to Daft's work, let's go through the principles that were suggestion by Covey to find out their possible application by the people of AGLR. Fascinatingly, the eight habits of highly effective people suggested by Convey (1990) can be divided into two main categories: habits that stress on 'from dependence to independence' and habits that deal with 'effective interdependence'.

While some Africans misuse the African concept of 'Ubuntu' to remain unfruitful and irrational because of excessively depending on others in their communities, some theorists of success find that as a barrier to success. The first habit of the first category is 'being proactive.' Daft (2015, p. 202) writes that "proactive peoples recognize that they have the ability to choose and to act with integrity. They do not blame others and life's circumstances for their outcomes." This statement may sound shocking for some people of the African Great Lakes Region who blames endlessly others for the consequences that the genocide and civil wars have in the countries of the region today.

Convey puts it clear that people cannot succeed with such mindsets and they cannot use their full potential of self-confidence to unlock the doors of possibities to welcome positive change. This habit can be part of people's successful leadership role in the region by the fact that it can assist in the process of taking new initiatives and knowing that their decisions are the primary factors for effectiveness in their lives. It can also assist in the process of to take serious responsibility for people's choices and being able to bear the consequences that will follow them. For example, every person in the AGLR is advised not to always be waiting for someone else to tell them what to do, how to do it, and when it.

No human being has the full right to tell others what to choose because the advisers have a little and sometimes no power over the consequences of the advised actions and choices. That is why the true discovery of 'self' can lead us effectively in the process of acting wisely by depending on our own thoughts, beliefs, reason, ability, will, and power. We don't to depend on others to act or to choose what to do in most life realities; we need to use our reasons or inner selves to guide us.

Likewise, the second habit suggested by Convey is 'Begin with the End in Mind' which means that people should be starting projects, journeys, battles, etc. with a clear image of their destination. This requires a knowledge of what is basic for people and a clear and reasonable distinction between what they want, and what they need so that their actions and choices may contribute to the accomplishment of their visions. This second habit is very important and completes the first habit of being proactive. When a person has original thoughts, beliefs, and actions, he or she appears to be himself or herself.

Any negative influence to people's thoughts and beliefs is likely to darken their true 'selves' and may fake their independence. And when that value is lost, it impacts people's original integrity. As a result, people's plans will run the risk of not having right ends. Why? People will be doing things they don't believe in strongly; they will not be ready or willing to bear the consequences of what they have done because they were just executing others minds. So, 'begin with the end in mind' can certainly assist in the process of planning with goals to reach with respect and consideration to all possible consequences of the actions that are directed by original thoughts and beliefs. It is a powerful habit that can lead people to self-discovery which is very important for self-awareness by putting a shed of light on their strengths and weaknesses in the process of achieving goals with clear knowledge of the end.

For example, planning to start a project without correct knowledge of its end, the goals assigned may run the risk of not being achieved. There will probably be a risk of not thinking of values and means assisting for the accomplishment the goals. And that is a failure for the person in charge who is supposed to be a good planner and achiever of goals as no one plans to fail. In addition, with this habit people will become able to want what they need to reach their objectives. This is important because sometimes it is difficult for some people to exactly want what they need. Adler (1997, p. 77-79) puts "Almost all of us want things that we do not need and fail to want things we do need. In the statement just made lies the crux of the matter. We ought to want the things we need. We ought not to want the things we do not need if wanting them interferes with our wanting – and acquiring – the things we do need."

So, if we begin with the end in mind, we will want the things we need to reach the planned end with success. We need to revisit the way we conceive our ideas and how we plan to put them into action. We may think of the late president Mobutu of Zaire (DRC today). Did this man plan to die in exile at the end of his political career? Was he working with the correct knowledge of where he was going? Possible not. Let's think about these other following leaders: Idi Amin late president of Uganda,

Habyarimana late president of Rwanda, and Michombero late president of Burundi.

With reference to the political histories of those political leaders, can we say that they really wanted what they needed? Can we say they wanted what people needed? Or they had lack of knowledge of the end of their careers? Were they good planners? Can they be 'good role model' of political leadership? Everyone who is knowledgeable of the thoughts, beliefs, and acts of these former leaders will agree with the reality that all of these personalities failed their plans and missions.

Moreover, the third habit of successful people is about 'Putting first things first.' Daft (2008, p. 202) writes about 'Put First Things First' putting 'it encourages people to gain control of time and event by relating them to their goals and by managing themselves." This habit is just recalling us that setting priorities always helps people to reach their ends that they have in minds. It put stress on time management and goal focusing. This is very important for developing countries in Africa where most of time we see some people wasting time in useless discussions, talks, and debates instead of being busy working to develop their communities. This habit also can help people to preserve and enhance their relationships while performing their duties in good and planned time.

That sounds reasonable because some conflicts may take place when people don't do what they said they will do at the time set for it. Or it can happen that people get into trouble when they concentrate on less important things rather than the more important. All the leaders and the population of the AGLR should be reminded that setting priorities wisely or putting first things first is very helpful for anyone who seeks durable peace and prosperity.

Time does not wait for human beings; time does not wait for change, and change does not change time; it remains the same and is endlessly running. If we do not act on time, it will act on us. We need to know that the future will one day accuse us if keep on wasting time on unimportant things while very important ones that can help our nations are left behind. No matter how what we do please us, if they do not get into the principle of 'putting first things first' the future will surely tell us that something went wrong.

If we want to get at the place we have in mind, if we want to reach the end we have our plans, we need always to be using 'reason' rather than 'feelings' when taking serious decision to act. I know that need a certain level of self-discipline and the discovery of the true self. Some conflicts in the AGLR have been nurtured by the inabilities of some leaders to use logical reasoning in their analysis the situations.

For example, a Leader who says publicly 'We must throw all the Tutsi people in the river to send them back where their ancestors came from', what logical reasoning is he using that make him ignore the history of his ethnic group showing clearly that this ancestors also came from somewhere... For him the priority of killing others because that is what comes first in his murderous plans! What kind of dirty mind and ugly plans? This kind attitude will always impede the development of the true self and as a result of durable peace and development will stumble. It can be agreed that when irrational opinions and actions dominate in a community, there cannot be any possibility of putting first things first.

The fourth habit of Convey which is the first one that deals with effective interdependence is 'think win-win.' About it, Daft (2008, p.202) writes that to "think win-win" means understanding that without cooperation, the organization cannot succeed. This is an excellent habit for workers of organizations who most of the time are asked to work in teams. It is also important for every member of a community because it does not allow people to be egoistic. The mentality of 'win alone' has characterized the relationship between the tribes and ethnic groups in the AGLR. When a member of ethnic group or tribe takes power, he tends to put aside all other people who don't belong to his or her ethnicity or tribe.

When a leader is from the Northern region, he or she gets rid of his or her office all other people who are from the Southern region. Selections after job interviews are not done according to the merit but to tribal belonging, ethnic belonging, and regional belonging! Where does this behavior leading the leaders of the AGLR? This is time to stop such a behavior; it is time to learn deeply about the habit 'think win-win'. It may assist in the leadership function of individuals to know or to be aware of the importance of good cooperation to the success of an organization or a team. Reminding us to avoid over-estimation of self and negative self-confidence is necessary for using our true inner self.

For example, people may avoid saying 'I can do it myself; I do not need the cooperation of others to achieve my goals because I am competent enough!' The habit 'think win-win' can make a team become more productive because it focuses on 'never gain alone'! Taking everything for oneself by ignoring the needs of others is what makes conflict alive in a community or a team. Therefore, effective conflict management is required during team cooperation.

Northouse (2007, p. 214) seems to mean the same by stating that "Teams that can manage conflict, collaborate well together, and build commitment will have good relation. Teams that are well connected to and protected from environment will also be more productive." Furthermore, for this habit of thinking win-win to be fruitful, leaders and followers should avoid negative stereotypes which constitute the barriers to a good cooperation. Knowing that modern organization do not hire workers on basis of their cultures but by their competence, it is advisable to have a positive intercultural communication in interaction and cooperation with others.

6.4. What do I know and believe about others in the African Great Lakes Region? Do I consider my tribe and ethnic group special with comparison to others? Do I consider myself as special and superior to other people?

These are the question that may have a negative impact on the habit 'think win-win.' What people think about themselves and others in the AGLR need to be addressed with very good enegry because that is part of negative racial stereotypes, and this seems to be a reality for many people in the world today; they seem to still have the grotesque colonial mentality of racial superiority. People need to correct that. Puwar cited by Wester (2008, p.60), talking about Britain, wrote: "In Britain, our colonial past stays with us like a sediment, where 'Black bodies' are represented as coming from uncivilized spaces, wilderness where people are savages and need training... whites are associated with spirit and mind, representing the flight from the body". This is an eloquent example showing how people stereotype others. These negative stereotypes may become barriers to good cooperation and should be avoided by today's organizations especially multinational having an employment of high cultural diversity.

Concerning the fifth habit Conveys 'seek first to understand, then to be understood', we may say that it convey the secret of the power of peaceful cohabitation. We live in societies where we are always with other people. Mostly and naturally, everyone needs to be understood first. And that sometimes result in quarrels and hates. So, this habit teaches us to understand first others' point of view before wanting them to understand ours. Even if we will not agree with them, we have moral obligation to listen to them and to understand what they say. This is a good skill of interpersonal communication that must be developed by people who are living or working with others.

Yusoontorn (Aug. 2011) talks about understanding others as his sixth habit for great leaders. He writes about of openness to new ideas by explaining that 'openness' means being open to new ideas even if they do not conform to the usual way of thinking. He inscribes "Good leaders are able to suspend judgments while listening to others' ideas, as well as accept new ways of doing thinks that someone else thought of." There are 'very good speakers' in the AGLR; they think they are better off because of too much impressive words that they use in their communications. Most of them are found in the Republic Democratic of the Congo. There, it is easy to find as many good speakers as possible.

Some people waste their time talking talking talking. They sometimes forget to do some work that may help them fight poverty. They move around the towns and the capital city looking for 'nice jobs' because some who are educated cannot do 'any jobs'. When they speak they make the impression of people who are very high as their clothes always suggest! And mostly, they only want to be heard themselves and judge severely and negatively criticize the opinions or acts of others. For such people, there is a need for positive change because such behavior does not lead to successful life; it does not guarantee durable peace and prosperity.

Again, the mentality of judging and gossiping is unhealthy and does not lead to harmonious and convivial state of mind. Scribd (2012) writes "From the Native American song to the Great Spirit – 'May I not judge my brother, until I have walked a mile in his moccasins.' Stephen Covey's Four Quadrants – once again this is just common sense – but it sure helps to have it laid out logically."

'Synergize' is the sixth habit of successful peoples suggested by Convey. It is the combined action that occurs when people work together to create new alternatives and solutions to their problems. It requires the moderation of the leaders' power or authority. From this, we can try think about how much the community and political leaders of the AGLR are willing to seek solutions to people problems by honestly taking into consideration their views. The dictatorship mindsets of some of those leaders do not allow suggestions that come from the people they are leading.

Durable peace and prosperity want us to be willing to welcome suggestions and to be open to different viewpoints of the other people. The 'synthesizing' habit calls to participative leadership because it sounds impossible to work in synergy when the leaders in the communities do not allow participation of their followers to the decision-making process. This habit is particularly addressed to all leaders and managers in the African Great Lakes Region.

Greiner (1973) cited by Western (2008, p. 115) engraves "Managers aren't authoritarians who manipulate their puppet sub-ordinates, neither do they accept participation as a blind ideology. Participative leadership is a sound general model if individual leaders can choose to be directive at will and if they can choose a variety of actions which fits their personal and career needs." Above and beyond, 'sharpen the saw', the seventh habit of Convey 'is a process of using and continuously renewing the physical, mental, spiritual, and social aspect your life." (Daft, 2008, p. 203). From this habit, we can understand that the human body needs good refreshments and strengthening exercises and practices to maintain and enhanced its fitness to complete a task. A bad spiritual, social, and physical health will surely have negative impact on professional outcomes of a leader or a follower. People should be paying much attention to their thoughts and beliefs because they dictate their habits. And habits make people's characters. Through characters, it is easy to predict a person's personality. And personality plays an important role in a person's leadership.

Much focus is to be put on women in the African Great Lakes Region who since long ago have been victims of some traditional customs of African cultures. Although they are natural agents of peace and prosperity of their families in the AGLR, many have been considered as people who cannot contribute efficiently to the progress of their nations. And that issue is to be seriously addressed because most women in Africa, in general, do not have a clear understanding of their inborn gifts and capacities. They are not given the chance of discovering what they are able to do for the positive development of their communities. We need to talk seriously about this issue because some women in the AGLR had been trained to perpetrate acts of genocide and civil wars.

Hogg (2010) shows, in her article Women's participation in the Rwandan genocide: mothers or monsters? In International Review of the Red Cross, that the propaganda organized by men in Rwanda affected the thoughts and beliefs of some women up to the extent of making them convinced to take part in the killings of the genocide of 1994. Some of the reasons that pushed them to kill are the perception of Tutsi to be associated with the RPF, the beliefs in the propaganda organized by men, the Hutu women were jealous of Tutsi women, the Hutu women were jealous of Tutsi' wealth.

Was it not the extremist Hutu propaganda that made some Hutu women involved in genocidal killings? Were these women aware of the power of their natural abilities to create riches for themselves instead of being jealous? How much trust did they put in men to accept what they were telling them without critical thinking or analysis? Were they educated enough to be able to use skills that comes from formal education?

The men of the AGLR should remember that educating a woman is to educate the whole family. Women are the ones that give children the first and most important foundation of education; so we need to give them chance to understand well and positively develop their 'selves.' We need to encourage them to go to school and to learn about themselves because it seems difficult for a woman who did not go to school to effectively encourage her child to go to school.

Also, it appears to be evident that a woman who does not know herself well will struggle to help a child to know herself or himself well. In today's aching and developing world, considering women as only second to men is like cutting slowly with a saw a sit on which you are sitting.

It is known that African women do hard and life-supporting works in African societies. Instead of leaving them without material and spiritual support, quality education, and professional opportunities, we ought to give them enough support. We need to remind that they are able to accomplish so many constructive and helpful projects for themselves and for the community.

Crawley (nd) gives ten essential steps to unshakable self-confidence to help women enhance their thoughts and beliefs to success. Her eleven steps are constructive; although they are addressed to women, men can also learn something from them. It can be agreed that women in Africa need to enhance their self-confidence by revisiting their inner state of mind to review or to correct their thoughts and beliefs.

Crawly writes that women should follow the following steps to reach unshakable self-confidence.

✓ Step 1 Develop positive self-esteem

'With greater confidence in yourself and your abilities, you will set yourself bigger goals, make bigger plans and commit yourself to achieving objectives that today you only dream about'. (Brian Tracy cited by Claudia Crawley p. 7)

"Positive self-esteem is the foundation stone of a confident personality. So what is self–esteem? It's the opinion you hold of yourself i.e. how much you like yourself. With high self-esteem, you'll like yourself; you'll feel comfortable in your own skin. You'll think positive thoughts and be highly motivated." (Crawley, p. 7)

"Your self -esteem is determined by your self-image…. Your self–image is shaped by your self-ideal, which is made up of your virtues, values, goals, hopes, dreams and aspirations". (Brian Tracy quoted by Crawley p. 8)

✓ Step 2 Replace your limitation beliefs with self-belief "There are two ways of meeting difficulties: you alter the difficulties, or you alter yourself to meet them." (Phyllis Battome cited by Crawley p. 10)

✓ Step 3 Use positive affirmation

"It's the repetition of affirmations that leads to belief. And once that belief becomes a deep conviction, things begin to happen." (Muhammad Ali cited by Crawley p. 13)

✓ Step 4 Visualize yourself being confident

"A social worker I knew visualized daily the house she wanted to buy, with its green front door, its bay windows and its neatly laid back garden. A couple of years later, she found it, her house with exactly the same front door, the bay window and back garden. It sounds too good to be true, but visualization is a technique used regularly and effectively by successful people. Tiger Woods used it on the golf course. Women use it to maintain their slender figures. It separates the really successful from the mediocre." (Crawley, p. 16 – 17).

✓ Step 5 Decide what you want and make it happen

"Things do not happen. They are made to happen." (John Fitzgerald Kennedy, the 35th US President, quoted by Crawley, p. 18).

✓ Step 6 Feel the fear

"We all have fears, whether fear of wild animals, fear of flying, fear of rejection. If it is rational and warns of impending danger, so that you take action (e.g. fleeing a fire), it can be a life saver. If imagined (e.g. fear of failure) or irrational (e.g. phobias), it can adversely affect your confidence and thereby limit your life chances." (Crawley, p. 20).

✓ Step 7 Look after your health

"Poor health can leave you completely stressed out. So learn to value and look after your health above all. Take time out to put yourself first and focus on your needs." (p. 23)

✓ Step 8 Dress to look and feel great

"Do you want to feel confident? Select clothes that make you look and feel great. Look after your hair. Ensure you are well groomed. Good grooming doesn't have to cost much, but it does require a little time and effort. When you're looking good, you'll feel good and others will compliment you and put their confidence in you." (Crawley, p. 25).

✓ Step 9 Surround yourself with the positive people

"Avoid negative people – they focus on bad news and problems. Their mood is infectious and influences you into negative thinking. If you were feeling good before meeting them, you'll feel down when you leave. Remember, the people you call friends says a lot about who you are. If you want to be successful and enjoy life hang out with successful people." (Crawley C. p.27).

✓ Step 10 Identify your strengths and acknowledge them

"Develop your confidence by taking an objective look at yourself and identifying and listing your strengths and your achievements to date.

✓ What are you good at?

✓ What do other people admire you for?

✓ What are your skills and talents?

✓ What awards have you achieved?

✓ What projects have you undertaken that have been successful?

List them all – I'm a good communicator; I dress well; I'm caring; I'm a good cook; I'm popular; I'm creative; I'm good at my job.......(Crawley C. p.29 – 30)".

✓ Step 11 The Essential bonus step – get a coach to work with you,

"If someone is going down the wrong road, he doesn't need motivation to speed him up. What he needs is education to turn him around." (Jim Rohn cited by Claudia Crawley p. 31)

It is obvious that in the AGLR, after many years of civil wars, there is scarcity of resources for millions of people. Women, in particular, suffer more the result of conflict. But successful initiatives that lead to durable peace and prosperity do not much mean or a lot of resources. What is proper does not need to get to the path of prosperity. It is what is in trouble that needs peace; it is what is in deficiency that needs prosperity. And that is why this book is written about AGLR, otherwise it could be a waste of time, energy, and resources addressing the serious needs of durable peace and prosperity where these rare and valuable facts already exist.

With strong and correct beliefs, from nothing may comes everything. "Don't complain about what you don't have. Use what you've got; to do less than your best is a sin. Every single one of us has the power for greatness, because greatness is determined by service – to yourself and to others." (Oprah Winfrey cited by Claudia Crawley, nd). That is true for people who believe it is.

Furthermore, back African women need to be careful about what people say they are; because it is not always true that they are what others say they are. And what is sad is that even in some of the countries where the black African women had been resettled they were and still considered as inferior today. Let's look at what happen in the United State of America for some African American women when interacting with some White American women. In the article of Marsha Houston, "When Black women talk with white women: Why dialogues are difficult", we learn that there is sometimes problem during White and Black women interaction in USA.

Marsha Houston illustrates how ethnicity can trump gender. After surveying 135 African American women and 100 White American women, she observed that communication between White and African American women was stressful, insensitive and in some cases even racist. Although it is usually more egalitarian and mutually supportive between women than between men, it remains unsatisfactory. Houston shows that in the US there are difficulties of interracial conversations between African American and White American women; but there is no genocidal propaganda or attempts to mass killing among them as it was the case in the AGLR.

In fact, according to Houston's survey, she had observed in the USA that, on one hand, when black women speak, they do it strongly and assertively by using a back experience in a white society. They also perceive white woman talks as arrogant, weak and submissive. On the other hand, white women perceive their own talk as varied, appropriate, and accent-free, and they hear black women using black dialect – saying things like "young'uns", "wif", and "wich you". This means that black women who speak both black dialect and general American speech are often perceived to speak only Black

English. Black and white speakers also notice different features of each other's language. A comment on this behavior of black and white women, when conversing in their American society, can push me to think about history.

It is known that the way most White American women arrived at the American continent is very different from the way most African American arrived. The first While Americans were businessmen, evangelists, missionaries, economic migrants from Europe, a continent which colonized Africa; and the second were mostly slaves sold in USA as manufactured goods. So, it seems to me that there is a certain complex of superiority in the brains of some White American women who consider the African American women like children of slaves from a 'Black

Dark Continent'. And if it really so, a positive mind make-up is strongly needed in that society by that group of white women. As it is urgently needed by some Tutsi women in Burundi, Rwanda, DRC, and Uganda. And so it is by some women in the Republic Democratic of the Congo, especially the highly educated women.

"However", writes Houston, "there are exceptions". The bleak picture painted by her survey ignores the successful and satisfying communication that can and often does occur between black and white women. This situation recalls the stereotyping and misunderstanding of European American students, in the article of Traoré (2003), who were considering African American students like 'Jungle bunny' coming from a 'Black Continent'. A Black woman graduate student cited by Houston

(Stewart, 2009, p.521) said that her conversations with white women of equal status involved much competition, aggression, and mutual lack of trust, intimacy, and equality.

Those exceptions are very important because they can serve as pioneers on behalf of black women to restore a positive consideration vis-à-vis to some white women who are still keeping some trances of racism in their minds. That is also true about the AGLR where there are some people who never think about themselves as support to other and who can be considered as 'role model' to teach lessons to others who think to be extremely high and important than others.

However, It can be assumed that there are no reasons to be considered good for people who experience difficulties in dialogues. Differences between people are not to be authors of separation. Instead, the differences between Black and White women in the USA are supposed to create a harmony between the two groups. In addition, what seems abnormal is that most of time the differences between people often creates a point of discord instead of creating a supplement for an effective harmony in the society. It is really a pity to see that things that could unite people are used to separate them. It is like human beings are refusing to learn from the natural reality of creatures.

Man is attracted to woman because they are naturally different; there is always attraction and easy cohabitation between positive and negative force. But negative does not mean weak or useless. People are different and they should be; that is why the world is very interesting and rich. They different in order to live together in harmony and peace; but they are equal. Difference does not mean inequality. Although there is attempts to genocide or ethnic civil wars in the USA as in the AGLR, it is uninteresting to notice that up to nowadays today the ideas of racism are still molding the behavior of some people in the US while I was thinking that it now belongs to the history. And what makes me to critically think of aspects of interpersonal communication are those difficulties in dialogues which could be overcome if the two groups could stop considering each other as talking in a negative way.

The challenge is that one group is accusing another group and vice-versa. Instead of accusing each other, they could accept each other. This is similar to many areas of AGLR where there is a total cease-fire. People are not killed by gun bullets or machetes any more in many areas of the AGLR; but there are too many acquisitions in the hearts and minds of some extremist people of different tribes, different regions, and different ethnic groups. And that is not only for women but for all the genders. That is why after discovering who people really are according to the Creator's design, there is a crucial need of positive change in order to welcome durable peace and prosperity for all.

In the process of discovering the 'true self' people should know that they may be unique but not superior or inferior to. When people think they are superior to others that means they haven't discovered their true 'selves'. There are no such words as 'inferior to' or 'superior to' in the true self; there are only two words which are 'equal to.' The 'self' should be discovered to be equal to the 'self.' There is no comparison between the 'self' and the 'other' because we are all different but equal in the Creator's eyes.

Furthermore, the true comparison or judgment about self is done with reference to self not to others. Some people think they are superior to others; some other think of themselves as inferior. In the AGLR, some of the reasons of that may be found in the policies of the colonialists; some in the precolonial period of the region; and some in the post-colonial period. We need to learn the true history of the African Great Lakes Region to help correct or discover our true 'selves.'

6.5. Do I know the history of African Migrations? Do I know the history of the people of AGLR? Do I know the impact of colonialism on Africa – on the AGLR?

The majority of the populations of the AGLR are Bantu. Most of them consider themselves as the sole owner of the lands of the region. While the history has a different view about that with clear explanation about Bantu migration, some Bantu people in the region consider themselves the owner of the countries of the AGLR by the fact that other people like the Nilotic met them there!

In Rwanda and Burundi, for example, during the civil wars and genocides, many Hutu people (belonging to

Bantu group) believed that the lands are theirs and the Tutsi (belonging to the Nilotic group) should leave those countries, to go back where they came from! This situation is so serious that it is still in the mind of millions of Hutu up to date. Some feel free to disclose and talk about that, and some do not. But what does the history of Bantu migrations in Africa has to tell about that situation.

In fact, the Bantu migration was strictly associated with agriculture and iron-working. The displacements of Bantu populations were motivated by the search of lands favorable for agriculture and for feeding their animals. After the overpopulation and the dying of Sahara region which turned into desert, their migration was facilitated by iron tools that they were making. So, the formation of early societies in sub-Saharan Africa where the AGLR is located was made by migrations.

Likewise, it is known that throughout their history on earth, human beings always look for places or areas that provide easy execution of their daily activities that make life possible. In the former time, people moved to find regions that were better for farming. Farming and fishing being the principal sources of food for Bantu, they needed more land-space to fight against food shortage resulting from overpopulation and drought that was attacking their region (Saharan desert today).

Korieh and Njoku (2012) write "Over and above the increase of population resulting from immigration from the Sahara, the development of agriculture seems to have brought about a substantial increase of population in at least one area, which led to Blacks beginning to settle in the southern half of Africa, where eventually they displaced or absorbed all other populations save only those in the extreme south-west" (p.53). They also write that from about 10,000 B.C. onward, the Saharan climate began to get appreciable drier, until ultimately the desert took over (p.51).

Nonetheless, it can be believable that the mass populations in the region attacked by drought couldn't stay there for a long time of history by the fact that the area had become unfit for an equable life. This reality is eloquent to show the impact of environmental factors on the migratory history of Africans. Herlin (2003) writes that "As is the case in other world regions, human history in Africa is closely linked to the favorable distribution of natural resources – particularly good soils and an adequate water supply.

Even today, this situation may still be convincing in some African countries due to the reality that people move from poor towns and regions towards rich ones to settle there for economical reasons. It is strongly believed that people need water to live; that is a true belief that seems to be irrefutable at any time. For example, some historians say that without the Nile River Egypt could be a desert. The Nile valley has played a crucial role in the process of immigration of peoples towards Egypt. That is why Herodotus described Egypt as "The Gift of the Nile". The agriculture which was one of the principal sources of foods of peoples was becoming impossible in the regions where drought predominated. This was also the case for the Bantu people who decided to immigrate in DRC, Rwanda, Burundi, Uganda, and in other countries of the Central and Southern Africa.

Equally, it is mentioned in the previous paragraphs, the lack of sufficient water was one of the main causes of the migrations of African peoples. Iron tools or kit tools facilitated their movements; without those tools, their migrations could be seriously challenged. The invention of iron tools allowed them to produce much food for reservation. Having enough food, people could surely have much time to move here and there. And by moving people there was the possibility of new experiences and discoveries that could lead to better lands.

Thus "the development of food production through agriculture had given time to spare for other pursuits, especially during the dry season between the harvest and the sowing." (Korieh and Njoku, 2012, p. 56). This sound logically acceptable because when a nation has a guarantee of food security, they tend to use their time in other domains; and that allows new discoveries important for their development. Those parents and guardians of the AGLR who are teaching their kids that they are the owner of the lands have to agree on the historical accounts of migrations in Africa that almost all the populations of the region were at a certain time economic migrants. They all came from somewhere.

What we need to do is to produce more food in order to be able to have enough for everybody so that we may have much time for new studies and discoveries that will help to make life more and more easier and better than today. If everybody should be sent back where they came from, as an ethnic group, those who came first should leave first. Thus, the pygmies should leave first, the Hutu people second, and the Tutsi third; that will allow animals and trees to enjoy their land in total calm in Rwanda and Burundi. This truth applies to other countries of the AGLR too.

We don't need to make our children inherit conflicts that are based on stereotypes and lies. Instead, we need to give them the spirit of entrepreneurship and scientific research in order that they may occupy their leisure time as our ancestors did for their youth when they wanted new lands. Korieh and Njoku put "Bands of restless young men might well use this new leisure to go on excursions into the unknown lands surrounding their villages and farms. Which supporting themselves by hunting and fishing, they would naturally keep their eyes on for empty lands and new resources which might offer further opportunities for themselves and their kinsfolk.' (Korieh and Njoku, 2012, p. 56).

We have to learn from history that we should not harm and destroy, but to heal and build together. We are to recognize that the issues that divide that are the ones that could unite us to work for common interests. African migrations have to be considered as movements of innovation by the fact that they have made the minds of some African peoples to be awakened. They are not to be considered as negative and destructive movements that always cause divisions, but we should see them as important by the fact that they may help us to be more aware of our selves. And the reality of human life on earth is that everybody is moving; no one is static.

Apart from African migrations, Europeans also migrated in Africa and their presence on the continent make a number of changes that we are going to talk about to see how they affected the 'self-awareness' for individual African. The arrival of Europeans in Africa made many transformations on the African Continent and in the Europe too.

When two different civilizations, cultures, or ethnic groups meet, there is always a win-win situation even if one may seem to be powerful than the other. The transformations or changes that occurred when Europe and Africa met could not be beneficial to both continent at the same level as Europeans considered themselves to be the 'civilizing agents' and Africans were thought to be in need of 'civilization'. There were surely the intended and unintended consequences of that encounter.

There were some positive and negative consequences of the European presence in Africa. That might have also been true when the Nilotic peoples met the Bantu peoples in the Sub-Saharan Region of Africa during the African historic migrations era. It might have been true when the Bantu people met the Pygmy peoples in the Sub-Saharan Region of Africa during their migrations. But what sounds unfair for some Bantu people is that they always complain publicly that Nilotic are the cause of their misery in the AGLR; while the Pygmy people never accuse the Bantu people who joined them and took possession of almost important parts of the land!

In fact, Africa suffered much from abusive European exploitation. One of the unintended outcomes of the arrival of Europeans in Africa is the slave labor. As it is known, the impact of Africa on the economy or the industrialization of Europe and America is very considerable. The growing demand for sugar in Europe influenced the demand for slaves from Africa who were transported to work in South America and in the West Indies.

Those slaves were mostly young persons. That means that Africa was losing its youth strength which could assist to ameliorate its economy. Korieh and Njoku write that those sold slaves were the young, most productive sector of the population, mostly aged between fourteen and thirty-five. And they were no longer treated as fellow human beings but rather as property, like domestic livestock, to be herded together, examined and bartered over (p. 172).

Also, the slaves were not the only African resources that were needed by Europeans. Minerals were also needed. Throughout its history, Africa has been exploited by Europeans colonialists to enhance their economies. We need to know this historical truth. Africans should not behave as such because Africa needs now to be set on the baths of durable peace and prosperity. Enough is enough; all people of AGLR should have good will to welcome peace for all. They should not accept to be used, as some of their ancestors were, in order to still what belongs to their neighbors. The people you exist to work for and help should not be the ones you still from!

Moreover, while slaves from Africa were used to develop European industries and economy, guns from Europe were used to deteriorate the African continent. In his Africa Video Series, episode 5 'The Bible and the Gun', Basil Davidson shows that the Europeans missionaries destroyed the African beliefs and in the conversion process guns were used. Korieh and Njoku write: "Wars in the West African interior may not have generally been waged deliberately just to produce captives for sale. But the presence of Europeans on the coast offering what appeared to be high prices for captives undoubtedly stimulated warfare. This was especially so in the eighteenth century when Europeans offered guns as their major trading item." (p. 172).

That really shows that guns from Europe assisted to organize wars. And wars were useful for slave trade because it produced a lot of slaves who were mostly captured prisoners of the wars. Mazrui also agrees with that by writing "The slave trade coincided with the gun trade. Africa slaves arriving in the Americas helped the West to be more productive; Western guns arriving in Africa helped Africans to be more destructive." (p. 160).

Those were some of the intended consequences of Europeans Explorers coming to Africa. Conversely, although the encounter of Europeans and Africans had some intended consequences, it also had some unintended ones. For example, the non-guns imported goods from West were surely needed in Africa. As a matter of facts, instead of looking at the movement of the sun to imagine the time, the African could learn to tell the time using watches imported from Europe.

Likewise, the colonial formal education which allowed Africans to be able to read and write was also positive and unintended outcome for Africa because it can be argued that the average African during the colonial period could not expect that. It can be believed that Africa could access to the modernization without suffering from the atrocities of slavery and racism. The AGLR can also have access to durable peace and prosperity for all without the use of weapons and violence to kill each other.

Africans could take advantage of European technology and education by using its minerals as payment without much suffering. And the big world companies that need the minerals of DRC may also have them without supplying guns to some rebel groups of the AGLR. The European imported goods were generally cheap and wanted but as mentioned in the previous paragraphs the guns were destructive. Korieh and Njoku inscribe,

> "Now the principal European imports into Africa were cheap manufactured goods – mainly cotton cloth and metal hardware, especially guns – in exchange for slaves. Indeed in the late eighteenth century the special manufacture of cheap, substandard guns for the African market became an important source of profit for the new British industrial city of Birmingham."

This is not far different from what is happening today in the AGLR. The mobile phones, computers, and other many manufactured goods are needed by the people of AGRL. And sometimes cheap in terms of price – money given to buy them in the shop – but they are very expensive in terms of values for they cost the lives of millions people of the region – the raw materials to make them are sometimes received by the manufacturers in exchange for guns to rebel groups and irresponsible political leaders.

Furthermore, it is known that the arrival of Europeans on African continent weakened the African craft industries. The more African peoples were interested to buy the European products the more they became disinterested in African craft industries. And it was declining progressively across the time. Because Africa did not develop their own industries that could compete the

European ones; there was and still is today an economic dependence of many African countries. Their economies depend mostly on the raw materials and minerals that they seem to export at cheap prices.

What seems to be unfair is that even for some raw materials and minerals the prices are mostly fixed by the buyers themselves. It is about 50 to 55 years of independence now, but the countries of the AGLR are still mainly depending on exportation of raw materials and on foreign aid to make their governments function! And in some countries like in DRC, in most of its provinces, the infrastructures left by the colonialists are still the ones which are used and never repaired or replaced.

May we say that the colonialists left a curse on the countries of the AGLR? Did they go with the brains of the political leaders of the AGLR? The region needs to deal seriously with the issue of political leadership in order to reach the true national economic resurrection. People should be very careful when voting the political leaders for their countries. We should make sure we are leaving good countries to our children. They should not suffer the consequences of our actions. They should not continue the colonization that was passed to us from our ancestors. We have all the ability to achieve that.

There is no need to look back in order to remain in the history; we have to restart with a powerful and constructive renewal of the national institutions of the countries of the AGLR. Read more about the history and the geography of the region if you've never do that and you will agree with me that the region has every necessary natural potential to overcome the problems it's facing today.

We need to discover our true 'selves' to accomplish what is good for us and the generations to come for that is the fundamental principle for durable peace and prosperity that we are talking about in this book. And discovering our true 'selves' will avoid us being the wrong persons at the right places because everybody will discover his or her gifts and use them to help the community to prosper in peace.

6.6. Do I know that the European Colonialists were over-estimated by some Colonized Africans who underestimated themselves and that delayed their fight for independence?
Do I know that many people in AGLR are still having the false view that some races or ethnic groups are superior to others?
Do I know the impact of Cold War on Africa – in the AGLR?

"People go to Africa and confirm what they already have in their heads and so they fail to see what is there in front of them." (Chinua Achebe)

Before the Second World War, Africans were trying to fight against European domination but failed. Taking into consideration the aim of European colonialism, it is clear that Europeans did not come to Africa with a good purpose of civilizing people. They tortured and massacred people up to the extent of selling them in slavery as if they were goods. Africans were not happy with European behavior. They wanted to be independent but missed the occasion of a general mobilization against Europeans.

The Second World War was to them a good opportunity to discover the weaknesses of white colonialists whom they thought were gods. So, the Second World War was a good opportunity for colonized Africans to discover 'who white colonialists were', and that gave them the courage in their process of asking independence. The same may also be possible for peoples of AGLR; the genocides and civil wars that happened in the region can be an occasion for the compatriots of the counties of the region to unveil the weaknesses and the worse tricks of some of their leaders and their international sponsors. And that may help them in their process of welcoming durable peace and prosperity which are necessary for economic independence in the region.

Taking into consideration all the sufferings that Africans endured due to inhuman attitudes and acts of colonialists such as disrespect, racism, torture, rape, and the slave trade, no one can agree with the fact that a 'civilizer' must behave like an exploiter, a sadist, and a killer in order to 'civilize' people. You cannot say you have come to civilize the people when you are forcing them to work without giving them enough and adequate food when they are hungry, and no rest when they get tired; without reaching the amount of work assigned to them, you kill them, or you punish them severely by cutting their hands or legs!

Korieh and Njoku (2012) write, "Men, women, and children in the Belgian Congo were forced to collect rubber from the wild rubber trees of the forest. And even though they were not paid for this, those who failed to comply had their hands cut off to teach them and others 'a sharp lesson'! Many were also massacred, as contemporary and historical accounts reveal" (p. 273). That was very sad, and it sounds shocking when we read about it in the books of history of Africa.

The Africans are not anymore colonized by the Europeans as it was the case before their official independence. But some of them have been perpetrating atrocious acts that more dangerous than the ones done by colonialists during colonial period. The forced labor continues to be practiced; the torture, the rape, the killing of innocents, and organized robbery continue as if the people of the African Great Lakes Region were created to suffer!

We may not even say that it is now the era of African colonialism in Africa because Europe colonialism in Africa had some positive impacts on the continent while the barbarisms of African rebels and fake leaders have no positive outcome for the populations. Some may say that the destructive behaviors of some leaders in Africa come from the lessons that the colonialists taught them, and from the hidden agendas of some western countries. While that may be considered as a reality, it is also clear that a mature, loving, and reasonable person cannot accept to be forced to murder his or her own people.

There is always a sole responsibility of the African compatriots who kill their brothers and sisters for power and money. They seem to believe that what they get from their atrocious activities is more valuable than the lives of millions of people that suffer the consequences. Their mindsets are not so different from that of Leopold II who preferred money and power than respecting and preserving the lives of millions of people in the DRC. That need to finish in the AGLR; even those who are still killing others silently and secretly must stop. They must cease that habit because human life is precious.

And it makes nonsense to kill people that are needed in the process of building durable peace and prosperity in the AGLR; even if they have killed your brothers and sister, killing them changes nothing to for sorrow instead it increases the number of unhealthy loads in your consciousness.

The history gives accounts that all over Africa most of African kings were hostile to the European domination that is why they refused to sign the treaties that were suggested to them. "Most treaties posed serious challenged to African independence, that is why most African rulers did not want to sign them. The treaties were initiated by Europeans after the Berlin conference to have control on the African lands." (Koriehand Njoku, 2012,p. 269). There were several African movements of resistance using 'Dawa' such as Maji Maji in Tanzania but they failed. The history of Africa never stops repeating, but the sad reality is that only the bad version of its which is always performed by the some of the children of Africa.

It sometimes hard to believe that some Africans of the DRC in a rebel movement in Itury (a new province of the DRC since 2015) committed very atrocious acts and killings; and after that, they ate the bodies of dad persons as 'good meat.' Can you image in the capital of the same country, Kinshasa, a mass of civilians in revolt against the soldiers of Rwanda, who helped Laurent Kabila to take power, burnt alive some Congolese people of the eastern parts of the country after accusing them of being from Rwanda! That was one of the consequences of hate propaganda initiated by some political leaders of Laurent Kabila's regime.

Unwise and violent acts have been committed in many parts of the AGLR; and the victims were most of time considered innocent. That is not how people should expect to build their nations; nations cannot be built on hatred, suspicion, fear, tribalism, regional discrimination, ethnical discrimination, and xenophobia that can reduce the number of foreign investors and even on tourists in the country who are one of the sources of foreign exchanges. Every country in the world needs foreigners because of their positive impact on national economy; and so does the AGLR.

However, the Second World War was considered as a catalyst of great transformation in the relationship between the colonialists and the colonized people of African. It made Europeans countries weak due to the spending of resources resulting from war and a new international consideration of colonialism and slave trade. With the formation of United Nation and its anti-colonialist orientation, the emergence of the US and the Soviet Union (S.U) as superpowers, and the Atlantic Charter declaration for the right of all people, the few African nationalists who were educated could have access to information from international forum criticizing colonial rule.

The colonies which were thought by Africans to have international support were losing it. That was a good occasion to educated Africans to reconstruct their identities more positively. Mazrui (1986), talking about the charter, inscribes "The Atlantic Charter between Roosevelt and Churchill was a declaration of new values. And yet, in spite of all this, imperial Britain and imperial Europe still resisted these forces of decolonization even in the midst of defending Europe's own liberties." (p. 279). That is to say that although international anti-colonialist convection was signed by the two world superpower countries after the Second World War, still Africans had to fight for their independence. Colonialists were not willing to give up although the international pressure on them.

It is also regrettable today that although the ceasefire and peace agreements some rebel leaders and political leaders of the AGRL are not willing to stop violation human rights; they are not willing to stop stilling things form their neighbors, killing, torturing, and raping people. The general populations who are always victims of such inhuman activities comparable to the ones to colonialists should wake up and claim their 'liberty' as their parents and ancestors did during colonial period.

So, laws and principles shall be used to bring the AGLR to durable peace and prosperity because machetes, knives, guns, and bombs have failed to do that. Because laws and principles are so powerful than machetes, knives, guns, and bombs,... we need to focus on them to be successful. As explained in previous paragraphs, the fact that Africans remained for a long time under colonial rule does not mean that they loved it, but they lacked occasion and force to match out the colonialists. This is also true for the majority of the population of the AGRL today; all the leaders who are involved in the inhuman business in the region should know it. The fact that most of populations of the AGRL remain under 'African colonialism in Africa' for a long time does not mean that they love it or they are happy to be living in such condition. The time is coming soon when people will stand up to build durable peace and prosperity by themselves, with themselves, and for themselves.

The impact of the Second World War on African compatriots who fought for political independence was passed to their children and grandchildren. It will soon be manifested in a different form in the AGLR. The era of a foolish and ingrate child killing her mother is soon over.

The time for some crazy African leaders destroying Africa is coming soon to an end. How can a person be sawing a chair on which he or she is sitting? How can a young man cut the breast that had fed him? Does such a guy 'know himself' well?

The image of a person cutting the breasts of his or her mother depicts the exact attitude and acts of some African leaders in Africa today. They may ignore that what they have been doing is similar to what is shown in the image but that is their way of acting. And some people in the AGRL are stilling trusting them; maybe because they are not informed about what their leaders do in secret, or about their true thoughts and beliefs concerning their interests, their communities, and the lives of the citizens.

Today in the AGRL people are in need of the knowledge that the first African freedom fighters got during the World War II. Their experience at home and at the battle during the Second World War played an important role to demystify the myth of colonial invulnerability. And that helped them to develop positively towards their goal. Korieh and Njoku (2012) put "World war II (1939 – 1945) also had a decisive impact on the course of political developments in Africa" (p. 392). At war, they noticed the weakness of Europeans and at home they have been promised to have a total reform socially, politically, and economically.

Many Africans were involved in that war. It was a general mobilization. Ferraton, M. (Dec 16, 2009) talking about African experience during the World War II, wrote this:

> "Africans who remained at home received promises of social, political, and economic reform such as those proposed at the Brazzaville Conference in 1944. Africans who served overseas received exposure to other cultures outside their own and witnessed firsthand European weaknesses. Their experiences resulted in the breakdown of the myth of colonial invincibility and created an environment of rising expectations of many Africans."

There are millions of people of the AGLR who believe that durable peace and prosperity of the region will never be achieved. They should know that there were also millions of Africans who did not believe that the colonialists will one day be removed from the African continent. There also people in the countries of the AGRL who think and believe that human rights will never be respected by the leaders of their countries; they do not believe that they can be able to suppress all the barriers for durable peace and prosperity for all. It can be assumed that, during the colonial era, there were millions of Africans who did not have hope that their counties could be ruled by their own brothers and sisters (the black Africans). Unfortunately, many of those black Africans leaders have deceived their own people due to their very bad leadership.

Moreover, when the colonialists were recruiting more Africans to serve their purpose during the Second World War, they did not know that the result of that will not be so beneficial to them at all. They seemed to ignore that the more people recruited the higher the number of revolted Africans will be, to make possible the fight for self-governance. The point is that when governments with no justice involve many people to serve their purposes, they are always ignorant of the fact that the same people there are illegally and unjustly exploiting may raise among them some leaders who will have access to some information that will arouse their anger to seek justice for all.

Korieh and Njoku (2012, p. 397) talk about the recruitment during the World War II by putting,

> "During World War II, European colonial powers intensified their exploitation of African human, agricultural, and mineral resources for the furtherance of the war. Large numbers of Africans were recruited into colonial armies and served in various parts of the world including Africa, Europe, and Asia. For instance, the British recruited 280,000 people from East Africa and 167,000 from West Africa. The French conscripted over 100,000 from West Africa alone. Thus, between these two colonial powers, nearly 500,000 Africans were recruited".

So, Africans were involved in the World War II without the freedom to refuse. Their contribution was considerable, but it paid back because the more African were involved, the more they had occasion to see how other people of the World enjoy their freedom like Japanese people at that time. From this historical reality of Africa and by the reality that history sometimes repeats itself, all the people of the AGLR who are involved in atrocious plans and acts have to feel sorry of what they have been doing so far. They need to fear and to stop so that the future of the region may be bear good fruits for all. We are not yet in the period of European colonialism in Africa and the World War II, but we have been experiencing the similar situations as a result of endless barbarisms and atrocities committed by Africans to their fellows in the AGLR.

Moreover, after the Second World War, the anger against colonial oppression increased in Africa. The movements seeking independence were created and intensified their fights. Most Africans fighters for independence were not prepared by their European colonialists. We need to have good knowledge of that true because most of the problems that we have in Africa started during the colonial periods; although some seem to be new, their roots or seeds belong to the historical eras. For example, the Belgian colonialists were not ready to give independence to Congolese in 1960 or to Rwanda and Burundi, although were forced to do so.

As a result, there was a significant involvement of Western countries in the post-independent African nations in the formation of their governments; the colonialists unwilling to leave the power to Africans for fear of losing their interests in Africa, did their best to influence the post-independent African leadership by corrupting and sponsoring the leaders who can serve their colonial interests and by eliminating those who seemed to be patriots.

The example of Patrice Lumumba of Congo (DRC) is eloquent to illustrate the colonial post-independent political strategy of corruption and elimination. I sometimes call it corruption-elimination strategy – 'CORELI Strategy'. That is what most leaders of AGLR are still using today – they have remained just like their colonial fathers – their role model – who taught them fake leadership. We really need a positive change because it is the same colonial mentality that brought Cold War to

Africa; a conflict opposed Eastern and Western blocs. The Cold War is over now, but it has been transformed into War Economy in the AGLR; innocent people's blood continue to be shed for egoistic interests.

In fact, after the Second World War, the international influence resulting from the formation of United Nations and the rise of the two superpowers, such as the USA and the Soviet Union, served as important catalysts for the Africans elites to fight for the independence. As European colonialists were not ready and willing to give African countries independence, they wanted to continue their colonial activities of exploitation in Africa although the pressures of the fighters for independence. Europe which had enhanced their industrialization and became more and more richer because of African slaves trade and imported minerals could have a new need to make Africa their market where to sell the manufactured goods from their industries.

As the Eastern bloc represented by the Soviet Union which was communist and the Western bloc represented by the USA was capitalist, after their independence some African countries chose to remain neuter to avoid any adherence to the Cold War. Each bloc wanted to increase the numbers of its members as much as it could and to make sure their interests in Africa are protected. That may be one of the reasons why Africa appeared as a fertile ground for the Cold War where it was possible to find some unaligned countries.

Likewise, western countries wanted to have authority over African leaders of the post-independence era as it is still the case today for some. They wanted to limit their autonomy, self-rule in order to serve colonialists' interests. And they knew very well that African leaders were not prepared enough to manage their respective new governments, so they helped African leaders to make Africa what it is today. Africa today still lives the negative consequences colonialism because during the colonization almost nothing was done to prepare African for effective self-rule.

For example in DRC, compared to other colonial powers, Belgium went to extremes in barring Africans from most educational opportunities and from all but the most menial positions in the colonial government (Korieh and

Njoku (2012). That was one of the serious mistakes made by European colonialists which could certainly push some post-colonial leaders like Lumumba to ask for assistance from communists to manage his government. And the history also tells that the lack of tertiary education was general to all colonies. "University education was totally ignored in all the colonies until the 1940s, and only one university was subsequently established for each colony". (Korieh and Njoku, 2012, p. 453).

Today, we may agree that there are many colleges and universities in the world that are teaching many Africans the knowledge of good leadership, but what kind of moral and virtues most of them have to accomplish successfully their roles. For example, most of the people with political leadership positions in the AGLR are formally educated; we may assume that most of them have attended universities and colleges. But what have they done so far with their education to make sure durable peace and prosperity have found a home in the AGLR?

Some of the fighters of independence who became the first political leaders after independence in the AGLR are reputed to have had good moral virtues and strong patriotism like Lumumba that many politicians of the region lack today. But they failed to build counties of durable peace and prosperity. While it is true that we need good leadership principles and good moral virtues and patriotism, it can be agreed that we need something else for the region to prosper in peace. What do we need?

This book gives answer to this question. We need to address it seriously to stop atrocious historical accounts of the AGLR from repeating.

In fact, the historian Basil Davidson, in his Africa Video Series, episode 8 'Legacy', shows that the European model of governance functioned well in Europe, but failed in Africa because it was conducive to separation in classes, associated to colonialism and corruption. Some Africa nationalist leaders at that time knowing that they should defend national interests as they were elected by the population, although impeded by the colonial power and the UN mission to perform well their duties, turned to Eastern Bloc for assistance to eradicate the civil unrest created by Western bloc implication in African governments.

An example of that reality can be found in the Congolese crisis of 1961 that caused the death of both Lumumba, the Congolese compatriot leader fighter of independence, and DAG, the UN Secretary-General. Cordier who was the UN Representative in the Congo crisis did not show really impartiality between the conflict of the President Kasavubu and the Prime Minister Lumumba. It can be believable that he served as a catalyst to put the two persons into conflict instead of assisting them to finish the Katanga cessation initiated by Chombe.

Korieh and Njoku (2012) write,

> "Cordier's barely three weeks stay in the Congolese capital of Léopoldville (now Kinshasa) coincided with a constitutional crisis: the reciprocal efforts of the Congo's President Joseph Kasavubu and its Prime Minister Patrice Lumumba to dismiss each other from office.

> Cordier's decisions effectively threw UN support behind Kasavubu and reinforced U.S. and Belgian efforts to oust Lumumba – seriously compromising the United Nations' impartiality." (p. 460).

Lumumba, who was dominated by nationalist ideology and elected by people to serve national interests, chose the Eastern communist bloc which was in conflict with Western capitalist bloc for partnership and assistance. Can it be argued that this kind of colonial scheme continues up to nowadays? Is the UN mission 'MONUC' in DRC making its work of pacifying the country or they are just plotting with some rebel leaders to make sure the conflicts continue? Are they saying 'No war, no job'?

Looking deeply and logically at the nature of the conflicts in the AGLR, one can believe that some African rebel leaders in the region are just like 'dogs on the trees'; naturally, a dog does not climb up a tree, if you find it on the tree you just assume that there is someone who put it there. And it remains on the tree not willing to jump down you can presume that being on the tree was one of its desires. It was just helped to fulfill one of its needs! This is the time for the populations of the AGLR to open eyes and see, to open ears and hears, to open minds and discerns to understand well what has been happening in the region since the colonial era.

We need to have a deep and correct understanding of 'ourselves' of – our history – our strengths – our weaknesses – our natural abilities and gifts – our natural riches – because the true information concerning those areas has been kept in hiding to our awareness since long ago. That is why most of us were ready to join any ideology or any militias or movements in order to uselessly destroy others' lives! Most of the people in the AGLR have been ignorantly used by some corrupt leaders to serve their egoistic interests. The time for that has to be over so that people may welcome durable peace and prosperity for all.

6.7. What is obedience to me? Up to what extent do I obey authorities or leaders?

There have been some categories of people who have lost their own lives and the lives of other people because of blind obedience to authorities in the AGLR. There have also been some other categories of people who had suffered the disastrous consequences of disobedience to authorities or leaders. Durable peace and prosperity for all in the AGLR will never be achieved if the followers of the 'extremist and fake leaders' of the region don't learn disobedience to violent and atrocious commands that they always receive.

It is also primordial for the followers of 'moderate and good leaders' to learn obedience to the peaceful and constructive commands that they are always given. But in both extreme, people need to be careful to what they are asked to do; people need to use their true and non-corrupt reason and sense of right and wrong because a good leader can sometimes produce bad ideas – when under anger for example – and a fake leader can sometimes give good principles or commands – when overjoyed for example.

That is why people should avoid being involved in a destructive ideology because of the readiness to obey the leaders or because of the group pressure. The three ethical problems of Milgram's work have made a powerful contrition to social psychology as a science. Milgram's work on the theory of obedience that has been evidenced in the society shows us how some people perform acts that are out of their consciences because of orders and commands given by leaders or people in authority.

Likewise, Stanley Milgram, after his obedience experiment, concluded that: "A substantial proportion of people do what they are told to do, irrespective of the content of the act, and without pangs of conscience, so long as they perceive that the command comes from a legitimate authority." (Milgram quoted by Blass T.,

2004, p. 100). It was believed that his experiment on obedience helped justify social psychology, a science some dismiss as unimportant, contributed to the understanding of humanity. Blass wrote that Milgram investigated a number of other areas including the "small-world phenomenon." This is the idea that two people, who do not know each other, can be connected by a small number of acquaintances. He made an experiment of the possibility of sending a letter to an unknown person through the known one. He also conducted a number of experiments on the urban life. These included differences between city and rural life, concluding that peoples living in the rural areas were more helpful than the one living in urban one.

The discovery of Milgram applies to what had happened in the AGLR during the genocides and civil wars. People who were followers of the leaders of the genocides and rebel movements were doing some violent acts out of their consciences. They could perform acts that were not in harmony with their true thought and beliefs. Were they used as machines? The time of 'blind manipulation' and 'blind obedience' should be over; people have been suffering for a very long time, and they now need durable peace and prosperity.

Moreover, the three ethical problems that allowed Milgram to reach his discovery consisted of the extreme emotional stress, lies to participants, and inflicted insight. The participants to his experiment suffered the consequences of these ethical problems. The participants considered as teachers to give electrical shocks to learners suffered from emotional stress. They could think of how harmful the shocks were to learners but could not stop administrating them. As the experimenter, Milgram did not tell his participants the truth about the experiment. The true reason of shocking learners electrically was not known and some participants were doing it out of their consciousness. Six years later (at the height of the Vietnam War), one of the participants in the experiment sent correspondence to Milgram, expressing his gladness to have participated. He puts,

> "While I was a subject in 1964, though I believed that I was hurting someone, I was totally unaware of why I was doing so. Few people ever realize when they are acting according to their own beliefs and when they are meekly submitting to authority... To permit myself to be drafted with the understanding that I am submitting to authority's demand to do

something very wrong would make me frightened of myself..." (Wikipedia - Milgram experiment. Retrieved 13th June 2012 http://en.wikipedia.org/ wiki/Milgram_ experiment#Ethics).

Surely, in many rebel movements, some people were taken by force or by lie to serve the rebel leaders' nonconstructive hidden aims. Some of those people are today suffering the consequences of doing atrocious acts based on lies and force. They have lost their inner peace and constitute a potential danger for future violence because of the psychological torments that they are still passing through. They need a cure in order to help build durable peace and prosperity for all.

Likewise, it is really ethically bad to make people execute thinks out of their conscious awareness. About 'inflicted insight', it can be accepted that it was a negative consequence for subjects that participated in the Milgram's experiment. It occurred when the subjects were given insight into their flaws through their participation in the experiment. It occurred unexpectedly and caused emotional pain. This happened because of the deception and frustration caused by the instruction to be obeyed by the participants in the experiment.

Davis and Palladino (2010) talking about the ethical aspect of the experiment write that: "After the initial 'shocks' were administered by the teacher, the learner protested and also indicated that he had a heart condition. In many instances the teachers became tense and faced a real conflict. They wanted to stop, but felt they could not. The stress they faced raised ethical issues about the conduct of this experiment." (p. 625). Most of the people of the AGLR have a natural sense of living together with others in harmony. Many of them are in need of peace that can last for generations to generations; even some of the people who have been using violence to get a lasting peace were not fully aware of the dangerous consequences of their acts because most were doing aggressive acts out of their true awareness.

That is why we put emphasis on 'discovering the true self' and using it in the process of establishing durable peace and prosperity. It is not easy to meet a person in the AGLR who is planning to live in poverty and insecurity; almost no one there can say that they need to be used as 'machines to perform destructive duties. That is why their leaders especially politicians often lie to them in order to use them. That is why rebel leaders, some traditional leaders or kings often use lies or force people to integrate their movements. Or they can untrue stories to create hate in the minds and hearts of the people of their tribes and ethnic groups to have them espouse their annihilative ideologies.

Milgram obedience experiment was important because it helps explain the behavior of peoples when they have to deal with the instructions or orders from authority figures. It shows the impact or influence of authority figures on the daily actions committed by people. What seems amazing is the degree to which humans execute the authority orders without critical thinking and without having a reason for their actions.

For example, peoples may start a massive killing of members of a given ethnic group or race only because an authority figure has given instructions no matter how silly they are. (for example Hitler to kill Jews, Extremist Tutsi leaders to kill Hutu during the 1972 genocide in Burundi, Extremist Hutu leaders to kill Tutsi during the 1994 genocide in Rwanda, Mobutu to kill the target opponents, Mzee Kabila to get out the country the Rwandan troops – which resulted in the death of some innocent Congolese from East of DRC, Idi Ami to get the Asians out of Uganda, etc.).

This situation always happens in many societies where political or military leaders instruct their followers to perform acts massively without having wise reasons for the instructions. An eloquent example may be seen in the genocide of Rwanda of 1994 where people of different tribes killed each other without no good reasons at all.

6.8. What do I know about racial discrimination during the colonial period of Africa?
Is it still shaping the way I consider the other races up to nowadays?
Are really black people inferior to other races?
Do I know the impact of African Stereotypes on Africans?
Do I know what is believed by some non-Africans about Africa today?

The attitude of consideration oneself or other people as special race, tribe, ethnic group, etc. is insanity. There are no special peoples on the planet earth. They are all mortal; they also come in this world using the same common way. People have different races, ethnic groups, and tribes but they are equal. The video of Davidson entitled 'Different but Equal' is thought-provoking. The history of colonization inscribes that European explorers believed that the colonialists and the colonized people were different because they were naturally unequal. They seemed to ignore the truth that being different from somebody doesn't mean being unequal to them. They stereotyped Africa and thought that this continent was inhabited by childish people having no intelligence to make a meaningful civilization.

Davidson has done a great job in his videos showing that Africans were intelligent enough and it wasn't correct to say that they had childish intelligence. One of the strong evidence their maturity was that they had built a civilization comparable to that of Medieval Europe. The peace and prosperity killing fact about some Africans is the attitude of underestimation that has penetrated the minds of millions in Africa and that has unfortunately been passed to generation after another. The ugly lies of some western historians and explorers have created a deep complex of inferiority in the minds of millions of Africans that is unhealthy for durable peace and prosperity that the AGLR need today.

Basil Davidson gives, in his videos, a clear and intelligible picture of what the stereotyped Africa is in reality. 'Different but Equal' is the title of the movie. After going through the various historical documents produced by western explorers and philosophers, the author observed that there are a lot of fallacies in them. Those people did not really understand Africa. It is manifestly believable that stereotypes and degrading declarations created by these Western explorers and philosophers damaged Africa's reputation. Friedrich

Hegel, a European philosopher, once said this about Africa, "This is the land where men are children. A land lying beyond the daylight of self-conscious history and enveloped in black color of the night. At this point, let us forget Africa for Africa is no historical part of the world".

Similarly, Samuel Baker, an early explorer in Africa wrote in his memoir, "Human nature viewed in its crudest state as seen among African savages is quite on the level of that of the brute and not to be compared with the noble character of the dog. There is neither a great pity, love nor self-denial. No idea of duty, no religion, nothing but covetousness, ingratitude, selfishness and cruelty". This is how some non-Africans have been portrayed Africans since the time of explorations. And some are still keeping the same images in their minds about Africa.

The self-awareness of millions of Africans seem to have been deteriorated by the beliefs in what the non-Africans said about Africa because of the positives and power that were behind their exploration and colonial activities. What is unfortunate is that a huge number of Africans are still negatively affected by the lies and negative stereotypes of some westerners. For example, it is not motivating and constructive to hear an African say 'I cannot live like a 'Muzungu' (a white person)', 'only white persons are able to do that!'; or to find a person who refuses to wash his hands before eating and who says 'that is for Bazungu (white persons), we black

Africans don't die by illnesses resulting from not washing hands!'

That kind of mindsets will never help people to fully use their natural abilities to positively transform their nations. That is what continues to kill many people's self-confidence and creativity that is necessary to transform the AGLR into a region of durable peace and prosperity for all. Black Africans can also create things of great contribution to the world. They are human beings of the same capacity as the people who innovate. But most of the time, most of them underestimate themselves and sometimes suffer the complex of inferiority that end up by killing their self-esteem and self-confidence preventing them to reach the discovery of their true selves. And they finally die in serious poverty because of not knowing who they really are and not using their true natural potential. Or they end up by killing each other because they have a serious ignorance of selves and only rely on what the world said and continue to say they are.

The time for that should be over in order to build durable peace and prosperity for all. We need to understand that any human being can make fantastic things that contribute to the durable peace and prosperity for all. We should not accept the viewpoints of some westerners who, trying to underestimate African peoples, deny that the Egyptian civilization was not held by people of African origin supposing that they are not clever enough to make some wonderful things such as pyramids.

Contrariwise, reacting to the views of Europeans about Africans during the colonial era, Davidson gives in his video some African historical facts which challenge their misconceptions of the African continent. He shows that wonderful kingdoms and empires existed and prospered in Africa as they did in Medieval Europe but historians have never recognized Africa's earliest civilization until recently.

The people of the medieval time were considered as different but equal but blacks almost everywhere are treated with inconsideration and ridicule nowadays. The history enlightens that when Europeans explorers came to Africa to look for gold they met a city in the heart of Africa built of stone hundreds of years ago. This means that Africans were also building houses as Europeans of medieval time.

It can be true as argued by Davidson that 'Racism' is a recent concept created and developed by white explorers aiming to degenerate Africans during the North Atlantic Slave Trade where black people were presented as less humanly important, objects for buying and selling like animals and to which any inhuman treatment was justified.

It can also be accepted that 'ethnic division', 'tribalism', and 'regionalism' are very destructive concepts in the AGLR that have been created by colonialists and adopted and propagated by some post-colonial leaders to serve their egoistic interests in detriment of the general populations. We have to understand that those kinds of leaders do nothing for the general interest of their nations; they do just work to serve themselves, but not the people as most of them claim. It is a pity to discover that the people who claim to have come to power to promote 'development' are the true hidden barriers durable peace and prosperity for all. Instead of developing their countries positively they are doing it very negatively – and they call it 'development'.

Besides, more evidence was given to prove that Africa has its own civilization and history with an identity different from that of explorers' continent. According to Davidson, modern science and history have proved the insights and early views about Europeans mistakes about Africa. Archaeology has proved that the first remains of species of Homo sapiens have been discovered in East

Africa. This reality may push to believe that culture and civilization as they are known nowadays originated in the African continent. Ancient African history also contains wonderful and interesting civilizations with facts and arts that have ever existed anywhere in Eurasia.

Also, in the Matopo hills of Zimbabwe, ancient carvings and art inscribed in stones portray messages of an advanced civilization. All these shown pieces of evidence indicate that Africa was not a childish continent. They are very eloquent to refute the explorers' views about African people. Africa was not an area inhabited by people of lower or equal consideration as dogs! Its people were able to make tools, pyramids, houses, etc.

Koreih and Njoku (2012) write that 'It is usually held that a useful distinction between man and all other animals is man's capacity to make tools, though recently this has become somewhat blurred by the discovery that some apes make what are in effect simple tools.' So, people of the AGLR should not think they are inferior or cannot do greater things that will benefit their region and the whole world; we are different but equal as that is shown by the historian Basil Davidson in his work about Africa. We need to renew our minds by taking courage – it is never later.

By taking courage, we should not ignore we are not exactly and totally what the world has been saying they are. Africans are not what the colonialists told them they were. That is very important to know for the discovery of the true 'self'. As mentioned in the paragraphs above, the true history of Africa may help us understand how Africans were negatively stereotyped; and that situation continues to take place up to nowadays. The lies that were created and propagated during the exploration and colonial eras have been accepted by Africans as truth and continue to prevail in some non-Africans minds today.

And what is unedifying is that some black Africans had accepted the ugly lies that they were an inferior race and taught it to their children making it a reality that is transmitted from a generation to another. Some European philosopher inscribed the following about Africa 'a land where people are children unable to do by themselves, a land of primitive, weak, and ignorant peoples, a place where people live in harmony with the nature and wild animals, a land where dangerous diseases exist, a continent of dangerous peoples, a black continent of death, decay, and poverty' (David Basilson Video).

That is what the some European colonialists taught their children about Africa and African people. That is what the some of the citizens of Western countries still strongly believe about Africa. That is what most Africans believe about themselves! There is no need of failing to recognize that fact that what was said about Africa in the past is still considered as true in by many westerns today, although sometimes that is unexpressed with words by many.

For example, Keim C. (2009), in his book "Mistaking Africa: Curiosities and inventions of the American mind", shows that in USA people are misinformed about Africa and its peoples. He states that the media such as Television and Newspapers negatively portray Africa. And the students he was teaching in the USA helped him create a list of words that come to their minds when talking about Africa. According to his experience, when you talk about traditional Africa, the following words come to minds of American students (p.4): native, hut, warrior, shield, tribe, savage, cannibals, jungle, pygmy, pagan, voodoo, and witch-doctor. And about Africa today, students mentioned some 'new words' such as coup, poverty, ignorance, drought, famine, tragedy, and tribalism.

When talking about 'change words' about Africa (words that show the impact of the western intervention for change in Africa), students mentioned: development, foreign aid, peacekeeping, and missionary. Do you see Africa with the eyes of those surveyed American students? Are all mentioned words stereotyped or some appear to be conveying the truth about Africa? Could Africa be thought of using such words before the colonial era? Were most of those words created during the colonial era? What have the post-colonial African leaders done so far to restore the image of Africa, and the dignity of its peoples? It can be said that most Africa leaders enforce the misconceptions about Africa instead of making strides towards clearing them in the minds of some non-Africans.

In addition, Keim (2009, p.5) writes that a survey by a major American museum on popular perceptions of

Africa had resulted in many misconceptions about African among them the following were mentioned:

- ✓ Africa is just one large country;
- ✓ Africa is all jungle;
- ✓ Africans share a single culture, language, and religion;
- ✓ Africans live in "grass huts";
- ✓ Africans mainly hunt animals for their subsistence;
- ✓ Africa has no significant history.

So, what is the truth in what many Africans think about Africa? What is the truth in what some westerners think about Africa? It is obvious that there is poverty, ignorance, and famine in Africa but it doesn't mean that all the Africans are poor, ignorant, and hungry. And it does not mean that there are no poor and ignorant people in Africa and in Western countries.

Likewise, the lies that have been conveyed about Africans aim nothing but keeping them enchained in the rooms of poverty, ignorance, and insecurity. Any African who believe in what the western western stereotypes about Africa will never develop his or her full natural potential, because of not being able to discover his or her true identity. His or her 'self-awareness' will remain erroneous. And the risk of dying unproductive will be too high for many if they don't pay much attention to that with a quick and effective reaction.

I know there may be many people in the AGLR, after reading this, who will say: 'I know very well who I am. I know very well what I know. I know I am not ignorant of myself. I know why I am a citizen of a country of the Great Lakes Region of Africa. I know the lies that had been publicized by the colonialists about Africa. I know these lies are considered as truth by some non-Africans and some Africans.'

'I know those lies played an important role in the determination of the status of the peoples of colonized countries. I know those lies were accepted as true by some colonized populations. I know those lies had molded negatively the colonized... I know those lies constitute a barrier to the development of some peoples, some regions, and some countries. I know those lies are still paying an important role in the international cooperation today', etc.

It is not bad to have too many 'I know's! But, it's time to know the very truth that will help the nations get on real paths of durable peace and prosperity for all; and that will never be possible if we don't act positively together. Everybody should know and act; not only just knowing. We should be able to know what to do and do it if we really need positive change in our communities! It is good to note that we are taking into consideration what is generally said about the whole African continent although we focus on the Great Lakes Region of Africa. The fact is that what is said about the whole Africa as a continent also applies to the African Great Lake Region.

Likewise, the history puts it clear that it was what the western colonialists and explorers said about Africa that is still being told to young people today. It is what they said about Africa that made most of Africans more and more ignorant of their true 'selves.' In fact, this seems to be one of the facts that paralyze the minds of some Africans and make them unable to compete successfully with other nations when they consider stereotypes to be true information about themselves and their land. It can also be one of the reasons some westerners support in a way or another the wars and rebellions in Africa.

Keim writes that: "Or, if we think of Africa only as a place of trouble, a large zoo, or a storehouse of strategic minerals rather than as a place where real people live real lives, we will likely be willing to exploit the continent for our own purposes."(Mistaking Africa.*Curiosities and Inventions of the American Mind.* 2nd ed., p.4). People of the Great Lakes Region of Africa should pay attention to any information that is transmitted to them by any source. A deep study and an examination of information are really needed regardless of its origins. Although some non-African overestimate themselves and underestimate Africa, still the true truth will remain unstoppable.

Moreover, the reality of the world today shows that even in the western countries Africans continues to be negatively stereotyped by the people of African origin. For example, when reading the article of Rosemary Lukens Traoré, we find that in the USA African and African American students are separated by a huge gulf which is sustained by myths, misperceptions and negative stereotypes. Although they share the same history and culture, collaboration is not easy between them while learning together in inner-city schools in the USA.

A recent study organized by Rosemary Lukens Traoré, of eight African American and nine African students at a high school in a large metropolitan city in the US, has shown that negative images of Africa and Africans resulted in pejorative characteristics such as "Jungle bunny", "heathen", and "savage". And this has contributed significantly to their hostile relationships with each other.

In that situation, we may be tempted to admit that the mindsets of some African American towards Africans is so erroneous not because of not having the same color but because of not being born in the same continent! This is an ugly situation full of lies that continue to put pressure on many Africans making them feel more and more inferior and less important than other people.

There is no need of demonstration for a situation which is already clear in itself. Traoré, in her article 'African students in America: reconstructing a new meaning to "African American" in urban education', talks about the non-harmonious relationships between African American and African students in the USA. She states that hostile relationships between African and African American students were developed in inner-city schools in the USA. This reality was evinced by some pejorative characteristics such as "jungle bunny", "heathen", and "savage". The mis-perception of African students was due to the ignorance of African American students about their origin, their culture and their ancestry.

The African American students did not know that their origin is Africa; that is why they considered Africa like a jungle which can only produce savage persons. Traoré (2003) puts that images that predominated in the minds of the African American students were Tarzan, wild animals, and the 'Dark Continent'; and that has made the 'Africans' something to be avoided or reviled. To comment this situation, I can say that in the mind of African American students there was a deplorable lack of knowledge about Africa. To say that Africa is a Dark Continent is totally untrue.

For example, can western companies that depend on raw materials from Africa say the same? Can they argue that what they need to make their companies work come from 'darkness'? The problem of Africa is not darkness of the minds or the land. People need to remember that Africa is sunny than any other continent in the world! People who believe that African continent is black have black minds about Africa. And we have the duty of pulling them from that mind-darkness by supplying them with accurate information about Africa.

We need to inform people; we need to re-educate some of the young people of Africa who really need to know the truth about themselves and their land. And most of them are willing to gain knowledge. "There is a prevailing thirst for knowledge that motivates students in Africa to attend school even when their circumstances are difficult. Students in Africa often must overcome great obstacles – long distances to walk, bad weather, sickness, hunger and much more – and yet they still consistently get to school" (Traoré, 2003, p. 247). In addition to what Traoré writes, it may be supposed that most of European colonialists were considering the uneducated African people like useless people who cannot think well, like people to be only used for hard jobs which do not pay good money to earn an ordinary living.

Durable peace and prosperity for all cannot be achieved with such situation in the AGLR. It will always darken people's natural ability to create ad think well and delay them in poverty and insecurity. That is a total ignorance of the true 'self.' Back to the African American students, I can say that the ignorance of their origin, their history, and their ancestry seemed to be the reason why they were stereotyping and mis-perceiving the African students.

Using a film as a method of putting them in good relationships at Jackson was an excellent way giving information to adolescents who ignore their origin. The film entitled '*The language You Cry In: The Story of a Mende Song*' had a positive impact on their daily behavior at school and in the society vis-à-vis to African classmates. Because some students discovered that they are coming from Africa and African students are now important – they can learn more from them – in their classrooms.

So, by that film African American students were connected to their history, to their culture. And I believe that it was the beginning of their disclosure which has the advantage of starting and deepening relationships between people. "One benefit of disclosure is that it can begin and deepen your relationships, whether at work, home, or school, it can also increase your self-awareness and your understanding of yourself." (Stewart, 2009, p. 253).

6.9. Do I recognize other people's potentials?
How much do I value them?
Or how much do I neglect or despise others?

It is important to know other peoples' values, potentials, and beliefs in order to live well with them. Some people are only interested in knowing people of high social status that live in their villages, avenues, or streets and seem to forget about the lower social status people who are most of time used in wars and genocides in the AGLR and are the most victims of conflicts in the region. The people who are supposed to attract more the attention of others so that the social justice prevails are the ones that mostly neglected.

Can a human being need peace and at the same time violate the principles that make it alive? Is it correct to say that you are in need of something that you are destroying? We need to know, recognize, and value others if we want to build durable peace and prosperity for all. Negligence, despise, discrimination, and hatred are destroyer of peace – they are able to transform things that are supposed to build into very destructive ones – and will never assure prosperity for all.

That is why recognition, respect, value, etc. should not be limited to some category of people – of high social status – but every human being deserves them. Every single individual can contribute outstandingly to durable peace and prosperity of a nation if taken with consideration by leaders and others in the communities.

That is why wise persons and particularly leaders should use adequately and regularly the potential of all their peoples; no one is to be despised regardless of their social status, their ethnic group, their religion, their age, their race, etc. It is ignorant to think that only rich and smart people are intelligent enough to contribute to the peace and development of Africa.

God gives wisdom to any person regardless of their social status. It can happen that a community or a nation is looking for solutions to its problems outside the country or in high standard rich peoples while the solutions are found in its poor general populations. It is good to listen to what people have to say even if they are poor and seem not smart. King Solomon had discovered that even in poor people there is great potential that can save even the whole country, and then he wrote,

> "There is something else I saw, a good example of how wisdom is regarded in this world. There was a little town without many people in it. A powerful king attacked it. He surrounded it and prepared to break through the walls. Someone lived there who was poor, but so clever that he could have saved the town, but no one thought about him, I have always said that wisdom is better than strength, but no one thinks of the poor as wise or pays any attention to what they say. It is better to listen to the quiet words of a wise person that to the shouts of a ruler at a council of fools, wisdom does more good than weapons, but one sinner can undo a lot of good." (Ecclesiastes 9:13-18).

In conclusion, people of the AGLR should revisit their conscience with the light from what has been discussed in the previous paragraphs to find true and edifying answers to the questions: Who am I?, Why am I here?, Why was I born in the AGLR?, What kind of thoughts and beliefs do I have?, What do I think about my tribe or ethnic group?, What do I think about other ethnic groups or tribes of my country?, Do I know the history of African migrations?, Do I know the history of the people of AGLR?, Do I know the impact of colonialism on Africa – on the AGLR?, What gift(s) or talent(s) do I have?, What goals do I have with reference to my gifts and beliefs? What do I like to do?; Is what I have been doing in accordance with what I was born to do?; What should I be doing from today?; etc.

We are optimistic that shedding light on people's minds with the suggested enlightening answers to these questions in Chapter 6 of this book (Volume I) will help in the process of establishing durable peace and prosperity for all in the AGLR. And that should lead our readers to Chapter 7 of this book (in Volume II) that contains the second fundamental for durable peace and prosperity in the AGLR which is 'Positive Change of Negative Mentality.'

References

Abbuco Gabson LLC. (ND). Family Farm (ABBUCO'S AGRI). Retrieved from http://www.abbuco.com/farmers

ACLED (2013). Armed Conflict Location & Event Dataset. Country Report: DR Congo. December 2013. Retrieved on 4th August, 2016 fromhttp://www.acleddata.com/wpcontent/uploads/2013/12/ACLED-Country-Report_DR-Congo_December-2013.pdf

AfDB, OECD, UNDP, UNECA (2012). African Economic Outlook 2012. Burundi 2012. Retrieved from http://www.afdb.org/fileadmin/uploads/afdb/Documents/Publications/Burundi%20Full%20PDF%20Country%20Note.pdf

AfDB. (2013). Democratic Republic of Congo 2013-2017 Country Strategy Paper. Regional Department Centre (ORCE/CDFO)

Africa.com (2016). Burundi Afripedia. Retrieved from http://www.africa.com/countries/burundi/afripedia/

African Security Analysis Program, ISS. (2009). Declaration of the PALIPEHUTU-FNL. Bujumbura, 9 January 2009. Draft Translation. Retrieved from https://issafrica.s3.amazonaws.com/site/uploads/FNLDECL9JAN09.PDF

768

All Africa. (ND). Arusha Peace and Reconciliation Agreement for Burundi. Retrieved from http://allafrica.com/download/resource/main/main/idatcs/00010127:d8c6a4de10b788affed1a5013e1d5d41.pdf

Amnesty International. (2014). Burundi: Locked Down. A Shrinking of Political Space. London: Amnesty International

Amnesty International. (2014). Burundi: Locked Down. A Shrinking of Political Space. London: Amnesty International

ANAPI (2016). Agriculture. Retrieved from https://investindrc.cd/en/sectors/agriculture

Atukunda, G. & Ahmed, M. (2012). Analysis of incentives and disincentives for fish in Uganda. Technical notes series, MAFAP, FAO. Rome: MAFAP & FAO

Ayebare, A. A. (ND). Peacemaking in Burundi – A Case Study of Regional Diplomacy Backed by International Peacekeeping and Peacebuilding. Retrieved from http://responsibilitytoprotect.org/favoritadonia.pdf

Baarabe, J. (2012). Energy Supply in Uganda. National Workshop on Promoting Sustainable Transport Solutions for East Africa. Wednesday 1 August, 2012. Retrieved from http://www.unep.org/transport/pcfv/PDF/icct_2012/ICCT_EnergySituation_JamesBanaabe_MEMD.pdf

Bagumire, A. (2009). Impact of the Global Economic

Crisis on LDCs' Productive Capacities and Trade Prospects: Threats and Opportunities. A Case Study: The fisheries sector in Uganda and United Republic of Tanzania. Impact of the Global Financial and Economic Crisis on the Fish Industry in Uganda and Tanzania. Vienna International Centre, Austria: UNIDO

Barnett, M. (2002). Eyewitness to A Genocide. The United Nations and Rwanda.

Barry, J. A. (1998). The Sword of Justice. Ethics and Coercion in International Politics. USA: Greenwood Publishing Group, Inc.

BBC (2016). Burundi Profile – Timeline. Retrieved from http://www.bbc.com/news/world-africa-13087604

BBC (December 2008). Rwanda: How the genocide happened. Between April and June 1994, an estimated 800,000 Rwandans were killed in the space of 100 days. Retrieved from http://news.bbc.co.uk/2/hi/1288230.stm

BBC News (15 November 2016). Democratic Republic of Congo profile – Timeline. Retrieved from http://www.bbc.com/news/world-africa-13286306

BBC News (2006). Kabila Declares Winner of Congo Vote. Retrieved from http://www.nbcnews.com/id/15736587/ns/world_news-africa/t/kabila-declared-winner-congo-vote/#.WF8c8hsrK00

BBC News (2016). Uganda profile – Timeline. Retrieved from http://www.bbc.com/news/world-africa-

770

14112446

BBC News. (2001). Burundi peace talks fail. Retrieved from http://news.bbc.co.uk/2/hi/africa/1190242.stm

BGR & KfW (April 2007). Les ressources naturelles en République démocratique du Congo – Un potentiel de développement? Brève étude sur la République démocratique du Congo réalisée par KfW Entwicklungsbank et l'Institut fédéral allemand des sciences de la terre et des matières premières (BGR). Retrieved from http://www.congoforum.be/upldocs/Ressources%20naturelles%20rapport%20Allemand%20avril%202007.pdf

Bridgland, F. (2007). Uganda: Leader of Holy Spirit Rebels Dies. The woman who was the spiritual inspiration of Uganda's Lord's Resistance Army dies in exile in Kenya. Retrieved from https://iwpr.net/global-voices/uganda-leader-holy-spirit-rebels-dies

Butera, J.B. & Rutangwenda, T. (2004). Plan Stratégique de Transformation de L'agriculture au Rwanda. Animal Production Sub-Sector. Kigali: Rwanda Ministry of Agriculture and Animal resources

Butunungu, L. (2013). Foot and Mouth Disease Sub Network Meeting, Entebbe 29- 30 August 2013. Country: Burundi

Byrnes, R. M. (1990). Uganda: A Country Study.

Retrieved from https://archive.org/stream/ugandacountrystu00 byrn_0/ugandacountrystu00byrn_0_djvu.txt

CAADP. (2013). *Democratic Republic of Congo Agriculture Investment Opportunities Brief CAADP Investment Facilitation Programme 2013.* Retrieved from http://www.abghq.com/downloads/DRC.pdf

Catholicrevelation.org (nd). *8 Visionaries Kibeho, Rwanda, Africa 1981-198*2 ("Mother of theWord"). Retrieved from http://www.catholicrevelations.org/PR/emman uel%20segatashya.htm

Centre for Humanitarian Dialogue. (2011). The AU and the search for Peace and Reconciliation in Burundi and Comoros. Geneva: Centre for Humanitarian Dialogue

Child War UK (2014). The Conflict in the Congo. Retrieved on 5th August, 2016 from http://www.warchild.org.uk/issues/conflict-in-democratic-republic-of-congo

Chossudovsky, M. (2010). The US was behind the Rwandan Genocide: Installing a US Protectorate in Central Africa. Retrieved from http://www.globalresearch.ca/the-us-was-behind-the-rwandan-genocide-installing-a-us-protectorate-in-central-africa/18540?print=1

CIA (2016). World Factbook. Africa: Democratic Republic of Congo. Retrieved from https://www.cia.gov/library/publications/the-worldfactbook/geos/print/country/countrypdf_cg.pdf

CIA. (2016). World Fact Book. Africa: Uganda. Retrieved from https://www.cia.gov/Library/publications/the-world-factbook/geos/ug.html

Coghlan, B. at al. (2006). Mortality in the Democratic Republic of Congo An ongoing crisis. Retrieved from https://www.rescue.org/sites/default/files/document/661/2006-7congomortalitysurvey.pdf

Collombat, B. & Servenay, D. (2014). "Au nom de la France". Guerres Secrètes. Paris: Éditions La Découverte

Dallaire, R. (2003). *Shake Hands with the Devil: The Failure of Humanity in Rwanda.* Canada: Random House Canada.

Davenport, D. (2014). International Criminal Court: 12 Years, $1 Billion, 2 Convictions. Retrieved from https://www.forbes.com/sites/daviddavenport/2014/03/12/international- criminal-court-12-years-1-billion-2-convictions-2/#c5ab1bd24053

Dembour, M. B. (2008). Recalling the Belgian Congo: Conversation and Introspection. New York: Berghahn Books

Documentary on 'Congo: White King, Red Rubber, Black Death' directed by Peter Bate. New

York: New York Daily News.

EACS. (2012). *East African Community Facts and Figures – 2012*. Tanzania – Arusha: EACS (East African Community Secretariat)

East African Community Secretariat. (September 2012). East African Community Facts and Figures – 2012. Tanzania – Arusha: EAC Secretariat

ECHO (2014). ECHO Factsheet – Democratic Republic of Congo – September 2014. Brussels: European Commission – Humanitarian Aid and Civil Protection

Ekitibwa kya Buganda (2013). Kanzu was already prominent in Buganda by 1925. Retrieved from https://ekitibwakyabuganda.wordpress.com/2013/01/12/

Enough (nd). The LRA in Congo, CAR, and South Sudan. Retrieved from http://www.enoughproject.org/conflicts/lra/congo-car-south-sudan

Ensign, M. M. & Bertrand, E. W. (2010). *Rwanda: History and Hope*. USA: University Press of America, Inc.

Failler, P. & Karani, P. & Seide, W. (2016). Assessment of the Environment Pollution and its impact on Economic Cooperation and Integration Initiatives of the IGAD Region; National Environment Pollution Report – Uganda. Retrieved from https://www.researchgate.net/publication/2994

42409_Assessment_of_the_Environment_Poll
ution_and_its_impact_on_Economic_Coopera
tion_and_Integration_Initiatives_of_the_IGA
D_Region_National_Environment_Pollution_
Report_-_Uganda#pfd

FAO (2004). Simple fish-drying racks improve livelihoods and nutrition in Burundi. Retrieved from http://www.fao.org/docrep/018/i2940e/i2940e10.pdf

FERN. (March 2006). Forest governance in the Democratic Republic of Congo. An NGO perspective. A report produced for FERN by Simon Counsell, March 2006. United Kingdom: FERN office.

Forges, A. D. (1999). "Leave None to Tell the Story" Genocide in Rwanda. New York, Washington, London, Brussels: Human Rights Watch

Fortune of Africa (2014). King Mwambutsa IV Bangiricenge. Retrieved from http://fortuneofafrica.com/burundi/king-mwambutsa-iv-bangiricenge/

Fortune of Africa. (2013). Minerals in Uganda. Retrieved from http://fortuneofafrica.com/ug/minerals-in-uganda/

Forum on Chine-Africa Cooperation (2009). History of Africa. Retrieved from http://www.focac.org/eng/zjfz/fzzl/t619148.htm

Gale, T. (2007). Burundi. *Worldmark Encyclopedia of*

Nations. Retrieved from http://www.encyclopedia.com/places/africa/bu rundian-political-geography/burundi

Genocide Watch. (2008). Genocides, Politicides, and Other Mass Murder Since 1945, With Stages in 2008. Retrieved from

Gettleman, J. & Sundaramaug, A. (2006). U.N. Brokers Cease-Fire as Congo Vote Turns Violent. Retrieved from http://www.nytimes.com/2006/08/23/world/af rica/23congo.html

Global Research (2008). UN to Send more troops to DR Congo. Retrieved from http://www.globalresearch.ca/un-to-send-more-troops-to-dr-congo/11068?print=1

Global Security (2006). Burundi 1993-1994. Retreived from http://www.globalsecurity.org/military/world/war/burundi3.htm

Gourevitch, P. (1998). *We Wish to Inform You That Tomorrow We Will Be Killed with Our Families.* USA: Farrar, Straus and Giroux

Grove, W. T. (2010). Greed Disguised as Humanitarianism:The Story of the Congo Reform Movement. Appalachian Spring Conference in World Historyand Economics. Retrieved from https://history.appstate.edu/sites/history.appsta te.edu/files/Tyler%20Grove-1.pdf

Hare, H. (2007). Survey of ICT and Education in Africa:

Burundi Country Report. ICT in Education in Burundi. May 2007. Retrieved from http://documents.worldbank.org/curated/en/29 3721468222603883/pdf/464080BRI0Box31di 010ICTed0Survey111.pdf

Hare, H. (2007). Survey of ICT and Education in Africa: Burundi Country Report. ICT in Education in Burundi. Retrieved from https://openknowledge.worldbank.org/bitstrea m/handle/10986/10697/464080BRI0Box31di0 10ICTed0Survey111.pdf?sequence=1

Hatungimana, A. & Theron, J. & Popic, A. (2014). Peace Agreements in Burundi: Assessing the Impact. Retrieved from http://www.guillaumenicaise.com/wp-content/uploads/2014/08/Hatungimana_Thero n_POPIC_Peace-agreements-in-Burundi.pdf

Hatzfeld, J. (2000). *Life Laid Bare: The Survivors in Rwanda Speak.* France: Edition du Seuil.

Hatzfeld, J. (2005). *Machete Season: The Killers in Rwanda Speak: A Report.* USA: Farrar, Straus and Giroux

Hill, A. C. & Kilson, M. (2014). Apropos of Africa: Sentiments of American Negro Leaders on Africa From the 1800s to the 1950s. New York: Routledge

History World (2016). History of Burundi. Retrieved from http://www.historyworld.net/wrldhis/plaintext histories.asp?historyid=ad25

Hivos (ND). Uganda: Energy Profile. Retrieved from https://www.hivos.org/sites/default/files/uganda_profile.pdf

Hochschild, A. (1999). King Leopold's Ghost. A Story of Greed, Terror, and Heroism in Africa. USA: Mariner Books Edition

Hogg, N. (2010). Women's participation in the Rwandan genocide: mothers or monsters? In *International Review of the Red Cross.* Volume 92 Number 877 March 2010 p. 86 – 88

HRW (2013). World Report 2013. Events of 2012. USA: Human Rights Watch (HRW)

HRW. (2013). World Report 2013: Burundi. Events of 2012. Retrieved from https://www.hrw.org/world-report/2013/country-chapters/burundi

http://ugandapeople.com/about/geography-and-climate

Human Right Watch (July 2013). ITURI: "COVERED IN BLOOD" Ethnically Targeted Violence in Northeastern DR Congo. New York: Woman Right Watch. Retrieved on 4th August, 2016 from https://www.hrw.org/reports/2003/ituri0703/DRC0703.pdf

Human Rights Watch (2009). DR Congo: Chronology. Retrieved from https://www.hrw.org/news/2009/08/21/dr-congo-chronology

Human Rights Watch (November, 25, 2008). "We Will

Crush You" The Restriction of Political Space in the Democratic Republic of Congo. Retrieved from https://www.hrw.org/report/2008/11/25/we-will-crush-you/restriction-political-space-democratic-republic-congo

Icirore C'amahoro. (ND). Burundi. Retrieved from http://www.icirore-camahoro.org/burund/

Ilibagiza, I. (2006). *Left to Tell: Discovering God Amidst the Rwandan Holocaust*. California, Carlsbad, London, Sydney, Johannesburg, Vancouver, Hong Kong: Hay House, Inc.

International Business Publications (2011). Global Logistics Assessments Reports Handbook. Volume 1. Strategic Transportation and Customs Information for Selected Countries. USA: International Business Publications

International Panel of Eminent Personalities (IPEP). Rwanda: A Priventable Genocide. Retrieved on 30th March, 2017 from http://www.refworld.org/pdfid/4d1da8752.pdf

IRIN (2016). Last rebel group signs cease-fire with government. http://www.irinnews.org/news/2006/09/07/last-rebelgroup-signs-cease-fire-government

Jeal, T. (2013). Livingstone: Revised and Expanded Edition. Format: ebook. Published by Yale University Press

Jennings, M. (2009). Uganda: Recent History, 1226 – 1253 pp *in Africa South of the Sahara 2009,*

38ᵗʰ Edition. Europe Surveys of the World. London and New York: Routledge Taylor & Francis Group

Kaji, S. (2013). Monolingualism via Multilingualism: A Case Study of Language Use in the West Ugandan Town of Hoima. *African Study Monographs, 34 (1): 1–25,* March 2013. Retrieved from http://www.kaowarsom.be/documents/KajiArt icleASM34-1.pdf

Kalyegira, T. (2005). Did Idi Amin really kill 300,000 people? Retrieved from https://www.mail-archive.com/ugandanet@kym.net/msg17848.h tml

UCA – Political Science (2014). 44. Uganda (1962-present). Retrieved from http://uca.edu/politicalscience/dadm-project/sub-saharan-africa-region/uganda-1962-present/

Kanyarukiga, S. G. (2004). *Strategic Plan of Agriculture Transformation Financing, Coordination and Monitoring and Evaluation in The Agricultural Sector.* Kigali: Ministry of Agriculture and Animal resources

Karimi, F. & Ntale, S. & Botelho, G. (2016). Uganda leader Museveni declared winner – despite issues, tensions. Retrieved from http://www.cnn.com/2016/02/20/africa/ugand a-election/

Karugaba, M. (2011). Heritage, Uganda Oil Case Starts in UK. Retrieved from http://www.ugandaoilandgas.com/blog/

Keane, F. (1997). *Season of Blood: A Rwandan Journey.* France: Penguin Putnam Trade

Kinzer, S. (2008). *A Thousand Hills: Rwanda's Rebirth and the Man Who Dreamed It.* USA & Canada: John Wiley and Sons, Inc.

Kiying, G. (2010). Forest Governance Reforms in Uganda Workshop organized by the Ministryof Water and Environment, and the World Bank Serena Hotel, Kampala, 15th – 16th June 2010. Workshop report. Retrieved from http://www.profor.info/sites/profor.info/files/docs/Forest-governance-workshop-Uganda2010.pdf

KPMG Global Mining Institute (2014). Democratic Republic of Congo. Country mining guide. Retrieved from https://www.kpmg.com/Global/en/IssuesAndInsights/ArticlesPublications/mining-country-guides/Documents/democratic-republic-congo-mining-guide.pdf

Kraemer-Mbula, E. & Wamae, W. (2010). Innovation and the Development Agenda. France: OECD Publishing

Kron, J. (2010). Opposition Calls Election in Burundi a 'Masquerade'. *New York Times*. Retrieved from http://www.nytimes.com/2010/07/01/world/africa/01burundi.html

Krueger, R. & Krueger, K. T. (2007). From Bloodshed to Hope in Burundi. Our Embassy Years During the Genocide. USA: University of Texas Press

L'Association Survie. (2007). La complicité de la France dans le génocide des Tutsi au Rwanda : 15 ans après, 15 questions pour comprend. Paris: L'Harmattan.

Leithead, A. (2015). Rwanda genocide: International Criminal Tribunal closes. Retried fromhttp://www.bbc.com/news/world-africa-35070220

Lemarchand, R. & Martin, D. (nd). Selective Genocide in Burundi. Report no. 20. London: Minority Rights Group

Lipschutz, M. R. & Rasmussen, R. K. (1986). Dictionary of African Historical Biography. Second Edition Expended and Updated. Berkeley, Los Angeles, London: University of California Press

LSE LAW. (2016). International Humanitarian Law Project: International Conference on the Great Lakes Region. Retrieved from https://www.lse.ac.uk/collections/law/projects /greatlakes/4.%20Humanitarian%20and %20Social%20Issues/4a. %20Programme/Final.HumSocPo %20Eng.Nov2006.pdf

Lugira, A. M. (1999). The Catholic Church And Development In Uganda. A Presentation at the Conference on Democracy For Truth, Justice, Peace and Development. A Tribute to the late

Hon. Benedicto Kagimu Mugumba Kiwanuka delivered at Georgetown University, McNeir Hall, Washington DC. December 4, 1999. Retrieved from https://www2.bc.edu/~lugira/churchdev.htm

Maula, J. (2012). The Jasmine Years: From My African Notebooks. USA: iUniverse

Ministere de l'Agriculture et de l'Elevage (2005). Evaluations des récoltes, des approvisionnements alimentaires et de la situation nutritionnelle. *Special report.* République du Burundi.

Ministry of Education. (2014). 2013 Education Statistical Yearbook. Kigali: Rwandan Ministry of Education

Morel, J. (2017). La France au cœur du génocide des Tutsi. Izuba Editions: Rwanda

MPSVE & ISSP/OU (2013). National Survey on the Situation of Out-of-school Children and Adolescents. DRC: Ministry of Primary, Secondary and Vocational Education and Higher Institute for Population Sciences of the University of Ouagadougou (ISSP / UO).

Mpuila, T. (2012). La colonisation belge avait ses stratégies et ses méthodes. Retrieved from http://www.udps.be/beluxx/viewtopic.php?t=2452

MTI (2009). *Rwanda Tourism Policy.* Kigali: Ministry of Trade and Industry.

MTI (2011). *Rwanda National Export Strategy (NES).*

Kigali: Ministry of Trade and Industry

MTWH & World Bank (2012). Uganda Tourism Sector Situational Assessment. June 2012.

Muhoro, P. N. (2010). Off-Grid Electricity Access and its Impact on Micro-Enterprises: Evidence from Rural Uganda. A dissertation submitted in partial fulfillment of the requirements for the degree of Doctor of Philosophy (Applied Physics) in the University of Michigan 2010. Retrieved from https://deepblue.lib.umich.edu/bitstream/handl e027.42/78822/pmuhoro_1.pdf?sequence=1

Murtis, M. (2017). Britain's Role in Rwanda's 1994 Genocide. Retrieved from http://www.globalresearch.ca/britains-role-in-rwandas-1994-genocide/5566703

Nation Unies – Conseil de Sécurité. (1999). *Rapport de la Commission Indépendante D'enquête sur les Actions de L'organisation des Nations Unies lors du Génocide de*

Nations Encyclopedia (2016). Congo, Republic of the (ROC) – Religions. Retrieved from http://www.nationsencyclopedia.com/Africa/C ongo-Republic-of-the-ROC-RELIGIONS.html

Nduwamungu, J. (2011). A Platform For Stakeholders In African Forestryafrican Forest Forum Working Paper Series Forest Plantations And Woodlots In Burundi. Volume I. Nairobi: African Forest Forum (AFF)

NEMA (2014). Fifth National Report to the Convention

on Biological Diversity. Uganda, Kampala: NEMA

New York: Cornell University Press

Nielsen, H. & Spenceley, A. (April 2010). The success of tourism in Rwanda – Gorillas and more* Background paper for the African Success Stories Study. Rwanda: World Bank and SNV (The Netherlands Development Organisation)

Nielsen, H. & Spenceley, A. (April 2010). *The success of tourism in Rwanda – Gorillas and more* Background paper for the African Success Stories Study.* Rwanda: World Bank and SNV (The Netherlands Development Organization)

NISR (2014). Fourth Population and Housing Census, Rwanda 2012. Thematic Report. Socio-cultural characteristics of the population January 2014. Rwanda: Ministry of Finance and Economic Planning

Nzioka, B. (2011). The Rwandan Genocide: Eye Witnesses to a Human Catastrophe. A Thesis submitted to the Faculty of the School of Continuing Studies and of the Graduate School of Arts and Sciences in partial fulfillment of the requirements for the Degree of Master of Arts in Liberal studies.Washington, D.C.: Georgetown University.

Nzongola-Ntalanja, G. (2002). Congo From Leopold to Kabila. A People's History. London & New York: Zed Books

Paulsworth, S. (2010). Uganda court dismisses treason case against opposition leader. Retrieved from http://www.jurist.org/paperchase/2010/10/uga nda-court-dismisses-treason-case-against-opposition-leader.php

Peace Maker. (2000). Arusha Peace and Reconciliation Agreement for Burundi. http://peacemaker.un.org/sites/peacemaker.un. org/files/BI_000828_Arusha%20Peace %20and%20Reconciliation%20Agreement %20for%20Burundi.pdf

Point, V. (2011). Genocide. The role of the West. Retrieved from *http://www.rwandanstories.org/genocide/role _of_the_west.html*

Preventing Genocide (2004). Africa. Retrieved from http://www.preventgenocide.org/prevent/news -monitor/2004jan.htm

PROfIT. (2007). Regional Investment Conference Tourism 27 to 29 June 2007. East Africa and the Indian Ocean. Country Profile: Burundi. Kampala: PROfIT

Promar Consulting. (2012). Agriculture, Forestry and Fisheries of Rwanda Fact-Finding Survey for the Support of Aid to Developing Countries (Fiscal Year 2011 Research Project). Supported by The Ministry of Agriculture, Forestry and Fisheries March 30, 2012. Tokyo: Promar Consulting

RAD & RDB. (nd). *Rwanda Ideal Conditions for High Value Products. Investment Opportunity:*

Fishery, aquaculture and animal feed production. Invest in Rwanda's Fishery, aquaculture and animal feed sub sector. Kigali: Agriculture Department, RDB

RDB (2012). *Rwanda Skills Survey 2012. Agriculture Sector Report.* Kigali: Rwanda Development Board (RDB)

Republic of Uganda (2010). National Development Plan. Vision: A Transformed Ugandan Society from a Peasant to a Modern and Prosperous Country Within 30 Years. Theme: Growth, Employment and Socio-Economic Transformation for Prosperity (2010/11 - 2014/15). Retrieved from http://npa.ug/wp-content/themes/npatheme/documents/NDP2.pdf

Reuters Africa (2009). DR Congo wins IMF loan, enters debt relief program. Retrieved from http://af.reuters.com/article/investingNews/id AFJOE5BB01I20091212

Rever, J. (2015). UN Appoints Rwandan General as Head of Darfur Peacekeeping Despite His Senior Rank During Rwandan-Backed Rebellion in Congo. Retrieved from http://www.foreignpolicyjournal.com/2015/12/19/un-appoints-rwandan-general-as-head-of-darfur-peacekeeping/

Revolvy, LLC. (2016). Transport in Burundi. Retrieved from https://www.revolvy.com/main/index.php?

s=Transport%20in%20Burundi

Riche, M. & Berwouts, K. (2014). DRC Elections: Will Kabila stay or go? And many other questions on the road to 2016. Retrieved from http://africanarguments.org/2014/06/24/drc-elections-will-kabila-stay-or-go-and-many-other-questions-on-the-road-to-2016-by-manya-riche-and-kris-berwouts/

Roest, F. (Nd). A Second Look at the Industrial Fisheries Data, Burundi, Lake Tanganyika (1973-1992). Retrieved from http://www.kaowarsom.be/documents/B_59_2 013/ROEST.pdf

Rufford (2009). *Eastern Gallery Forest Conservation Project Biodiversity survey. A Final Research report to the Rufford Small Grant Foundation, UK.* Retrieved from http://www.rufford.org/files/12.02.08%20Deta iled%20Final%20Report.pdf

Rule, S. (1986). Rebel Sworn in as Uganda President. In *New York Times.* Retrieved from

Rwanda Agriculture Department, RDB. (nd). *Rwanda Ideal Conditions for High Value Products. Investment Opportunity: Fishery, aquaculture and animal feed production.* Invest in Rwanda's Fishery, aquaculture and animal feed sub sector. Kigali: Agriculture Department, RDB

Rwanda Development Board (RDB). *Rwanda Skills Survey 2012. Energy Sector Report.* Kigali:

RDB
Rwanda Ministry of Trade and Industry. (2009). *Rwanda Tourism Policy*. Kigali: Ministry of Trade and Industry

Rwanda Ministry of Trade and Industry. (2009). Rwanda Tourism Policy. Kigali: Ministry of Trade and Industry

Save the Children. State of the World's Mothers 2014. Saving Mothers and Children in Humanitarian Crises. USA: Save the Children Federation, Inc.

Sebarenzi, J. & Mullane, L. A. (2009). God sleeps in Rwanda. A Journey of Transformation. New York: ATRIA Books A Division of Simon & Schuter, Inc.

Sèbe, B. (2008). The French Betrayal of Rwanda. Bloomington and Indianapolis: Indiana University Press, 2008. 330 pp. in *H-France Review Vol. 8* (October 2008), No. 133)

Sebushahu, T. (2008). Poultry Sector Country Review. Version of 15th September 2011. Bujumbura: FAO Animal Production and Health Division

Sida. (2014). Division for Eastern and Western Africa. A Strategic Conflict Analysis for the Great Lakes Region. Retrieved from http://www.sida.se/contentassets/c30494ada89 f4783b789e6290b635ccb/a-strategic-conflict-analysis-for-the-great-lakes-region_437.pdf

Snow, H. K. (2005). Rwanda's Secret War. U. S. -backed destabilization of Central Africa. Retrieved from http://www.thirdworldtraveler.com/Africa/Rw anda_Secret_War.html

SNSA. (2012). L'agriculture Congolaise en Quelques Chifres. Retrieved from http://agriculture-rdc.net/agri/documents/statistiques/agriculture rdc_en_chiffres.pdf

State House. (1995). Constitution of the Republic of Uganda, 1995. Arrangement of the Constitution. Retrieved from http://www.statehouse.go.ug/sites/default/files /attachments/Constitution_1995.pdf

Stedman, S. J. & Tanner, F. (2003). Refugee Manipulation. War, Politics, and the Abuse of Human Suffering. Washington, DC: Brookings Institution Press

Straus, S. (nd). *Rwanda and RTLM Radio Media Effects*. Madison: University of Wisconsin, Department of Political Science

Tardif, T. (2001). *To avoid a horrible war Conversion, prayer, penance, fasting Messages of Our Lady of Sorrows in Kibeho, Rwanda These Apparitions have been officially recognized by the Church in 2001 In Kibeho, Our Lady had precited, in 1984, the horrible war of 1994.* Retrieved from http://www.michaeljournal.org/kibeho.htm

Telegraph Media Group Limited (2015). African presidents' dilemma: Should I stay or should I go? Retrieved from

http://www.telegraph.co.uk/news/worldnews/a
fricaandindianocean/burundi/11614000/Africa
n-presidents-dilemma-Should-I-stay-or-
should-I-go.html

Terence Co (2013) The Second Congo War 1998 – 2002
in *MODERN WAR. SEP–OCT 2013* p.31
retrieved   from
http://modernwarmagazine.com/wp-
content/uploads/2013/07/MW7-sample.pdf

The Associated Press (June 11, 2000) The Forces of
Rwanda and Uganda Fight in Congo.
Retrieved   from
http://www.nytimes.com/2000/06/11/world/th
e-forces-of-rwanda-and-uganda-fight-in-
congo.html

The Combat Genocide Association. (nd). Burundi 1972.
Retrieved from https://combatgenocide.org/?
page_id=893

The Commonwealth (2011). Uganda Presidential and
Parliamentary Elections 2011: Interim
Statement.   Retried   from
http://thecommonwealth.org/media/news/ugan
da-presidential-and-parliamentary-elections-
2011-interim-statement

The Commonwealth (2017). Uganda: History. Retrieved
from   http://thecommonwealth.org/our-
member-countries/uganda/history

The Editors of Encyclopedia Britannica (2013). Mwanga.
Kinga of Buganda. Retrieved from
https://www.britannica.com/biography/Mwan

ga

The Gale Group (2010). Uganda. The Great Soviet Encyclopedia, 3rd Edition (1970-1979). © 2010 The Gale Group, Inc. Retrieved from http://encyclopedia2.thefreedictionary.com/Ugandan

The Resolve (nd). The LRA Crisis. Key Statistics. Retrieved from http://www.theresolve.org/the-lra-crisis/key-statistics/

The Ugandan Space Agency (nd). Timeline of Events in Uganda ...From the Past to the Future. Retrieved from http://www.hudsonfla.com/auganda.htm

Tourism Reawakening. Uganda: MTWH & World Bank

Trading Economics (2016). Mineral rents (% of GDP) in Burundi. Retrieved From http://www.tradingeconomics.com/burundi/mineral-rents-percent-of-gdp-wb-data.html

Trial International (2016). Kyungu Mutanga. Retrieved from https://trialinternational.org/latest-post/kyungu-mutanga/

Triposo (ND). Burundi History. Retrieved from http://www.triposo.com/loc/Burundi/history/background

Turner, B. (2014). The Statesman's Year Book 2015. The Politics, Cultures, and Economies of the

Twagilimana, A. (2016). *Historical Dictionary of Rwanda. Second Edition*. London: Rowman & Littlefield Publishers.

Twagiramungu, F. (2006). Environmental Profile of

Rwanda. Rwanda: European Commission &
Twagiramungu, F. (July 2006). *Environmental profile of Rwanda*. Kigali: European Commission & Republic of Rwanda

UBOS (2008). The National Livestock Census Report 2008. Kampala, Uganda: UBOS

UBOS (2013). Uganda National Panel Survey 2010/2011. Wave II Report. Kampala: UBOS

Uganda Bureau of Statistics (2014). 2014 Statistical Abstract. Retrieved from http://www.ubos.org/onlinefiles/uploads/ubos/ statistical_abstracts/Statistical_Abstract_2014. pdf

Uganda Bureau of Statistics (UBOS). June 2013. Uganda National Panel Survey 2010/2011 – K Wave II Report. Kampala, Uganda: UBOS

Uganda Bureau of Statistics. (2012). Agricultural Sector. Gender Statistics Profile. Kampala, Uganda: UBOS

Uganda Bureau of Statistics. (2014). National Population and Housing Census of 2014 – Provisional Result. November 2014. Revised Edition. Kampala: UBOS

Uganda Bureau of Statistics. (2016). The National Population and Housing Census 2014 – Main Report. Kampala, Uganda: UBOS

Uganda Chamber of Mines and Petroleum. (2016). What Minerals Exist in Uganda? Retrieved from

http://www.ucmp.ug/details?
imgt=news&cid=30&name=%20what
%20minerals%20exist%20in%20uganda?
&typ=news

Uganda People (2012). Uganda Geography and Climate.

Uganda Recent History 1226 – 1253 pp. in Africa South of the Sahara 2009, 38th Edition. Europe Regional Surveys of the World. London and New York: Routledge Taylor & Francis Group

Uganda Wildlife Society (UWS). (2010). Uganda's Environment and Natural Resources: Enhancing Parliament's Oversight. Norway: Printed at Birkeland Trykkeri

UN Security Council (2005). Press Release. Security Council Extends Democratic Republic of Congo Mission until 31 March 2005, Authorizes Additional 5,900 Troops, Police. Retrieved from http://www.un.org/press/en/2004/sc8203.doc.htm

UN Security Council (2015). Press Release. Security Council Democratic Republic of Congo Sanctions Committee Updates Sanctions List. Retrieved from https://www.un.org/press/en/2015/sc11772.doc.htm

UNESCO & IBE (2010). World Data on Education. 7th Edition. VII Ed. 2010/11. Uganda. Retrieved from http://www.ibe.unesco.org/fileadmin/user_upload/Publications/WDE/2010/pdf-versions/Uganda.pdf

Unicef & FIDA Uganda (nd). Collection of Children laws. A Simplified Hand Book on International and National Laws & Policies on Children. Retrieved from https://www.unicef.org/uganda/collection_of_ children_laws_finale_110711.pdf

US Department of State (2005). Burundi (10/05). Retrieved from https://www.state.gov/outofdate/bgn/burundi/ 54278.htm

US Department of State (2005). International Religious Freedom Report 2005. Burundi. Relesed by the Bureau of Democracy, Human Rights, and Labor. Retrieved from https://www.state.gov/j/drl/rls/irf/2005/51453. htm

US Department of State (2005). U.S. Department of State Country Report on Human Rights Practices 2004 – Burundi. Retrieved from http://www.refworld.org/docid/4226d9672f.ht ml

US Department of State (2008). International Religious Freedom Report 2004. Burundi. Relesed by the Bureau of Democracy, Human Rights, and Labor. Retrieved from http://www.classbrain.com/art_cr/publish/buru ndi_religious_freedom_report.shtml

US Department of State (2010). Burundi 2009 Country Reports on Human Rights Practices. March 11, 2010.Retrieved from

https://www.state.gov/j/drl/rls/hrrpt/2009/af/1
35941.htm

US Department of State. (2013). Democratic Republic of
the Congo 2013 Human Rights Report.
Country Reports on Human Rights Practices
for 2013 - United States Department of State •
Bureau of Democracy, Human Rights and
Labor. Retrieved from
http://www.state.gov/documents/organization/
220312.pdf

USAID (2010). Burundi. Water and Sanitation Profile.
Retrieved from
http://www.washplus.org/sites/default/files/bu
rundi2010.pdf

USHMM (2002). A Good Man in Hell: General Roméo
Dallaire and the Rwanda Genocide.
Retrieved from
http://www.ushmm.org/confront-
genocide/speakers-and-events/all-speakers-
and-events/a-good-man-in-hell-general-
romeo-dallaire-and-the-rwanda-genocide

USIP (nd). International Commission of Inquiry for
Burundi: Final Report. USA: USIP – United
States Institutes of Peace

UWS. (2010). Uganda's Environment and Natural
Resources: Enhancing Parliament Oversight.
Norway: Birkeland Trykkeri

Virtual Knowledge Africa (2016). Burundi Agriculture.
Retrieved from
http://www.virtualknowledgeafrica.info/index.
php/country-programs

Vision Group Uganda (2015). A brief history of elections in Uganda. Retrieved fromhttp://www.elections.co.ug/new-vision/election/1000257/brief-history-elections-uganda

Wallis, A. (2013). *Silent Accomplice: The Untold Story of France's Role in the Rwandan Genocide.* London & New York: I.B. Tauris & Co. Ltd

Ward, K. (ND). A History of Christianity in Uganda. Dictionary of African Christian Biography. Retrieved from http://www.dacb.org/history/a%20history%20of%20christianity%20%20uganda.html

Whitelaw, K. (nd). The CIA, Belgium and the Assassination of an African Hero. Retrieved on 18th March, 2017 from http://www.thenewblackmagazine.com/view.a spxindex=598

Wikivisually (ND). Early history of Uganda. Retrieved from

World Atlas (2016). Burundi History Timeline Retrieved from http://www.worldatlas.com/webimage/country s/africa/burundi/bitimeln.htm

World Bank (2016). Access to electricity (% of population). Retrieved fromhttp://data.worldbank.org/indicator/EG.E LC.ACCS.ZS?locations=BI

World Relief. (2014). World Relief: Burundi Introductory Report 2014 – 2018. Retrieved from http://oldsite.colonialchurch.org/wpcontent/up

loads/2013/08/World-Relief-Burundi-Introductory-Report.pdf

World Without Genocide. (2015). Democratic Republic of the Congo. Retrieved on 6th August, 2016 from http://worldwithoutgenocide.org/genocides-and-conflicts/congo

Worldometter (2016). Burundi Population. Retrieved from http://www.worldometers.info/world-population/burundi-population/

WTTC. (2014). Travel & Tourism. Economic impact 2014. Burundi. London: World Travel & Tourism Council – The Authority on World Travel & Tourism

Yaa-Lengi (2015). My Fellow Americans: The Millions Killed and Being Killed in Congo D. R.Weigh Heavily on us and our Governments! Part One: Russ Feingold says "Success" while Bank-Ki-Moon says "Failure!". Retrieved from https://congocoalitionblog.wordpress.com/2015/03/06/my-fellow-americans-the-millions-killed-and-being-killed-in-congo-d-r-weigh-heavily-on-us-and-our-governments-part-one/

Yager, T. R. (May 2013). The Mineral Industry of Burundi. 2011 Minerals Yearbook. Burundi [Advance Release]. USA: USGS Science for a Changing World - U.S. Department of the Interior

54100982R00444

Made in the USA
San Bernardino, CA
08 October 2017